Springer Series on **Behavior Therapy and Behavioral Medicine**

Series Editors: Cyril M. Franks, Ph.D., and Frederick J. Evans, Ph.D.

Advisory Board: John Paul Brady, M.D., Robert P. Liberman, M.D., Neal E. Miller, Ph.D., and Stanley Rachman, Ph.D.

Raymond C. Hawkins II, Ph.D., received his doctoral degree in 1975 from the University of Pennsylvania. He joined the Department of Psychology at the University of Texas in 1975 as an Assistant Professor and conducted research on developmental psychopathology, in particular adolescent onset eating disorders in women. For the past year, Dr. Hawkins has served as a clinical psychologist at the Austin Regional Clinic and maintains a private practice in behavior therapy at the Austin Stress Clinic.

William J. Fremouw, Ph.D., received his doctoral degree from the University of Massachusetts in 1974. He joined the faculty at West Virginia University in 1975 and is currently an Associate Professor in the Department of Psychology. His research interests include anger control, anxiety reduction, and eating disorders.

Pamelia F. Clement, Ph.D., obtained her doctoral degree in clinical psychology from the University of Texas in 1980. For the past three years, she has served as a clinical psychologist in the Renaissance Program, Shoal Creek Hospital, an inpatient substance abuse program in Austin, Texas. In addition to bulimia, Dr. Clement's research interests are in family intervention for substance abusers.

THE BINGE–PURGE SYNDROME

Diagnosis, Treatment, and Research

Raymond C. Hawkins II, Ph.D.
William J. Fremouw, Ph.D.
Pamelia F. Clement, Ph.D.
Editors

SPRINGER PUBLISHING COMPANY
New York

No part of this publication may be reproduced, stored in a retrieval system, or transmitted in any form or by any means, electronic, mechanical, photocopying, recording, or otherwise, without the prior permission of Springer Publishing Company, Inc.

Springer Publishing Company, Inc.
536 Broadway
New York, N.Y. 10012

85 86 87 88 / 10 9 8 7 6 5 4 3 2

Library of Congress Cataloging in Publication Data

Main entry under title:
The Binge–purge syndrome.
  Includes bibliographies and index. 1. Bulimarexia. I. Hawkins, Raymond C., II. Fremouw, William J. III. Clement, Pamelia F. [DNLM: 1. Anorexia nervosa. 2. Appetite disorders. W1 SP685NB v.14/WM 175 B613]
RC552.B84B56 1983   616.85′2   83-20178
ISBN 0-8261-4020-3

Printed in the United States of America

Contents

Introduction

In December 1980, Dr. Fremouw organized a symposium on binge eating, presented to the Association for the Advancement of Behavior Therapy in New York City. The response to the symposium, in terms of both attendance and continuing professional exchanges, was the impetus for this book. Many professionals are interested and concerned about bulimia, but little systematic research has been available to help guide diagnosis and treatment efforts. This book provides recent research and perspectives on the binge-purge syndrome with the hope that it will stimulate further understanding of this serious eating disorder.

Part I. Differential Diagnosis: Bulimia, Anorexia Nervosa, and Obesity

At the symposium that provided the inspiration for this volume, the prevalence estimates for binge eating varied from 5 to 90 percent of young adult women. This wide disparity is attributable to several factors: unclear definitional criteria, different populations sampled, and variations in the self-report instruments used. In Chapter 1, entitled "The Definition and Prevalence of Bulimia," Drs. Hamilton, Gelwick, and Meade are concerned with reviewing the diagnostic criteria for bulimia, with one aim being to arrive at a more precise prevalence estimate. Besides their own data from two colleges, the authors compare data from several other samples. This chapter provides a necessary first step for developing sufficiently precise diagnostic criteria for research collaboration and clinical assessment. Hamilton and colleagues suggest that the *DSM-III* definition of bulimia as a psychiatric disorder (APA, 1980) be adopted whenever possible, to reduce diagnostic confusion. They also recommend a standardized assessment battery and offer suggestions as to the components it should contain.

The authors of Chapter 2, Dr. Garfinkel and Dr. Garner, have reported recently that about 50 percent of their large sample of female clients with anorexia nervosa exhibited alternating periods of fasting and binge eating, while the remaining half of their sample showed the classic fasting pattern (Garfinkel, Moldofsky, & Garner, 1980). This provocative clinical finding raises the question of the degree of similarity between anorexia nervosa and bulimia, despite the differences in body weight. This chapter, entitled "Bulimia in Anorexia Nervosa," summarizes this differential diagnostic problem, along with the important etiological and prognostic implications of these two subtypes of anorexia nervosa.

Many but not all obese individuals show bulimic behavior. In Chapter 3, entitled "The Obese Binge Eater: Diagnosis, Etiology, and Clinical Issues," Dr. Gormally describes the incidence of bulimia in a large sample of obese individuals. First he distinguishes "indulgers," who overeat with enjoyment, from "bingers," who display negative thinking patterns when overeating. Then he discusses the treatment implications for the distinction between the compulsive and addictive aspects of bulimia. His cognitive–behavioral perspective provides an excellent transition from the diagnostic–definitional focus of the first part of this volume to the treatment section that follows in Part II.

Part II. Assessment and Treatment

These six chapters provide comprehensive, in-depth information on "state-of-the-art" interventions for bulimia. Our intent is to provide assessment and treatment recommendations that are linked closely and based systematically upon clearly articulated theoretical predictions, mostly from the cognitive–behavioral perspective, but also including the psychodynamic, phenomenological, social–experiential, and neurological–psychopharmacological points of view.

In 1976, Dr. Boskind-White coined the term "bulimarexia" (Boskind-Lodahl, 1976), defined as an eating disorder purported to be common among female undergraduates, characterized by alternating episodes of binge eating and rigid dieting and accompanied by low self-esteem, poor body-image acceptance, and a fear of rejection in heterosexual relationships. A popularized version of this paper (Boskind-Lodahl & Sirlin, 1977) stimulated much of the research reported in this volume. In Chapter 4, entitled "An Experiential–Behavioral Treatment Program for Bulimarexic Women," Dr. White and Dr. Boskind-White provide an excellent example of group treatment recommendations based on a careful conceptualization of the binge eating syndrome in a circumscribed population with an explicit etiologic reference (i.e., a feminist perspective on the socialization of women in our society today).

The most common way to assess bulimia and ascertain its characteristics is through self-report procedures. The "Restraint Scale" (Herman & Mack, 1975; Herman & Polivy, 1975) was the first laboratory-validated self-report measure of restrictive dieting tendencies and fear of loss of control of eating. This scale has been used to predict when overweight or normal-weight subjects would exhibit "counterregulation" or "disinhibition" of dieting restraint during laboratory manipulations of perceptions of calories ingested. In Chapter 5, entitled "Restraint and Binge Eating," Drs. Polivy, Herman, Olmstead, and Jaswinski compare their construct of restraint with the related but not equivalent phenomenon of binge eating. They propose that restrictive dieting ("restraint") is necessary and sufficient to explain the occurrence of binge eating in most cases. This theory has important implications for not only the treatment of bulimic individuals but also the prevention of the binge-eating syndrome's developing in the first place.

Dr. Rau and Dr. Green, in Chapter 6, "Neurological Factors Affecting Binge Eating: Body over Mind," provide a contrast to the psychological theories of bulimia emphasized in the other chapters of this volume. These investigators have published several studies from this perspective of the neuropsychological status of individuals manifesting compulsive eating behavior. Their thesis is that there exists a subtype of bulimic whose compulsive eating may be associated with brain seizure activity, treatable by anticonvulsant medication. The neuropsychological findings of Dr. Rau and Dr. Green constitute an exciting challenge for theory building and future research leading toward an integrated, brain-behavior conceptualization of bulimia, subsuming complex and subtle idiosyncratic interrelationships among binge behaviors, nutritional choices, interpersonal perceptions, cognitions and affects, and brain functions and biochemistry.

Chapter 7, by Dr. Orleans and Dr. Barnett, entitled "Bulimarexia: Guidelines for Behavioral Assessment and Treatment," continues the emphasis on carefully conducted clinical assessment, in this instance from the cognitive–behavioral perspective with the addition of the Minnesota Multiphasic Personality Inventory (MMPI). These investigators describe a new, structured interview device, the "Personal Data Questionnaire," which facilitates a functional analysis of the client's bingeing–purging habits and, more importantly, provides a direct linkage to specific intervention procedures, which then are reviewed and integrated with the preceding behavioral assessment.

Dr. Loro (Chapter 8, "Binge Eating: A Cognitive–Behavioral Treatment Approach") outlines a broad-spectrum, multimodal treatment program for bulimia in which each treatment component is linked directly to assessment categories (as described in Chapter 7). Particularly noteworthy is Dr. Loro's detailed description of his innovative "programmed binge" technique. Programmed binge eating involves countercontrol tactics such as paradoxical injunctions and intentions to gain control over binge behaviors. Dr. Loro has found this procedure to be useful early in the treatment of "rebellious" binge eaters, in that it neutralizes the battle for control and clears the way for more direct and straightforward antecedent and consequent control approaches.

Programmed bingeing may illustrate the efficacy of procedures based upon the "relapse-prevention" model developed by Dr. G. Alan Marlatt (Marlatt & Gordon, 1980). Approximately two-thirds of "slips" or relapses experienced by dieters, drinkers, and smokers occur under conditions of negative emotional arousal or social pressure. There is an obvious relationship between bingeing (and the accompanying self-deprecatory thoughts and feelings of loss of control) and the "abstinence violation effect" postulated in the relapse-prevention model. This model therefore provides a theoretical framework for a set of interventions that are designed to assist the client in recognizing high-risk situations for relapse and in learning coping skills with which to handle these dangerous situations without succumbing to the "one-bite myth." This model represents the most popular psychological formulation of the dynamics of behavioral addictions. It serves as an excellent counterpoint to Dr. Rau and Dr. Green's neurological–psychopharmacological model.

The battle for control alluded to by Dr. Loro in his use of programmed bingeing with "rebellious" binge eaters is stated more explicitly in Dr. Coffman's chapter, "A Clinically Derived Treatment Model for the Binge–Purge Syndrome." Theorizing from within the tradition of relationship-focused, interpretive, and purposive psychotherapy, Dr. Coffman developed his step-by-step treatment program to assist the bulimic client in building a "cognitive map" of the problem, using a "master–slave" model as a heuristic metaphor. The crucial step in the sequence is a direct interpretation to the client that her bingeing behavior is a symbolic statement of determination and integrity. The expectation is thus conveyed that, when the client asserts personal control over important life decisions and makes choices, the binge–purge behavior no longer will serve a useful purpose and slowly will disappear.

Part III. Research and Theory

This section describes recent research studies that have been conducted to operationalize and measure the construct of "bulimia." The major purpose of this research has been to corroborate the clinical description of bulimia, develop reliable measurement instruments, estimate the prevalence of the binge eating syndrome in various populations, and test the validity of the preliminary theories of the etiology and treatment of bulimia. This particular section will be useful to research investigators as a sampling of "state-of-the-art" studies, with the advances and limitations clearly indicated. Although the intervention section may have more direct appeal to the practicing clinician and lay person, sound treatment, just like sound research, requires careful operationalization and theory construction.

In Chapter 10, entitled "Binge Eating: Measurement Problems and a Conceptual Model," Dr. Hawkins and Dr. Clement deal with another possible reason for the wide disparity in prevalence estimates for bulimia. They contend that an adequate conceptual model should specify the necessary and sufficient components of the binge eating syndrome, as well as etiological and prognostic factors. Is the individual who admits to occasional binge episodes—involving breaking a diet by eating a single brownie—experiencing a similar condition as someome who daily consumes 3000 to 5000 or more calories in 20 minutes? Does engaging in more extreme forms of purgation after binge (e.g., fasting, self-induced vomiting, use of laxatives) constitute bulimia of clinical severity? Must there be evidence of compulsive overeating alternating with rigid dieting, or can the bulimic individual exhibit one or the other pattern for long periods of time? These questions involve more than differences in assessment instruments. Hawkins and Clement offer a preliminary conceptual framework in which binge eating behavioral tendencies form a continuum from a mild, prevalent preoccupation with food and body weight that is influenced by prevailing sociocultural role stereotypes related to feminine socialization, to a more severe "eating neurosis" or clinical bulimia, associated with fear of loss of control of eating and weight, a negative body image, self-deprecatory thoughts and feelings after a binge, and the like. The model analyzes these component pathways to bulimia, offering suggestions for measurement of each component and intervention–prevention implications.

Next, Dr. Fremouw's and Dr. Heyneman's chapter, entitled "A Functional Analysis of Binge Episodes," best exemplifies the convergent-measures approach to the construct validation of the bulimia syndrome. These investigators have studied binge eating by individual self-report measures, behavioral observations of actual eating behavior, and even laboratory manipulations precipitating minibinge episodes under scientifically controlled conditions (Spencer & Fremouw, 1979). This approach may be the most promising method for determining the functional relationships between binge episodes, antecedent stimuli, and consequences. In their detailed comparison of binge and snack episodes of obese binge eaters these investigators found that binge episodes were distinguished from snacks by the higher stress levels and more negative self-statements and moods that preceded the binge episodes.

In the final chapter "Toward the Understanding and Treatment of Binge Eating," Dr. Wilson discusses and integrates the theoretical and empirical contributions of the authors of this volume. Therapists will value Dr. Wilson's careful behavioral analysis of the addictive and compulsive aspects of bingeing and purging. Counselors, students, and theoreticians will have ample food for thought in considering the relative merits of the direct, symptom-focused, response-prevention, exposure-therapy procedures advocated by Dr. Wilson (e.g., Mavissakalian, 1982; Rosen & Leitenburg, 1982), as contrasted with the more indirect approach of interpreting the meaning of binge-purge behaviors within the broader psychosocial context of a client's life situation and search for identity (e.g., Coffman's model). Considering the present limited state of knowledge in this area, a creative synthesis of these opposing perspectives is undoubtedly possible, even desirable, from the practical standpoint of best treating the bulimic individual. The more important advances in our understanding of the determinants of binge eating behavior and its treatment, however, will come from carefully designed empirical research studies based upon clearly formulated theoretical predictions. Dr. Wilson summarizes the experimental designs suitable for evaluating treatment outcome. In view of the apparent pervasiveness of binge–purge behaviors in the general female population, these controlled-treatment-outcome studies should be augmented by programmatic laboratory and naturalistic, cross-sectional, and longitudinal studies of the development and natural course of dieting and binge eating behaviors over the life span.

In conclusion, we wish to thank the contributors to this volume and the many colleagues and interested persons who have expressed encouragement and support for the completion of this book. Additional thanks go to Catherine M. Allensworth and Eileen G. A. Allensworth for their assistance in typing and organizing the manuscripts.

Raymond C. Hawkins II
William J. Fremouw
Pamelia F. Clement

References

American Psychiatric Association. *Diagnostic and Statistical Manual of Mental Disorders,* 3rd. ed. Washington, D.C.: American Psychiatric Association, 1980.

Boskind-Lodahl, M. Cinderella's stepsisters: A feminist perspective on anorexia nervosa and bulimia. *Signs: The Journal of Women in Culture and Society,* 1976, *2,* 342–356.

Boskind-Lodahl, M., & Sirlin, J. The gorging–purging syndrome. *Psychology Today,* 1977, *11,* 50.

Garfinkel, P. E., Moldofsky, H., & Garner, D. M. The heterogeneity of anorexia nervosa: Bulimia as a distinct subgroup. *Archives of General Psychiatry,* 1980, *37,* 1036–1040.

Herman, C. P., & Mack, D. Restrained and unrestrained eating. *Journal of Personality,* 1975, *43,* 647–660.

Herman, C. P., & Polivy, J. Anxiety, restraint, and eating behavior. *Journal of Abnormal Psychology,* 1975, *84,* 666–672.

Marlatt, G. A., & Gordon, J. R. Determinants of relapse: Implications for the maintenance of behavior change. In P. Davidson & S. M. Davidson (eds.), *Behavioral Medicine: Changing Health Lifestyles.* New York: Brunner/Mazel, 1980.

Mavissakalian, M. Anorexia nervosa treated with response prevention and prolonged exposure. *Behavior Research and Therapy,* 1982, *20,* 27–31.

Rosen, J. C., & Leitenburg, H. Bulimia nervosa: Treatment with exposure and response prevention. *Behavior Therapy,* 1982, *13,* 117–124.

Spencer, J., & Fremouw, W. J. Binge eating as a function of restraint and weight classification. *Journal of Abnormal Psychology,* 1979, *88,* 262–267.

Contributors

Linda R. Barnett, Ph.D., Department of Psychiatry, Duke University Medical School.

Marlene Boskind-White, Ph.D., Psychology Service, George Junior Republic.

Pamelia F. Clement, Ph.D., Renaissance Program, Shoal Creek Hospital, Austin, Texas.

David A. Coffman, Ph.D., Counseling Center, University of Texas at Austin.

William J. Fremouw, Ph.D., Department of Psychology, West Virginia University.

Paul E. Garfinkel, M.D., Department of Psychiatry, University of Toronto.

David M. Garner, Ph.D., Department of Psychiatry, University of Toronto.

Beverly P. Gelwick, Ph.D., Counseling Center, University of New Hampshire at Durham.

James Gormally, Ph.D., Department of Psychology, University of Maryland.

Richard S. Green, M.D., Department of Psychiatry, Long Island Jewish–Hillside Medical Center.

M. Kathryn Hamilton, Ph.D., Department of Psychology, Southern Illinois University.

Raymond C. Hawkins, II, Ph.D., Austin Stress Clinic, Austin, Texas.

C. Peter Herman, Ph.D., Department of Psychology, University of Toronto.

Nicholas E. Heyneman, M.S., Department of Psychology, West Virginia University.

Carol Jazwinski, M.A., Department of Psychology, University of Toronto.

Albert D. Loro, Jr. Ph.D., Department of Psychiatry, Duke University Medical Center.

Charles J. Meade, Ph.D., Department of Psychology, Southern Illinois University.

Marion P. Olmsted, M.A., Department of Psychology, University of Toronto.

C. Tracy Orleans, Ph.D., Department of Psychiatry, Duke University Medical School.

Janet Polivy, Ph.D., Department of Psychology, University of Toronto.

John H. Rau, Ph.D., Department of Psychiatry, Long Island Jewish-Hillside Medical Center.

William C. White, Jr., Ph.D., Garnett Medical Clinic, Cornell University.

G. Terence Wilson, Ph.D., Department of Psychology, Rutgers University.

I.

Differential Diagnosis: Bulimia, Anorexia Nervosa, and Obesity

1

The Definition and Prevalence of Bulimia

M. Kathryn Hamilton
Beverly P. Gelwick
Charles J. Meade

The writer attempting to summarize current conceptualizations of bulimia and its assessment techniques is faced with an intriguing quandary. Despite enormous attention in the popular press and in professional circles, there is a very small and fragmented body of literature specifically discussing bulimia and related entities. The recency of the initial use of the term and the fact that only in 1980 was it officially designated a psychiatric disorder (APA, 1980) are the causes of this situation. From informal and nonpublished sources of information it can be understood safely that there is a great deal of work being done investigating the identification, assessment, and treatment of persons variously identified as bulimic, bulimarexic, compulsive eaters, or binge eaters. Much of that work will be summarized in this volume. The purpose of the present chapter is to draw together existing thinking regarding the problems of defining and assessing bulimia and the related problem of discovering its prevalence, thought by many to be widespread in American culture today.

Historical Antecedents of Bulimia: Anorexia Nervosa

The history of the disorder bulimia is tied inextricably to the history of two other major eating disorders: anorexia nervosa and obesity. Cases of self-starvation closely resembling the modern definition of anorexia nervosa have been noted since antiquity (Bliss & Branch, 1960). Its history has been detailed well by Bruch (1973). Enough attention has been given to this disorder that various well-developed conceptual and treatment approaches have been found, ranging from the psychodynamic approach, probably best represented by the work of Bruch (1973) to the family systems approach, typified by Minuchin (1974) and Palazzoli (1974). Behavioral approaches to treatment (Bemis, 1978) have been prominent. Physiological explanations for the development of anorexia nervosa enjoyed a brief period of prominence in the early part of the century (Bruch, 1973), then faded, only to reappear in recent years with a focus on endocrine and metabolic explanations (Beumont, Carr, & Gelder, 1973). Recently, several authors have postulated a multifaceted disorder that is multiply determined (Hamilton & Meade, Note 3; Garner & Garfinkel, 1980). This latter approach appears to hold much promise for a more sophisticated means of understanding, classifying, and treating individuals suffering from anorexia.

Development of the Concept of Bulimia

Bulimia does not enjoy a similarly substantial body of literature. Bulimia (or a similar syndrome given a different label) has been mentioned infrequently until recent years and appears in the literature before the 1970s primarily as a symptom of anorexia nervosa (Bliss & Branch, 1960; Bruch, 1973; Dally, 1969), as a rare variant of a hysterical neurosis (Lindner, 1971), or as a syndrome usually called compulsive eating or binge eating (Ondercin, 1979; Rau & Green, 1975). Descriptions of the latter two terms have varied enormously.

Early Case Histories

Several classic case histories bear mentioning, as they represent essentially the only early writing about bulimia. Stunkard's article, published in 1959, delineated three kinds of eating patterns in obese individuals, one of which is called binge eating. This was typified by irregular "orgiastic" binges, somewhat dissociative in nature, which involve consumption of large amounts of food quickly, ending with physical discomfort and subjective feelings of guilt and self-criticism. Stunkard (1976) also described bulimic episodes in obese patients. Lindner (1971) described his treatment of a young woman who also had severe binges that were seen as dissociative in nature and eventually were thought to be a response to an unresolved Oedipal conflict in which she wished symbolically to bear her father's child. Bruch (1973), in her writing about anorexia nervosa and obesity, mentioned binge eating as a part of the syndrome for some anorectic and some obese individuals, but did not discuss bulimia as a separate syndrome. She did describe a pattern exhibited by individuals she termed "thin fat people," in which the individual maintains a thin or normal body weight but does so by constant self-denial and preoccupation with food and weight. She cited bulimia (sometimes with vomiting) as associated with this problem for many patients.

Recent Descriptive Studies

Within the past 10 years, several terms have appeared that seem to address the problems of describing bulimia and the beginning efforts to hypothesize its etiology. We will review and compare the most prominent.

In 1980, the third edition of the American Psychiatric Association's *Diagnostic and Statistical Manual of Mental Disorders* (*DSM-III*) described bulimia thus:

> . . .the essential features are episodic binge eating accompanied by an awareness that the eating pattern is abnormal, fear of not being able to stop eating voluntarily, and depressed mood and self-deprecating thoughts following the eating binges. The bulimic episodes are not due to anorexia nervosa or any known physical disorder. [p. 69]

In addition to these characteristics, three of the following must be present for the diagnosis:

> (1) consumption of high-caloric, easily ingested food during a binge; (2) inconspicuous eating during a binge; (3) termination of such eating episodes by abdominal pain, sleep, social interruption, or self-induced vomiting; (4) repeated attempts to lose weight by severely restrictive

diets, self-induced vomiting, or use of cathartics or diuretics; (5) frequent weight fluctuations greater than ten pounds due to alternating binges and fasts. [P. 71]

This official definition is beginning to be used and cited by researchers; however, several competing terms also dot the literature, adding to the complexity of the definitional picture.

The term "bulimarexia," coined by Boskind-Lodahl & White (1978), refers to a cyclical eating disorder in which women alternately binge and then purge themselves, using vomiting, fasting, a laxative, or amphetamine abuse. The binging is followed by guilt and a compulsion to rid themselves of food. The authors also cite a distorted body image in which the woman perceives herself as too fat, even though this perception may not be shared by others. Obviously, this description is quite similar to the *DSM-III* description. One implicit weakness of the bulimarexia definition is that it ignores the existence of some males with essentially identical symptoms.

Palmer (1979) described a syndrome he calls the "dietary chaos syndrome," which was typified by a grossly disordered eating pattern with some or all of the following: vomiting, periods of abstinence from food, purgative abuse, bulimia, unusual choice of food, mastication of food without swallowing, secret eating, and eating confined to special circumstances, such as when driving a car. Patients were extremely preoccupied with food and eating and sometimes with weight. Eating impulses were experienced as uncontrollable, and failure to control eating was followed by guilt. There sometimes was erratic behavior and emotional instability. In general, weight was within or above normal limits. This syndrome was thought by Palmer to have a poor prognosis and often to have a chronic course. Ondercin (1979) also described a pattern of what she called "compulsive eating" in college women, in which the characteristics were uncontrollable eating episodes unprompted by hunger, in which patients consumed much food and following which they felt guilty and remorseful.

Russell (1979) suggested the title "bulimia nervosa" for a syndrome diagnosed by these criteria: an irresistable urge to overeat, sometimes alternating with periods of abstinence, often with self-induced vomiting or purgation. He also cited (from data gathered on a sample of 30 patients selected for their history of overeating episodes followed by self-induced vomiting, purging, or both) abnormal fear of fatness and preoccupation with body size as determined by unrealistically harsh standards, patients having relatively normal weight, and the majority of patients having previously experienced anorexia nervosa. He saw it as closely related to anorexia nervosa.

Rau & Green (1975) distinguished between "binge eating" (which they described as ego-syntonic, similar to a drunken celebration or spree) and "compulsive eating" (which they regarded as ego-dystonic, alien, and uncontrollable). They acknowledged that their use of these terms was nearly the opposite of the usual connotation (e.g., as described by Bruch, 1973, and Stunkard, 1959), in which binge eaters experience their bingeing as negative and in which compulsive eaters usually are described as being individuals who consistently overeat and occasionally binge rather than as having a problem with episodic excessive eating that is specifically a source of depression and self-criticism. Rau & Green justified adding to the semantic confusion by alleging that what they called compulsive eating had its etiology in a primary neurologic disorder. Two cases are presented that illustrate their hypothesis that some compulsive eaters can be successfully treated with anticonvulsant medication. A small group of studies by these investigators and others gave both positive (Davis, Quaills, Hollister, & Stunkard, 1974; Green & Rau, 1974) and negative (Weiss & Levitz, 1976) evidence regarding the possibility that this treatment may be successful for some individuals with compulsive eating problems. While this approach appears to hold some potential for identifying the etiology of at least a subgroup of bulimia suffers, the confusion generated by essentially reversing the usual use of two common terms is considerable.

Summary

It is clear that the preceding attempts to identify and label bulimic-like patterns represent a response to a problem that is challenging many clinicians today. Given the recency of several of the proposed labels, one wishes that the *DSM-III* description had been widely available a few years earlier! Though no two of the preceding "syndromes" are described identically, the degree of overlap is substantial. It is clear that for some time research on bulimia will be burdened with lack of definitional clarity and the use of more terms than are necessary or helpful. We propose, therefore, that the use of the *DSM-III* definition be adopted whenever possible in continuing research on bulimia, for the following reasons:

1. The definition is now a widely available one, part of the most widely accepted psychiatric nosology in use today, and the result of extensive field work and information integration.
2. It is the most encompassing definition; none of the others cited are as thorough.
3. It is the most parsimonious definition, having little to say about etiology, dynamics, or subtypes.

The latter point is also a weakness in that there is little direction given for further understanding of one or more coherent, specific patterns. The *DSM-III* description is also valuable in that it acknowledges bulimia as a unique, separate psychiatric disorder that is not necessarily a part of (or even related to) anorexia nervosa. This should encourage more investigation into it as a problem in its own right, instead of as an unfortunate but less-important symptom of anorexia nervosa or obesity.

Current Research Relating to Bulimia

The difficulty in establishing precise diagnostic criteria for psychiatric syndromes has been well documented (Matarazzo, 1978). Numerous examples exist of the at best mixed success in demonstrating interrater reliability for various diagnoses (Cooper, Kendall, Gurland, Sharpe, Copeland, & Simon, 1972). Though primary anorexia nervosa may be diagnosed more easily than some other entities, as we have seen, systematic use of distinct criteria in the case of bulimia has not begun yet. There is not even consistent use of bulimia as a diagnostic term.

Establishing and following prescribed diagnostic criteria for a given syndrome is one of the major problems in epidemiological psychiatry (called the case definition problem). A second problem is finding the cases that exist (case identification problem) (Williams, Tarnopolsky, & Hand, 1980). The present section will address each of these problems. First, several self-report instruments that provide direction for conceptualizing and measuring bulimic symptoms and cognitions will be reported. Next, several studies will be discussed that report particularly relevant data about binge eating and its concomitants in several contexts. Treatment aspects of these studies will not be discussed. Finally, a small number of studies will be reviewed that begin to address the question of prevalence. The latter work is of particular importance in view of the fact that the *DSM-III* notes that there is "no information" available on familial patterns, prevalence, or predisposing factors.

Self-Report Instruments Relating to Bulimia

Several of the instruments described here focus on the assessment of binge eating characteristics. One was developed for use in assessing characteristics of anorexia nervosa, and one is a derivative of a general personality measure, the Minnesota Multiphasic Personality Inventory (Hathaway & McKinley, 1970).

Binge Scales.   Gormally, Black, Daston, & Rardin (1982) constructed scales to assess the severity of binge eating among the obese. The Binge Eating Scale (BES) contains 16 items to identify the behavioral characteristics of a binge and the feelings/cognitions that cue or follow a binge. The Cognitive Factors Scale (CFS) was developed to assess both standards for setting a diet and efficacy expectations about being able to adhere to a diet.

Hawkins and Clement (1980) developed the Binge Scale (BS), a nine-item questionnaire designed to measure the behavioral and attitudinal parameters of bulimia. In addition, they attempted to quantify bulimic tendencies along a severity continuum. Items were constructed specifically to attempt to tap behavioral and psychological characteristics as described in the *DSM-III* (APA, 1980), for example, length of binge episodes, presence of vomiting, and antecedent and consequent emotional states.

Ondercin (1979), attempting to assess what she calls compulsive eating, constructed a self-report instrument, the Compulsive Eating Scale (CES), which includes information on emotional states related to eating, specific aspects of bingeing behavior, and some information about physical stature (e.g., weight, height, and bone structure). The scale, revised to include 32 items (Dunn & Ondercin, 1981), appears to discriminate between individuals with regard to degree of compulsive eating. Though limited by being a general self-report measure, which does not allow information to be gathered about specific aspects of specific binges, it does generate general information about types of food eaten during binges, frequency of binges, alternating of binges with dieting or fasting, and emotional responses after bingeing, all of which are diagnostic criteria from *DSM-III*. With specific instructions (e.g., "describe the most recent binge you experienced"), the scale may have potential for more precise assessment of behavioral patterns in bulimia.

Anorexia Nervosa Scale.   Garner & Garfinkel (1979) developed a 40-item self-report instrument, the Eating Attitudes Test (EAT), which serves as an index of symptoms and attitudes found in anorexia nervosa. Preliminary studies (Garner & Garfinkel, 1979, 1980) showed that the EAT is valuable in identifying anorectic symptoms and that it appears to be sensitive to clinical remission (Garner & Garfinkel, 1979). Given the close association between anorexia and bulimia in the clinical literature, and the proposed similarities in concern for body shape and weight (APA, 1980), an instrument such as the EAT might be of considerable use in understanding the relationship between bulimia and anorexia. In fact, the EAT has been used specifically in one study of bulimic symptoms (Clement & Hawkins, Note 1).

Addictive Tendencies Scale.   Recently, some authors have suggested that there may be "common personality or behavioral syndromes in persons with different types of addiction problems" (Leon, Kolotkin, & Korgeski, 1979). These investigators administered the MacAndrew Scale (MacAndrew, 1965) (developed originally to differentiate alcoholic patients from other psychiatric patients) to groups of obese, anorectic, and smoking patients and a group of normal controls. The scale did not differentiate between eating-disordered groups, nor between those groups and the smokers or the controls. However, the scale was found useful in another study (Leon, Eckert, Teed, & Buchwald, 1979) in which massively obese persons (more than 100 pounds overweight) scored close to the addictive range. Thus, the scale may be tapping some common personality patterns among persons prone to various addictive behavior syndromes.

Summary.   Though all of the instruments cited have potential for contributing to the assessment of bulimia, none has been created specifically for the identification and explication of bulimic symptoms except the Binge Scale (Hawkins & Clement, 1980). There is probably some worth in continuing to use the better-validated scales in combination with one another to assess the interrelationships and the implications for improved understanding and diagnosis of bulimia. However, the lack of a more detailed means of including attitudinal, cognitive, and behavioral parameters of bulimia in a single measure is unfortunate. The MacAndrew Scale (MacAndrew, 1965) probably deserves more trials as a possible predictor of binge eating tendencies.

Descriptive Studies Relating to
Conceptualizing Bulimia

There is almost no research that was designed specifically to study bulimia; however, a number of investigators have examined binge eating from a variety of perspectives, and this work is useful as a beginning framework for more focused research on bulimia. Some researchers working in the treatment of obese and overweight patients have contributed to the understanding of binge eating in self-referred inpatient and outpatient populations; representative studies will be discussed here. Next, a group of studies examining the relationship between anorectic and bulimic symptoms will be reviewed. A third context in which binge eating has been conceptualized is neurological; one study that has implications for etiology will be discussed. Finally, a small group of studies that can be categorized only as miscellaneous will be discussed for their individual contributions to defining and understanding bulimia.

Studies with Obese Patients. Loro and Orleans (1981) reported on 280 obese and overweight adults, 230 females and 50 males, admitted to the Dietary Rehabilitation Clinic at Duke University Medical Center from September 1977 to December 1978. Data were gathered from pretreatment self-report questionnaires and clinical records. The authors reported several interesting patient characteristics. First, although binge eating usually has been reported as a problem primarily for women, Loro and Orleans found no significant difference between the sexes in this behavior pattern. Although these results will require replication, one might speculate that the cultural norm for slender women and the readily accepted expectation that women may ask for help has made self-referral to clinics more of an option for women than for men. Second, the authors reported that 68 percent of the frequent bingers and 74 percent of the regular bingers noted childhood or adolescent onset of obesity. Third, the unreliability of anecdotal data on the intensity of binge eating was documented by the extreme range of caloric intake, ranging from 1000 to 10,000, depending upon considerable individual situational differences.

Finally, Loro (Note 5) reported additional data about response characteristics of binge eating. The time range for binge episodes was brief, with more than half lasting less than an hour. Most binge eating occurred when the clients were alone (82%) and at home (78%). Locations preferred for bingeing were the kitchen if at home and in an automobile or fast-food restaurant. Most clients preferred to binge in the early or late evenings. Many clients (44%) reported being consciously aware that they were bingeing but feeling that they could not or would not stop during the episode.

Gormally et al. (1982), using two samples of overweight persons seeking treatment (Sample 1, N = 65; Sample 2, N = 47), found that at least three populations may be represented by the way obese subjects report behaviors/feelings characteristic of bingeing. Twenty-two percent were identified as "indulgers" with little emotional response to their overeating. They enjoyed eating and did not feel that they were lacking in control. The majority of subjects (55%) were judged to have moderate problems with binge eating, mostly episodic periods of poor control. These people appeared to be more tolerant of their responses than the third type, "severe bingers" (23%). The "severe bingers" felt a complete lack of control leading to a constant struggle to avoid a binge. This loss of control led to extreme guilt and self-hate. The authors further differentiated the "severe bingers" from the other two groups. Severe bingers, having "high dieting standards" but "low personal efficacy," were more likely to experience a minor loss of control in a "high-risk" situation. Following the minor slip, severe bingers were likely to internalize the lapse as being due to a self-described "lack of willpower" and then to further lose control and have a binge.

Gormally (Note 2) also did an outcome study of 38 participants who had lost at least 15 pounds during a 16-week treatment. Of these participants, 16 were successful maintainers and 22 were relapsers. He found four who regularly monitored body weight and eating behavior and participated in planned exercise. They were good at problem solving, both in regard to everyday activities and to eating behavior. Gormally differentiated four maladaptive cognitions that interfere with problem solving for the relapsers: (1) self versus situation attributions, (2) either/or thinking, (3) lack of prioritizing, and (4) magical thinking.

Studies with Anorectic Patients with Bulimic Symptoms. Strober (1981) studied 44 adolescent females with anorexia who had been admitted to the children's service of a psychiatric hospital. Using two matched samples, he distinguished the subgroups of those with and without the syndrome of bulimia:

> In comparison to nonbulimic anorectics, bulimics evidenced higher levels of core anorectic symptomatology and were more likely to show affective disturbance and alcohol use. Bulimia was more strongly as-

sociated with affective instability and other signs of behavioral disturbance during childhood. The family environment of bulimics was characterized by significantly greater conflict and negativity, less cohesion, and less structure . . . , and bulimics experienced more stressful life changes prior to illness onset than did nonbulimic patients. Parents of bulimic anorectics also reported significantly higher levels of marital discord, were rated as more emotionally distant from their daughters, and exhibited greater psychiatric morbidity and physical health problems. [p. 28]

In an earlier extensive study of body image disturbance in 18 anorectic females and 24 female controls, Strober, Goldenburg, Green, and Saxon (1979) found that the presence of vomiting as a symptom was associated with higher scores on the Fisher Body Distortion Questionnaire (Fisher, 1970). This 82-item instrument measures aberrations in perception of body image and produces a "total distortion score." The authors linked this finding to their clinical experience, suggesting that vomiters "harbor more bizarre notions about food and bodily processes" (p. 700).

A third study (Beumont, George, & Smart, 1976) differentiated between "dieters" and "vomiters and purgers" in a group of 31 patients with primary anorexia nervosa. Dieters were described as those who had achieved weight loss solely because of dieting and exercise; vomiters and purgers had used other means to lose weight, such as vomiting and the abuse of purgatives. They suggest that "clinical psychiatric differences" exist between these two subgroups of anorectic patients. Premorbid personality traits, possible precipitating factors for the illness, and interviews were used to elicit information leading to the identification of differences between groups. Vomiters and purgers were more likely to exhibit histrionic personality traits, to have heterosexual relationships (for the majority, including sexual intercourse), to have been obese prior to onset of symptoms, and to have a less favorable prognosis than those patients who had merely dieted. The authors suggest that there are two subtypes of anorectic patients and that vomiters/purgers are more likely to have a longer, more complicated course of illness.

Beumont, Abraham, and Simson (1981) also differentiated between "dieters" (N = 15) and "vomiters or purgers" (N = 16) in a study of psychosexual histories of 31 female adolescent and young-adult patients with anorexia nervosa. Age at menarche was not different, nor was time of first special heterosexual relationship or first intercourse. The age of onset of illness was significantly lower in "dieters," and they were less likely to use tampons during menstruation. Also, a higher proportion of "vomiters or purgers" had "experienced intercourse, indulged in oral genital sex and had more than one sexual partner." This may be in part because of the later age of onset for these patients. Because a table giving all raw data for each subject was not available, questions such as this were not answerable.

Another comparison of 21 bulimic anorectic patients to nonbulimic anorectic patients (here called "habitual vomiters," N = 9; and "pure abstainers," N = 12) found no substantial personality or symptomatic differences between the two groups (Ben-Tovim, Marilov, & Crisp, 1979).

In contrast, Garfinkel, Moldofsky, and Garner (1980) found several differences between bulimic and nonbulimic anorectic patients. Bulimics were more likely to have been obese prior to symptom onset, to abuse alcohol and other drugs, and to report suicidal symptoms.

The proportion of patients with anorexia nervosa who vomit was estimated by Sours (1980) as at least 25 percent of all cases. Halmi (1974) reports bulimia in 10 percent of a sample of 94 anorectics, with regular vomiting in 33 percent. Bruch (1973) estimates that 25 percent of patients with primary anorexia nervosa exhibit bulimic episodes. The presence of this symptom (including vomiting) is associated with a poorer prognosis by several authors (Crisp, Hsu, & Stonehill, 1979; Garfinkel, Moldofsky, & Garner, 1977; Morgan & Russell, 1975).

There is obviously new attention being given to differences between anorectics who vomit and those who do not; this may shed light on the definitional questions regarding bulimia. One difficulty with several studies is the lack of clarity regarding categorization of patients. Some (Beumont, Abraham, & Simson, 1981; Beumont, George, & Smart, 1976; Strober et al., 1979) denote the presence of vomiting alone as an adequate criterion for dividing the anorectic group. Strober (1981) uses a history of binge eating as the major apparent criterion for selecting bulimics. In future research it will be important to use more precise criteria for differentiating these subgroups of anorectic patients to provide meaningful interpretations of differences and to allow valid comparisons among studies.

Research Addressing Neurological Components of Bulimia.
Only one study will be cited here. Rau and Green (1975), as discussed previously, believe that some individuals who have severe,

ego-dystonic, uncontrollable eating episodes (a pattern they term "compulsive eating") have a neurologic disorder that causes the bulimic symptoms. Following several experimental treatment studies (Green & Rau, 1974; Rau & Green, 1975), they reported a descriptive/treatment study (Rau & Green, 1978) that focused assessment on identifying neurological "soft signs" in compulsive eaters. Thirty patients had a complete EEG and a structured interview to assess the presence of 10 neurological soft signs: rages, frequent headaches, dizziness, stomachaches, nausea, paresthesias, history of convulsions, perceptual disturbances, other compulsions, or a family history of epilepsy. Twenty-three patients received treatment with an anticonvulsant; of those, 12 improved and 11 did not. The 10 signs were summed and the EEG added as an eleventh for each patient. The sum of the 11 signs was significantly correlated with improvement, though no sign or smaller combination of signs predicted improvement. This study is of interest in the support it lends to a possible neurological etiology for some bulimia patients.

Research on Personality Characteristics and Cultural Factors. Most research on bulimia has used instruments designed to assess problems with eating behavior, cognitions or attitudes about food, or body-image perceptions. There is little information about broader aspects of personality in nonanorectic bulimic individuals. Dunn and Ondercin (1981) investigated personality variables related to compulsive eating in college women with the following findings: (1) compulsive eaters (as defined by the Compulsive Eating Scale developed by Ondercin in 1979) showed "higher inner tension, greater suspiciousness, and less emotional stability" on the Sixteen Personality Factor Test (Cattell, Eber, & Tatsuoka, 1970) than low-compulsive eaters; and (2) there was also a higher masculine self-ideal as measured by the Bem Sex Role Inventory (Bem, 1974) in the high-compulsive-eating group.

Research on bulimia with purging that is not defined as a subgroup of anorexia nervosa is described by Boskind-Lodahl and White (1978) and called "bulimarexia." These authors take a feminist perspective, speculating that cultural factors are predominant in the etiology of this syndrome. This study represents one of the few treatment reports written. Unfortunately, no control (or comparison) group was included.

One further study bears mentioning because of its implications for conceptualizing bulimia. Herman and Polivy (1975) defined restrained eaters as those obese *or* normal-weight individuals who restrain their eating to keep their body weights or body fat below biological "set-point." This view proposes that many obese individuals with excesses of fat cells are "relatively deprived" of food. In order to maintain their weight below set-point they usually eat in a restrained fashion. This description is similar to Bruch's description of "thin fat people," who maintain a normal-range weight by constant restraint or by cycles of bingeing and purging or extreme dieting. Thus, relative deprivation may be the "most viable conceptualization underlying individual differences in eating behavior," particularly when considering nonobese subjects. Herman and Polivy also cited the "relative hyperemotionality" of restrained normal-weight people; this characteristic is mentioned frequently in descriptions of bulimic patients (Casper, Eckert, Halmi, Goldberg, & Davis, 1980). Unfortunately, Herman and Polivy did not inquire about specific bulimic symptoms in this study; however, one might speculate readily that some of their normal-weight restrained eaters had bulimic symptoms.

Prevalence Studies

In psychiatric epidemiological research there is always the problem of agreement upon a definition for the type of case being sought. If and when there is agreement on what is sought, a continuum problem still esists. As cited by Williams et al. (1980), in a quote from Barker and Rose (1976) ". . . in the general population, disease behaves as a continuously distributed variable. The question is not so much 'has he got it?' as 'how much of it has he got?' " This question may be particularly of relevance in discussing the prevalence of bulimia and bulimic-like behaviors in women, since as many as 85 percent (Clement & Hawkins, Note 1), and 78 percent (Ondercin, 1979), of college women self-reported at least occasional bingeing. Differentiating clinical cases of bulimia from this larger group is one problem. A second problem, beyond the scope of this chapter, is the need to understand and differentiate among the nonclinical groups of women reporting problems with binge eating and its concomitants, in order to assess need for preventive intervention (to *prevent* worsening of bulimic behaviors) or developmental intervention (with women who may not become clinical cases but whose eating concerns interfere with their full enjoyment of life and personal development). The following studies, done on normal college populations, provide a beginning toward true prevalence studies of bulimia.

Clement and Hawkins (Note 1) gathered data from three normal-weight samples (N = 231, N = 277, N = 161, including 41 males) and from a weight control program (N = 86). Of the approximately 85 percent of the normal-weight women reporting binge eating, only about 6 percent of them reported inducing vomiting after a binge. Normal-weight women who reported *no* bingeing described themselves as having a more positive self-image, had less fear of loss of control of eating, were less neurotic, were more assertive, and had dating competence. Between 11 percent and 15 percent of the normal-weight females obtained EAT (Garner & Garfinkel, 1979) scores of at least 30 (the clinical anorexia nervosa cutoff score). These subjects also showed a significantly more negative self-image, more binge eating tendencies, more dieting "restraint," more neuroticism, and more depression than those whose EAT scores were less than 30. The overweight women reported more pronounced binge eating tendencies, but the frequency of self-induced vomiting among the clinically obese women was lower than for the normal-weight women (3.7 percent). They noted that there was a relationship between EAT scores exceeding 30 and severe compulsive eating as measured by their Binge Scale (Hawkins & Clement, 1980), and urged further investigation into the question of the relationship between anorexia nervosa and bulimia in their "subclinical manifestations in a college population."

Svendsen and Cusin (Note 6) administered the EAT (Garner & Garfinkel, 1979) to a control group of men and women college students who used a university health service and compared their scores with groups of sorority women, dance majors, and clinically diagnosed bulimic women. Significant differences were found among the groups. The following percentages of the subject groups scored above the clinical cutoff on the EAT: Student Health Service men (2%), Student Health Service women (9%), sorority women (17%), dance women (22%), and bulimic women (77%). They concluded that particular sociocultural factors relating to body shape and size are significant contributors to the development of an "anorectic attitude." Dancers and/or sorority women are expected to be strongly influenced by such factors.

Much has been made in this chapter of the lack of true epidemiological studies of bulimia. At this point, we do not have accurate data on either incidence or prevalence of bulimia as defined by *DSM-III* or of less severe, but still troubling, eating and appetite disorders (e.g., an eating pattern of bingeing and severe dieting). We ourselves have made an initial foray into this area, however, and we shall discuss briefly the methodology and results of our study here.

There appears to be both anecdotal and research evidence to suggest that women in late adolescence and their early twenties may be the group at highest risk for developing bulimia and its variants (Clement & Hawkins, Note 1; Bruch, 1973). In our investigation (Hamilton, Meade, & Gelwick, Note 4), we were interested in attempting to determine the incidence of various eating disorders in a subgroup of such women, those who are in college.

Three instruments, the Eating Attitude Test (EAT) (Garner & Garfinkel, 1979) and the Compulsive Eating Scale (CES) (Ondercin, 1979), both of which had been previously validated, and a demographic and family and personal health questionnaire, were mailed to a random sample of 10 percent of the female students at Southern Illinois University and a random sample of 50 percent of the female students at Stephens College (Columbia, Missouri). Return rates were substantial, approximately 80 percent for the SIU sample and approximately 50 percent for the Stephens sample.

Between 10 and 15 percent of the sample scored in the clinical range on the EAT and a similar percentage scored above the cutoff score previously established for the CES. Of these subjects, approximately 5 to 8 percent scored above the cutoff on both instruments. Thus, these latter subjects have attitudes and behaviors similar to both anorectics and compulsive eaters and are certainly a group of prime candidates for developing bulimia. One would not wish automatically to conclude that 8 to 10 percent of the women on large campuses have an eating disorder that would fit *DSM-III* criteria for bulimia; rather, this would seem to represent an upper limit on the prevalence of bulimia among these women. These data appear to be consistent with those reported by Clement & Hawkins (Note 1), who found that about 6 percent of their combined sample of normal-weight college women stated that they had engaged in self-induced vomiting.

We have interpreted our data in two ways. First, there seems to be a group of college-age women who clearly fit the diagnostic criteria for bulimia. The number of women in this group does not exceed approximately 8 pecent of the total female undergraduate population. This figure seems alarmingly high (even assuming that the true figure for *DSM-III*-type bulimia may be 1 to 2 percent). Second, there is a very large number of women who exhibit many of the same attitudes and behaviors as bulimics, even though they currently do not exhibit a clinical disorder. This group certainly contains a significant number of individuals who either are at risk to develop bulimia or who have done so already.

Summary. Though the studies just discussed are preliminary and not replicated, they indicate support for the possibility that bulimia and related syndromes are prevalent problems. Several clinical impressions of widespread bingeing and vomiting in college women (Boskind-Lodahl & White, 1978; Bruch, 1973; Sours, 1980) have warned of this possibility. Recent reports of relatively high prevalence of primary anorexia nervosa (Crisp, Palmer, & Kalucy, 1976; Kendall, Hall, Hailey, & Babigan, 1973), as well as findings such as those just cited, give credence to those who cite sociocultural factors in Western culture as contributing to a rise in incidence of eating problems, particularly in women (Boskind-Lodahl & White, 1978; Bruch, 1973).

Research on Bulimia: Summary and Limitations

It is impossible to summarize the varied studies discussed in this chapter in the way that one would summarize an integrated body of literature organized around a single concept, trait, or theoretical problem. Most of the studies discussed were not designed specifically to address the problem of bulimia. Many of them addressed it only within the limited context of anorexia nervosa and its manifestations. Still, it seems apparent that there is a syndrome being described that has some unique identity. Allowing for significant individual variations among studies, most authors seem to be discussing a syndrome that has as its major characteristic cyclic binge eating, solitary in nature, usually not pleasurable, with a feeling of being out of control. This is associated with feelings of guilt, self-criticism, low self-esteem, and/or depression. Vomiting, laxative abuse, extreme dieting or fasting, and drug and alcohol abuse are cited frequently as concomitants of the binge eating. This composite description is very close to the *DSM-III* diagnostic criteria. Binge eaters, bulimic anorectics, compulsive eaters, or bulimarexics are described frequently as having one or more of the following characteristics: to be affectively overreactive, more sexually and socially mature than classic anorectics, impulsive, likely to have been obese, more difficult to treat in terms of behavior change than anorectics, histrionic, to have a tendency toward compulsive stealing, to be suicidal or seriously depressed, and to be tense. This intriguing overlap and similarity in description gives credence to the idea that there is a clinical entity, perhaps a very complex one, that needs to be understood better.

The original intent in outlining this chapter was to provide a critical comparison of the various research studies relating to assessing, defining, and discovering the prevalence of bulimia. Though each of these questions can be addressed here, it is impossible with any degree of appropriateness to compare descriptive studies that, for example, are attempting to describe clearly related, perhaps identical syndromes, but syndromes that the investigators have defined and labeled differently. This is the first, and the primary, limitation in the studies that have been cited. Not only is there no clear agreement about using the official *DSM-III* definition of the syndrome, but most authors do not even use the term bulimia in their work, though what they are describing definitely appears to be a bulimic or bulimic-like syndrome (Boskind-Lodahl & White, 1978; Palmer, 1979; Russell, 1979). Until there is agreement on a diagnosis of that term, there can be no unified research on bulimia.

The second limitation is that there is minimal information about the discrete parts of the diagnostic criteria for bulimia given in the *DSM-III,* the definition we recommend be adopted for the present time. Only Clement & Hawkins (Note 1) have attempted to begin purposefully to tie assessment procedures to the *DSM-III* procedure. The parameters and degrees of a bulimic episode must be identified better. Though the definition specified that the episodes must not be due to any known physical disorder, there are indications (Rau & Green, 1975) that at least some bulimics may have a predisposing neurological condition. No clear guidelines exist for ruling out this possibility, though their more recent investigation (Rau & Green, 1978) does give some direction to assessment procedures allowing differential diagnosis of bulimic patients with a neurological disorder.

The third limitation that we would note is the vast lack of clarity about the relationship of bulimia to anorexia nervosa. While bulimia is not supposed to be diagnosed if the episodes are due to anorexia nervosa, it is true that several of the few studies of bulimic behavior in existence were conducted using anorectic patients with bulimic episodes (Beumont et al., 1976; Strober, 1981). At this stage in our understanding of bulimia, it seems as premature to separate it artificially from anorexia nervosa as to minimize it as only a subtype of anorexia. The relationship is complex and must be explored further before meaningful conclusions can be drawn.

This brings us to the fourth problem in bulimia research. Even given the very few studies specifically focused on bulimia, there is some indication that there may be more than one subtype of bulimic patients. No study to date has compared bulimics to one another to begin to identify various subpatterns of the disorder. Within-group differences may be more instructive than between-group differences at this stage of our knowledge about the eating disorders, particularly with regard to quesions of etiology. Specifically, it might seem reasonable to hypothesize that the etiology of bulimia in obese individuals would differ from the etiology of individuals who initially were diagnosable as having primary anorexia nervosa. In addition, there are probably important differences between bulimics who exhibit vomiting and those who do not. The presence of vomiting has been noted by anorexia researchers to worsen the prognosis for the disorder (Beumont et al., 1976; Morgan & Russell, 1975), be associated with a more lengthy course (Morgan & Russell, 1975), be correlated with greater instability (Russell, 1979), and to predict a larger disturbance in body image (Strober et al., 1979) in anorectic patients.

Fifth, most of the studies cited here that even indirectly address the question of prevalence do so without following established epidemiological procedures for case definition and case identification. Without more systematic procedures, without the use of large, random samples, it will not be possible to develop baselines for the presence of the disorder(s) that we will have defined, once we correct the other four deficiencies in the research.

Conclusions and Suggested Directions for Future Research

Fortunately, there are severe limitations on length of this chapter, for it is tempting to engage in a "binge" of recommendations about future research needs in this barely explored clinical area. Given the current assumed prevalence of this serious disorder, it seems incumbent upon researchers in the area to give all attention to following the most rigorous methods in order to hasten our understanding and ability to treat—even to prevent—bulimia. We have not addressed treatment research or made recommendations for treatment research. Each of the following recommendations, however, seem quite relevant for anyone considering investigations into treatment of bulimia.

1. Since diagnosis is clearly the subject of some controversy, diagnosis in research studies should be based on the *DSM-III* criteria. Specific criteria should be defined operationally, and every effort should be made to make information about eating patterns as behaviorally based as possible. The work of Clement and Hawkins (Note 1) is a good example of the kind of procedures that appear to hold promise for more meaningful diagnosis and assessment.

2. Since there is virtually no information about etiology, family dynamics, social class, or the presence of other metabolic or addictive problems in the family, any study of individuals diagnosed as bulimic should gather as much of those types of information as is reasonably possible in order to begin building data bases that allow meaningful comparison across studies.

3. There do appear to be some promising instruments for the assessment of eating behaviors and attitudes. We would recommend consideration of a full and standardized test battery containing at least the following: the Eating Attitude Test (Garner & Garfinkel, 1979), the Binge Scale (Hawkins & Clement, 1980), and the Compulsive Eating Scale (Ondercin, 1979). Since there is little information about premorbid personality, and since there are some indications (Dunn & Ondercin, 1981) that sex-role identity may be an issue for some women who develop bulimia, we recommend that the Minnesota Multiphasic Personality Inventory (Hathaway & McKinley, 1970) and the Bem Sex Role Inventory (Bem, 1974) also be given. If there is time, it is possible that the standardized interview of Rau and Green (1978) for assessing neurological soft signs would add useful data about the prevalence of such signs among the bulimic population.

4. Prevalence studies, following appropriate epidemiological procedures of case definition and case identification, are necessary to learn more about the incidence of clinically diagnosable cases of bulimia. Such studies must be rigorous and must include adequate assessment and follow-up with possible cases, in order to provide valid information about prevalence.

5. There is some indication (Russell, 1979) that bulimia may become an intractable, chronic pattern relatively quickly and that there may be some "contagion effect" with sus-

ceptible individuals modeling bulimic behaviors (Bruch, 1973). In view of that and in view of the possible high prevalence of the disorder, research is needed on assessment of an intervention with individuals showing early phases of the syndrome. Being able to predict who is at risk for this problem appears to hold much promise for early intervention and perhaps for primary prevention.

Reference Notes

1. Clement, P. F., & Hawkins, R. C. Pathways to bulimia: Personality correlates, prevalence, and a conceptual model. Paper presented at the 14th annual convention of the Association for the Advancement of Behavior Therapy, New York, 1980.
2. Gormally, J. Factors associated with weight loss maintenance. Paper presented at the 88th annual convention of the American Psychological Association, Montreal, 1980.
3. Hamilton, M. K., & Meade, C. J. A theoretical framework for appetite disorders in women. Paper presented at the 88th annual convention of the American Psychological Association, Montreal, 1980.
4. Hamilton, M. K., Meade, C. J. & Gelwick. B. P. Incidence and severity of eating disorders on two campuses. Paper presented at the 88th annual convention of the American Psychological Association, Montreal, 1980.
5. Loro, A. D., Jr., Binge eating in overweight populations: A clinical–behavioral description. Paper presented as part of a behavior therapy symposium, "Emotional Factors in Etiology and Treatment of Obesity," 14th annual convention of the Association for Advancement of Behavior Therapy, New York, November 1980.
6. Svendsen, D., & Cusin, J. Eating disorders in college students: Anorexia and bulimia. Paper presented at the annual meeting of the American College Health Association, San Diego, 1980.

References

American Psychiatric Association. *Diagnostic and Statistical Manual of Mental Disorders,* 3rd. ed. Washington, D.C.: American Psychiatric Association, 1980.

Barker, D. J. P., & Rose, G. *Epidemiology in Medical Practice.* London: Churchill Livingstone, 1976.

Bem, S. L. The measurement of psychological androgyny. *Journal of Consulting and Clinical Psychology*, 1974, *42*, 155–162.

Bemis, K. M. Current approaches to the etiology and treatment of anorexia nervosa. *Psychological Bulletin*, 1978, *85*, 593–617.

Ben-Tovim, D. I., Marilov, V., & Crisp, A. H. Personality and mental state (p.s.e.) within anorexia nervosa. *Journal of Psychosomatic Research*, 1979, *23*, 321–325.

Beumont, P. J. V., Abraham, S. F., & Simson, K. G. The psychosexual histories of adolescent girls and young women with anorexia nervosa. *Psychological Medicine*, 1981, *11*, 131–140.

Beumont, P. G. V., Carr, P. J., & Gelder, M. G. Plasma levels of luteinizing hormone and of immunoreactive oestrogens (oestriadol) in anorexia nervosa: Response to clomiphene citrate. *Psychological Medicine*, 1973, *4*, 219–221.

Beumont, P. J. V., George, G. C. W., & Smart, D. E. "Dieters" and "vomiters and purgers" in anorexia nervosa. *Psychological Medicine*, 1976, *6*, 617a–622.

Bliss, E. L., & Branch, C. H. H. *Anorexia Nervosa*. New York: Hoeber, 1960.

Boskind-Lodahl, M., & White, W. C., Jr. The definition and treatment of bulimia in college women—a pilot study. *Journal of the American College Health Association*, 1978, *27*, 84–86, 97.

Bruch, H. *Eating Disorders: Obesity, Anorexia and the Person Within*. New York: Basic Books, 1973.

Casper, R. C., Eckert, E. D., Halmi, K. A., Goldberg, S. C., & Davis, J. M. Bulimia: Its incidence and clinical importance in patients with anorexia nervosa. *Archives of Central Psychiatry*, 1980, *37*, 1030–1035.

Cattell, R. B., Eber, H. W., & Tatsuoka, M. M. *Handbook for the Sixteen Personality Factor Questionnaire (16 PF)*. Champaign, Ill.: Institute for Personality and Ability Testing, 1970.

Cooper, J. E., Kendall, R. E., Gurland, B. J., Sharpe, L., Copeland, J. R. M., & Simon, R. *Psychiatric Diagnosis in New York and London*. London: Oxford University Press, 1972.

Crisp, A. H., Hsu, L. K. G., & Stonehill, E. Personality, body weight and ultimate outcome in anorexia nervosa. *Journal of Clinical Psychiatry*, 1979, *40*, 332–335.

Crisp, A. H., Palmer, R. L., & Kalucy, R. S. How common is anorexia nervosa? A prevalence study. *British Journal of Psychiatry*, 1976, *128*, 549–554.

Dally, P. J. *Anorexia Nervosa*. London: Heinemann, 1969.

Davis, K. L., Quaills, B., Hollister, L. E., & Stunkard, A. J. EEG's of "binge" eaters (letter to editor). *American Journal of Psychiatry*, 1974, *131*, 1409.

Dunn, P. K., & Ondercin, P. Personality variables related to compulsive eating in college women. *Journal of Clinical Psychology*, 1981, *37*, 43–49.

Fisher, S. *Body Experience in Fantasy and Behavior.* New York: Appleton-Century-Crofts, 1970.

Garfinkel, P. E., Moldofsky, H., & Garner, D. M. Prognosis in anorexia nervosa as influenced by clinical features, treatment and self-perception. *Canadian Medical Association Journal*, 1977, *117*, 1041–1045.

Garfinkel, P. E., Moldofsky, H., & Garner, D. M. The heterogeneity of anorexia nervosa: Bulimia as a distinct subgroup. *Archives of General Psychiatry*, 1980, *37*, 1036–1040.

Garner, D. M., & Garfinkel, P. E. The Eating Attitudes Test: an index of the symptoms of anorexia nervosa. *Psychological Medicine*, 1979, *9*, 273–279.

Garner, D. M., & Garfinkel, P. E. Socio-cultural factors in the development of anorexia nervosa. *Psychological Medicine*, 1980, *10*, 647–656.

Gormally, J., Black, S., Daston, S., & Rardin, D. The assessment of binge eating severity among obese persons. *Addictive Behaviors*, 1982, *7*, 47–55.

Green, R. S., & Rau, J. H. Treatment of compulsive eating disturbances with anti-convulsant medication. *American Journal of Psychiatry*, 1974, *131*, 428–432.

Halmi, K. A. Anorexia nervosa: Demographic and clinical features in 94 cases. *Psychosomatic Medicine*, 1974, *36*, 18–25.

Hathaway, S. R., & McKinley, J. C. *Minnesota Multiphasic Personality Inventory.* New York: The Psychological Corporation, 1943, 1951, 1967, renewed 1970.

Hawkins, R. C., & Clement, P. F. Development and construct validation of a self-report measure of binge eating tendencies. *Addictive Behaviors*, 1980, *5*, 219–226.

Herman, C. P., & Polivy, J. Anxiety, restraint, and eating behavior. *Journal of Abnormal Psychology*, 1975, *84*, 666–672.

Kendall, R. E., Hall, D. J., Hailey, A., & Babigan, H. M. The epidemiology of anorexia nervosa. *Psychological Medicine*, 1973, *3*, 200–203.

Leon, G. R., Eckert, E. D., Teed, D., & Buchwald, H. Changes in body image and other psychological factors after intestinal surgery for massive obesity. *Journal of Behavioral Medicine*, 1979, *2*, 39.

Leon, G. R., Kolotkin, R., & Korgeski, G. MacAndrew Addiction Scale and other MMPI characteristics associated with obesity, anorexia and smoking behavior. *Addictive Behaviors*, 1979, *4*, 401–407.

Lindner, R. *The Fifty-Minute Hour.* New York: Bantam, 1971.

Loro, A. D., Jr., & Orleans, C. S. Binge eating in obesity: Preliminary findings and guidelines for behavioral analysis and treatment. *Addictive Behaviors*, 1981, *6*, 155–166.

MacAndrew, C. The differentiation of male alcoholic outpatients from non-alcoholic psychiatric patients by means of the MMPI. *Quarterly Journal of Studies on Alcohol,* 1965, *26,* 238–246.

Matarazzo, J. D. The interview: It's realiability and validity in psychiatric diagnosis. In B. B. Welman, (ed.), *Clinical Diagnosis of Mental Disorders.* New York: Plenum Press, 1978.

Minuchin, S. *Families and Family Therapy.* Cambridge, Mass.: Harvard University Press, 1974.

Morgan, H. G., & Russell, G. F. M. Value of family background and clinical features as predictors of long-term outcome in anorexia nervosa: Four-year follow-up of 41 patients. *Psychological Medicine,* 1975, *5,* 335–371.

Ondercin, P. Compulsive eating in college women. *Journal of College Student Personnel,* 1979, *20,* 153–157.

Palazzoli, M. P. *Anorexia Nervosa.* London: Chaucer, 1974.

Palmer, R. L. The dietary chaos syndrom: A useful new term? *British Journal of Medical Psychology,* 1979, *52,* 187–190.

Rau, J. H., & Green, J. S. Compulsive eating: A neuropsychologic approach to certain eating disorders. *Comprehensive Psychiatry,* 1975, *16,* 223–231.

Rau, J. H., & Green, R. S. Soft neurological correlates of compulsive eaters. *The Journal of Nervous and Mental Disease,* 1978, *166,* 435–437.

Russell, G. Bulimia nervosa: An ominous variant of anorexia nervosa. *Psychological Medicine,* 1979, *9,* 429–448.

Sours, J. *Starving to Death in a Sea of Objects: The Anorexia Nervosa Syndrome.* New York: Jason Aronsen, 1980.

Strober, M. The significance of bulimia in juvenile anorexia nervosa: An exploration of possible etiologic factors. *International Journal of Eating Disorders,* 1981, *1,* 28–43.

Strober, M., Goldenberg, I., Green, J., & Saxon, J. Body image disturbance in anorexia nervosa during the acute and recuperative phase. *Psychological Medicine,* 1979, *9,* 695–701.

Stunkard, A. J. Eating patterns of obese persons. *Psychiatric Quarterly,* 1959, *33,* 284–292.

Stunkard, A. J. *The Pain of Obesity.* Palo Alto, Calif.: Bell, 1976.

Weiss, T., & Levitz, L. Diphenyl-hydantion treatment of bulimia (letter to editor). *American Journal of Psychiatry,* 1976, *133,* 1093.

Williams, P., Tarnopolsky, A., & Hand, D. Case definition and case identification in psychiatric epidemiology: Review and assessment. *Psychological Medicine,* 1980, *10,* 110–114.

2

Bulimia in Anorexia Nervosa*

Paul E. Garfinkel
David M. Garner

Symptoms and Progression of Anorexia Nervosa

Anorexia nervosa is a syndrome characterized by the relentless pursuit of a thin body shape (Bruch, 1970). It is associated with an exaggerated dread of weight gain and fat, often in spite of emaciation and to the detriment of other physical and psychological aspects of the individual's life. The person with anorexia nervosa begins dieting in an attempt to lose weight. Over time, achievement of ever-decreasing weight becomes a sign of mastery, control, and virtue. The drive for a thinner shape is secondary to concerns about control and/or fears about consequences of achieving a mature shape. The pursuit of thinness becomes necessary for the individual to feel a sense of mastery or control over her body. It is our view that anorexia nervosa is a syndrome that is the product of forces interacting among the individual, her family, and culture. What is known about the pathogenesis of the illness and its perpetuation will not be reviewed here but has been described elsewhere (Garfinkel & Garner, 1982).

*This work was funded by the Ontario Mental Health Foundation (Research Grant 810/81–83). Dr. Garner is a research scholar, Medical Research Council (Canada). The authors wish to acknowledge M. O'Shaughnessey for her technical assistance.

The anorexic's pursuit of thinness begins with dieting, like that of many adolescents, but it evolves from roots that antedate the diet. Typically, the patient has been slightly overweight and may begin to diet in response to comments about her size from family members, peers, or a boyfriend. A particular part of her body (e.g., her stomach, thighs, or buttocks) may feel too large. The initial intent is to "lose a few pounds." At first she will cut out sweets, desserts, and high-calorie snacks; this often is met with approval by family and friends, particularly in our health- and nutrition-conscious society where this behavior has come to represent being more "in control" in a more general sense. However, when her weight goal has been attained, she still feels somewhat overweight and then gradually decides to further restrict her intake of foods. Usually this takes place over several months and goes unnoticed by those around her. By the time others do notice it, she is stubbornly refusing to eat normal amounts of food. Usually the intake is limited to about 600 to 800 calories per day. There is some variability in what these young women eat, but in general, they will select high-protein, low-carbohydrate foods that are presumed to be low in calories. Many patients will develop extreme rigidity in their eating habits in an effort to control their weight.

While anorexia nervosa patients have an overriding drive to be thin, they often do not offer any explanation for this; they merely state that they will feel better if they are thinner. The drive for thinness is ego-syntonic and is not viewed as abnormal or something they would like to see changed (Theander, 1970). Central to the concept of the distorted drive for thinness in anorexia nervosa is a disturbance in body image that has been described clearly by Bruch (1962): In spite of the severe and progressive weight loss, many anorexics are unaware of their emaciated state. They may deny several aspects of the disorder but especially the fact that their changed bodies are not healthy or beautiful. The disturbance of body image is an overvalued idea and is of near or actual delusional proportions. As described by Garner and Garfinkel (1981), it can take several specific forms: (1) most commonly patients either deny the extent of the weight loss or feel that, while they have lost weight generally, a particular body part remains far too large; (2) strong feelings of self-loathing are the usual emotional component to the body image; and (3) some patients may display a fleeting emotional reaction of pleasure toward their new, thinner shape.

According to Bruch (1973) the lack of body awareness goes beyond the recognition of body size and extends to a variety of inner feelings, including fatigue. Instead of being exhausted while starving, these young women enjoy boundless energy until late in the illness. Gull (1874) wrote, "It hardly seemed possible that a body so wasted could undergo the exercise which seemed so agreeable" (reprinted in Kaufman & Heiman, 1964, p. 133). The exercise is, in part, directed to burning up calories and losing further weight. As with the dieting, however, with time the exercise eventually becomes an issue of self-discipline; anorexics cannot allow themselves to miss even one day of the exact amount of self-prescribed activity.

While the term "anorexia" implies a loss of appetite, this does not usually occur until very late in the starvation process (Garfinkel, 1974; Theander, 1970). Hunger may be absent if the patient fasts totally and ketosis develops (Dally, 1969). Most patients report normal awareness of hunger but express terror at giving in to the impulse to eat. Because of the intense hunger some patients are driven to misuse appetite suppressants such as amphetamine or other "diet pills" or drink large quantities of fluid. Others reinterpret their hungry state as a sign of their self-discipline. By contrast, satiety perception is extremely distorted. Patients report severe bloating, nausea, and distension after eating even small amounts of food, and they do not feel rested or satisfied after eating, as most people do. Instead, there is usually a marked sense of guilt for having "given in" to the biological urge to eat. It is not yet certain how much, if any, of this satiety disturbance is related to altered gastrointestinal function subsequent to starvation. Constipation is a regular feature due to the restricted food intake and starvation, which in turn leads to further symptoms of bloating and reduced dietary intake. Some patients begin to treat themselves with laxatives or enemas. From this point, others develop the idea of using laxatives to prevent the absorption of foods and thus prevent further weight gain.

Amenorrhea is a constant feature in female patients with anorexia nervosa. The amenorrhea indicates the complexity of many of the anorexic's symptoms: It appears largely, but not entirely, to be the product of weight loss and starvation. It has been observed repeatedly that, for many women (70%), amenorrhea develops shortly after the onset of the weight loss (Fries, 1977). However, in a significant proportion (estimates vary between 7 and 24%) amenorrhea actually appears to precede the weight loss (Fries, 1977). At present it is not known whether the patients' emotional distress or other independent hypothalamic dysfunction triggers the amenorrhea (Garfinkel, Brown, & Darby, 1981).

Bulimic Anorexics

A large subgroup of anorexics alternate between not eating and bulimia, a condition that has been recognized for a long time. In 1874 Gull wrote, "Occasionally for a day or two the appetite was voracious" (reprinted in Kaufman & Heiman, 1964, p. 133). The bulimic patients are usually more distressed by their behavior. They alternate between an intense sense of self-control, while dieting, and a sense of total lack of control and self-loathing, when bulimic. When busy they usually restrict food intake, but during solitary leisure time they will overeat to the point of exhaustion. During the bulimic episode, foods that are "forbidden" (but not disliked) by the self-prescribed dieter are consumed ravenously: rich cakes, desserts, and ice cream.

Enormous quantities of food may be eaten during these periods; dozens of doughnuts may be consumed at one sitting. Following the binge some patients will restrict their food intake for several days while others will begin to vomit or misuse laxatives for the purpose of preventing weight increases. The bulimia–vomiting cycle may last for many hours, and an individual may vomit several times over the course of one evening. A considerable amount of money may be required to buy these foods, and some patients begin to steal to support this behavior. The bulimic patients have many characteristics that differentiate them from restrictive anorexics. In our view, they represent a distinct subtype of the anorexia nervosa syndrome (Garfinkel, Moldofsky, & Garner, 1980), and the evidence for this will be developed throughout this chapter.

Subtypes of Anorexia:
A Review of the Research

There have been previous attempts at distinguishing subtypes of anorexia nervosa (Dally, 1969); however, these earlier classifications relied heavily on whether or not hunger was retained and on personality and other features that were often quite inconsistent. More recently Beumont and his group (Beumont, 1977; Beumont,

George, & Smart, 1976) pursued an earlier suggestion by Meyer (1961) that clinical differences existed between those anorexia nervosa patients who lost weight by restricting food intake (dieters) from those in whom vomiting is a major symptom (vomiters and purgers). All female patients seen by Beumont and colleagues over a two-year period who met rigorous criteria for primary anorexia nervosa were reviewed. A number of clinical differences were observed between the groups; specifically, the vomiters and purgers were likely to have been obese premorbidly, to be more sexually active, and to have histrionic personalities. When a subgroup of these patients was studied using psychometric tests (Beumont, 1977), both groups were observed to be highly obsessional, but the dieters were characterized by introversion. Vomiting, which is a poor prognostic sign in anorexia nervosa (Garfinkel, Moldofsky, & Garner, 1977), may be related to the duration of illness; that is, patients may present first with caloric restriction and only as the illness becomes chronic will they vomit or abuse laxatives. While this occasionally occurs, the differentiating features between groups that Beumont documented, with regard to premorbid obesity and sexual activity, predate the onset of anorexic symptoms.

While the presence or absence of vomiting may be used to subclassify anorexia nervosa, the Pathology of Eating Group (Garrow, Crisp, Jordan, Meyer, Russell, Silverstone, Stunkard, & Van Itallie, 1975) distinguished one group of chronic anorexia nervosa patients that seemed to display many aspects of addiction; that is, they habitually overate and vomited large quantities of foods, usually in secret. They retained a terror of weight gain and had a need to control their weight, yet they had a psychological craving for food. Metabolic consequences of their vomiting and diarrhea (e.g., fluid and potassium depletion) were thought to further stimulate their ingestive behavior, thereby perpetuating this cycle. Other features of this group included use of drugs known to facilitate weight loss and the use of alcohol for sedative effects. They frequently smoked to excess, possibly to control appetite. No data were provided to support the description of this group or whether the group could be discriminated satisfactorily from anorexic patients who tended to restrict their caloric intake and never engage in bulimia. Similarly, Boskind-Lodahl (1976) described women with bulimia and called them "bulimarexic," although clinical features to distinguish them from bulimic and restricting anorexic patients were not provided.

Russell (1979) reported recently on a group of 30 patients with

(1) an irresistible urge to overeat, (2) followed by self-induced vomiting or purging, and (3) a morbid fear of becoming fat. He used the term "bulimia nervosa" to describe these individuals; Russell's detailed account stressed the close association between bulimia and vomiting or laxative misuse and reviewed the possible complications of this disorder. The metabolic and emotional consequences were observed to differ between bulimic and restricting anorexics. In particular, hypokalemia, impaired renal function, convulsions, and depression were more common in this bulimic group. While he recognized a core set of features to this disorder, he suggested that it was premature to consider this a distinct syndrome except in its most narrow sense of shared signs and symptoms. He felt, however, that this syndrome did not imply a common etiology; in fact, he stressed that the etiology was largely unknown. Of the 30 patients studied, 24 met his criteria for a past history of anorexia nervosa and six displayed these symptoms without any history of weight loss and therefore could not be classified as having anorexia nervosa. This led him to conclude that bulimia nervosa might be a disturbance with different causes, one of which is anorexia nervosa. At present it is not known how commonly bulimics have had frank episodes of anorexia nervosa, since Russell's patients were probably self-selected to overrepresent anorexics, given his longstanding interest in the illness.

In a large, multihospital collaborative study of anorexia nervosa (Casper, Eckert, Halmi, Goldberg, & Davis, 1980), 105 patients were divided into two groups, according to the presence or absence of bulimia, and then compared on a variety of clinical, developmental, and psychosocial parameters. Forty-seven percent of the sample had been bulimic periodically, 16 percent on at least a daily basis. The bulimic patients were significantly different: clinically they were more likely to vomit than dieting restricters, to admit to a strong appetite, and to engage in compulsive stealing. Socially, the bulimic patients were said to be more outgoing, more interested in sex, and to have had some heterosexual experience. On psychological tests, they displayed higher depression and somatization scores. Bulimic patients also tended to be older; they clustered in the over-18-year-old group, but mean ages at onset did not differ between the groups (Casper et al., 1980; Halmi, Casper, Eckert, Goldberg, & Davis, 1979). With regard to this last point, these investigators suggested that bulimia may therefore be a sign of chronicity or that a "certain degree of . . . maturation is a necessary requirement for bulimia to develop."

Current Research by Garfinkel and Garner

In a similar effort to determine whether these anorexic patients who repeatedly overingested foods ("bulmic") were a distinct subgroup within the primary anorexia nervosa syndrome, we reviewed our consultation files on all our anorexic subjects who met criteria that have been described elsewhere (Garfinkel & Garner, 1982). We were careful to exclude nonanorexic patients with bulimia, as bulimia may exist in obese or other nonanorexic disorders.

From 1970 to 1981, we had consulted on or treated 335 patients who met these criteria, who were known to be either bulimic or not bulimic at the time of consultation, and whose data from these consultations were coded using a standard format. This provided the clinical base of information for each patient. Bulimia was defined as an abnormal increase in one's desire to eat, with episodes of excessive ingestion of large quantities of food which the patient viewed as ego-alien and beyond her control. Bulimic episodes were characterized by the eating of large quantities of food, usually high in carbohydrates. This usually was done secretly when the individual was alone. The duration of the eating was highly variable but could take several hours or more. Crisp (1980) has estimated that the mean daily caloric intake of bulimics is between 4000 and 5000 calories per day, but it is not uncommon to see patients whose ingestion during bulimic periods far exceeds this.

We have collated data from these 335 patients, who consulted with us over a period of several years and who were seen during various phases of their illness and with varying degrees of chronicity (on average, about 4 years after the onset of amenorrhea). Of the total sample, 178 experienced bulimia at the time of initial consultation and 157 did not. Of the bulimic patients, 50 percent experienced episodes of excessive ingestion of food at least on a daily basis. Both groups of patients showed similar social characteristics, with the upper and middle social classes being overrepresented in comparison with the general population. There were no differences between the bulimics and restrictors in age of onset, marital status, sex distribution, or religion.

Duration of illness did not differ significantly from the findings of Casper et al. (1980). This suggests that bulimia for our series is not simply a manifestation of chronicity. Of patients who developed bulimia, the onset of bulimic episodes occurred at varying phases of the disorder. In some patients, it preceded or was coincidental with the weight loss. For those patients, on whom these data were available in an earlier study, we found that the mean time of onset of bulimia was 19.2 ± 8.0 (m ± SEM) months after the onset of dieting (Garfinkel et al., 1980). Russell's (1979) "bulimia nervosa" patients also developed bulimia relatively early after the onset of the dieting behavior; in 18 out of the 30 patients the overeating commenced within one year of beginning the diet. Similarly, 14 of Dally's 23 patients who were bulimic developed this complication within 18 months of beginning to diet (Dally, 1969).

There were major differences between our bulimic and restricting groups on weight-related clinical features (see Table 2–1). Bulimic patients had a history of weighing more; in fact, over 35 percent were obese premorbidly. By contrast, obesity was less common in the restricters. Similarly, bulimic patients weighed significantly more at the time of our initial contact and at their minimum weights. Casper et al. (1980), however, were unable to find premorbid- or minimal-weight differences in their sample. In agreement with our weight data, both Russell (1979) and Beumont (1977) reported higher than expected weights in their bulimic and "vomiter-purger" samples.

The bulimic and restricter groups studied in our series showed similarities as well as clear differences in the methods they used to lose and maintain a low weight. The restricters avoided meals

Table 2-1. Weight-Related Clinical Features in Two Groups of Anorexia Nervosa Patients.

	Bulimic (N = 178)	Restricting (N = 157)	Level of Statistical Significance*
Maximum premorbid weight (kg)	62.1 ± 1.0	55.9 ± 1.0	$p < 0.001$
Percent of average	104.8 ± 1.2	96.6 ± 1.3	$p < 0.001$
Premorbid obesity	36%	23%	$p < 0.02$
Minimum weight (kg)	40.9 ± 0.6	37.3 ± 0.6	$p < 0.001$
Percent of average	69.5 ± 0.9	63.8 ± 0.9	$p < 0.001$
Weight at consultation (kg)	47.6 ± 0.8	40.5 ± 0.8	$p < 0.001$
Percent of average	80.3 ± 1.0	69.2 ± 1.0	$p < 0.001$
Height (cm)	163.4 ± 0.5	162.5 ± 0.6	NS
Menarche (yrs)	12.8 ± 0.2	12.8 ± 0.1	NS

*χ^2

whenever possible, and when this was not possible, selected low-carbohydrate foods. They also hid foods frequently and engaged in vigorous compulsive exercising aimed at burning calories. The bulimic patients pursued all of these behaviors but also frequently vomited and misused laxatives. Vomiting was present in 62.8 percent of bulimics, versus 20.3 percent of the restricters ($p < 0.001$). Laxative misuse for the deliberate purpose of weight loss was surprisingly common in both groups but much more so with bulimics (49.4%) than restricters (23.4%) ($p < 0.01$). Diuretic misuse occurred in 9.4 percent of bulimics, versus only 2.6 percent of restricters ($p < 0.01$). Similarly, both Russell (1979) and Casper et al. (1980) have reported that their bulimic patients relied heavily on devices other than starvation for weight control.

The bulimic groups differed from the restricters on a variety of impulsive behaviors (see Table 2–2). Bulimics had misused street drugs and alcohol and had stolen significantly more frequently than restricters. Suicide attempts and deliberate acts of self-inflicted injury without suicide intent were more common in the bulimic group. Lability of mood was more frequent in bulimics, as determined in the mental status examination. These findings are supported by Russell (1979), who described subjective depression to be common in his bulimic patients; 11 of his 30 patients also had attempted suicide.

Sexual and social characteristics of the two groups also were different. The restricting group tended to be relatively isolated and formed few friendships. Less than one-fifth of these individuals were involved in social relationships and found them satisfying. Bulimics less commonly were isolated and more frequently en-

Table 2-2. Impulse-Related Clinical Features in Two Groups of Anorexia Nervosa Patients.

	Bulimic (N = 178)	Restricting (N = 157)	Level of Statistical Significance*
Street drug use	30.0%	12.9%	$p < 0.01$
Alcohol use (weekly or more)	18.1%	8.7%	$p < 0.05$
Stealing	16.6%	0.7%	$p < 0.001$
Self-mutilation	9.4%	2.7%	$p < 0.05$
Suicide attempts	20.6%	7.4%	$p < 0.01$

*χ^2

gaged in transient and nonsatisfying relationships. Patients in the bulimic group were more sexually active and more likely to use oral contraceptives; however, they did not describe their sexual relationships as pleasant. Crisp (1967) had observed that this group "rushed into one relationship after another . . . in the mistaken belief that they would then feel secure and wanted" (p. 128). He noted that their sexual relationships frequently were characterized by fellatio and that this was followed by vomiting. Russell (1979) also noted the increased social and sexual behavior of "bulimia nervosa" patients, as have Beumont et al. (1976) and Beumont, Abraham, and Simpson (1981) in their studies of anorexics who vomit.

The family histories of our patients showed that the mothers of bulimic patients more frequently were obese (47% versus 30% in the restricting group; $p < 0.05$). No difference was found in the history of parental mental illness between the groups. Previously, using these clinical factors, a discriminant function analysis had been found to be accurate in predicting group membership in 79.2 percent of the subjects (Garfinkel et al. 1980); that is, 85.9 percent of restricters and 72.4 percent of bulimics were classified accurately. These data indicated that there were real differences between the groups.

Data such as these that rely on historical information must be treated with some caution. It must be recognized that patients with anorexia nervosa frequently deny aspects of their illness or are poor historians. Furthermore, these results were obtained at one point in time (our first consultation); it is possible that further symptoms may appear in any given patient as the illness evolves. Clearly a patient who displayed no bulimia or vomiting when first seen may develop these symptoms later. The fact that we have seen each of these patients ourselves, that we have utilized a standard assessment technique and independent raters to extract the relevant data, and that most patients were seen after they had been ill for several years may help to reduce these deficiencies. A further problem with all studies by people who are particularly "interested" in a disorder is that of the referral or selection bias. Our sample is not necessarily representative, since we only investigate subjects referred to us. In large measure our sample is composed of rather chronically ill people who often have failed in therapies elsewhere. In this regard, bulimics—in particular, severely ill bulimics—are likely overrepresented. Just how common bulimia is in anorexia nervosa is not known. While studies such as those by Casper et al. (1980), Hsu, Crisp, and Harding (1979), and ourselves report figures of 44 to 55 percent, these are highly selected samples. Other investigations have found bulimia to be less frequent; for example, Theander (1970) found 16 percent, and Rollins and Piazza (1978) found 27 percent. Crisp and colleagues' (1980) estimate of bulimia occurring at some point in the illness in about 30 percent of anorexic patients is probably reasonable, if one discounts the selection biases we have been discussing.

Differences between Restricting Anorexics and Bulimics

In spite of the limitations of this type of study, significant differences between bulimic and restricting anorexics have been observed. In our patients these differences were in the areas of premorbid obesity, weight-, food- and impulse-related problems during the illness, and maternal obesity, all associated to a greater degree with the bulimic patients than with restricting anorexics. Taken together, these characteristics suggest a specific group of women who are predisposed to develop the bulimic type of anorexia nervosa. These women frequently have been premorbidly obese, and their mothers also have been obese, as had been suggested by Garrow et al. (1975). The 47-percent prevalence for obesity in our bulimic patients' mothers is even more striking when one considers the reduced frequency of obesity in North American women of upper social classes relative to other classes (Stunkard, 1975). Premorbid obesity and a family history of obesity highlight the conflicts these individuals face. As Ellen West described it, "Fate wanted me to be heavy and strong but I want to be thin and delicate" (Binswanger, 1944).

Stordy, Marks, Kalucy, and Crisp (1977) have shown recently that the thermic response to a carbohydrate meal differs in anorexics who were previously obese: they gain weight more readily. To achieve their desired degree of thinness they must inflict greater dietary restraint upon themselves or resort to vomiting and laxatives, but they never reach as low a weight as other anorexics. Others may use pharmacologic agents such as amphetamines to reduce appetite, or diuretics to reduce bloating. For example, Ellen West misused thyroid pills to the point of developing hyperthyroidism.

Bulimic patients often are sexually active but usually feel misused and unable to enjoy sex. They often report that a feeling of being out of control, sexually, exacerbates the bulimia. As in their eating and other areas of self-control, they do not know "in betweens" in sexual behavior. Moreover, their moods are labile and frequently feel out of control. They behave in harmful, impulsive ways; for example, 20 percent of our bulimic patients previously had attempted suicide and 16 percent were involved in stealing. Crisp, Hsu, and Harding (1980) have reported that stealing occurred in 14 out of 102 anorexic patients seen by them; in 13 of the 14 cases stealing occurred in conjunction with bulimia. Abuse of alcohol by some bulimic anorexics, observed in our study, also has been described by others (Brosin, 1941; Casper et al., 1980).

We found that 9 percent of the bulimics previously had engaged in self-mutilation. Several other authors have observed the association of self-mutilation, particularly genital self-mutilation, with disturbances in eating (French & Nelson, 1972; Goldney & Simpson, 1975; Rosenthal, Rinzler, Wallsh, & Klausner, 1972; Simpson, 1975). For example, in Rosenthal and colleagues' (1972) series of 24 wrist-cutting patients, 15 described either compulsive overeating or severe anorexia or both, while 18 of 24 self-mutilators in Simpson's (1975) study experienced such eating problems, versus only two subjects in a control group. Goldney and Simpson (1975) went so far as to link the occurrence of genital self-mutilation, eating disturbance, and hysterical personality under the title of "Caenis syndrome." There is no clear rationale for delineating such a syndrome, but these symptoms all are indicative of the degree of disturbance in psychosexual identity experienced by this group of patients. These studies highlight the frequency of disturbances in eating behavior, and possibly of anorexia nervosa, in groups of self-mutilators.

Selvini-Palazzoli (1974) has described differences in psychological characteristics between bulimics and restricting anorexics. Using Rorschach test responses, she observed that her bulimic patients displayed serious disorders in thought and communication not present in restricters. She also felt that families of bulimics, like the patients themselves, were more chaotic, demonstrating "psychotic confusion, violence and a complete breakdown of family communication" (p. 205). These findings, however, were impressionistic, and Bruch (1973) was unable to confirm such differences using a similar scoring technique. With regard to the families of bulimics, Crisp, Harding, and McGuinness (1974) described excessive obsessionality in the fathers. Their standards for performance and self-control were considered to be important factors in this group's bulimia. However, controlled studies comparing the family characteristics of bulimics and restricting anorexics have not been conducted yet.

On psychometric tests the bulimic patients display differentiating characteristics. These relate largely to their reduced impulse control, increased extroversion, and mood variability. Casper et al. (1980) administered a variety of psychometric tests to their large sample. These included the MMPI, the Hopkins Symptom Checklist, and the Raskin Mood Scale. Bulimic patients experienced increased anxiety, depression, and guilt and reported more somatic preoccupation. Those patients who were bulimic every day displayed more significant psychopathology as evidenced by elevations on the MMPI subscales for schizophrenia, depression, psychopathic deviance, paranoia, and psychasthenia. Strober (1980) studied a smaller number of young subjects (all less than 17) and found "bingeing–vomiters" had reduced self-control but were more psychologically minded and flexible on the California Personality Inventory. In this small sample, restricting and bulimic groups were observed to share a variety of psychological features. By contrast, Stonehill and Crisp (1977) and Hsu and Crisp (1980) administered the Crown-Crisp Experiential Index and found that anorexic patients who vomited had significantly more psychopathological symptoms, especially depression, than the restricting group. This finding persisted when patients were retested on follow-up. Finally, we recall Beumont's (1977) findings regarding increased extroversion in vomiting patients, which have been described already.

We also have administered a series of psychometric tests to our group of anorexic patients; the details of these have been described elsewhere (Garner & Garfinkel, 1981). Body-size estimation, using a distorting photograph technique (Garner, Garfinkel, Stancer, & Moldofsky, 1976), was found to differ significantly in the bulimic group with the most pronounced symptoms (see Table 2–3). Of the 197 patients tested, 36 percent were "marked overestimators" (> +10%) of their body sizes. This degree of overestimation was significantly more common in people who were bulimic, and as the frequency of bulimic episodes increased, so did the distortion in body image. Using other techniques to assess body size, patients with cycles of bulimia and vomiting, when compared with restricting anorexics, were found to be more inaccurate in self-estimates of their body sizes (Button, Fransella, & Slade, 1977). They also showed more severe and refractory body image disturbances (Strober, Goldenberg, Green, & Saxon, 1979), which may be indicative of the severity of psychopathology.

Table 2-3. Body-Size Estimates in Two Groups of Anorexia Nervosa Patients Using a Distorting Photograph Technique.

	*Body Size Estimates**	
	Greater than +10%	*Less than +10%*
Restricting Anorexics	26 (36%)	62 (49%)
Bulimic anorexics		
bulimia less than weekly	2 (3%)	11 (9%)
bulimia weekly but not daily	12 (17%)	25 (20%)
bulimia daily	31 (44%)	28 (22%)
Total	71 (36%)	126 (64%)

*$p < 0.01$ (x^2 with 3 degrees of freedom); the rationale for the division of body-size estimates into these groups has been given elsewhere (Garner & Garfinkel, 1981)

Our bulimic anorexics also display other significant differences from the restricters. For example, when asked to estimate their preference for ideal body size on the distorting photograph technique, they preferred to be much thinner ($-5.5 \pm 1.2\%$ versus $+4.2 \pm 1.4\%$ for restricters; $p < 0.001$), but this may reflect in part their heavier weights. In keeping with both the body-size overestimation and desire for thinness they display significantly more body dissatisfaction (Berscheid, Walster, & Hohrnstedt, 1973) than restricters (76.1 ± 2.0 versus 70.3 ± 1.9; $p < 0.05$). They also feel more externally controlled as measured by Reid and Ware's (1974) three-factor Locus of Control Scale (17.4 ± 0.6 versus 15.1 ± 0.6; $p < 0.01$), and this is reflected largely in their sense of a lack of self-control (5.8 ± 2 versus 4.4 ± 0.2; $p < 0.001$). Bulimics' subjective sense of depression is also evident by their elevated scores on the Beck Depression Inventory (26.6 ± 1.6 versus 21.8 ± 1.8; $p < 0.05$). Other tests we have utilized, including the Hopkins Symptom Checklist (Derogatis, Lipman, & Rickels, 1974), the Janis Field Scale (Janis & Field, 1959), and the EAT (Garner & Garfinkel, 1979) do not differentiate between these two anorexic groups. As a whole, these data suggest that the bulimic anorexics display greater psychopathology characterized by body image disturbances, subjective sense of feeling out of control, and depression. These characteristics may not necessarily precede the bulimic state but may be sequelae to it.

The fact that bulimics display certain ominous clinical features, have metabolic complications due to electrolyte losses, and appear to be more psychologically disturbed than restricting ano-

rectics may be reflected in the repeated observation of a poor outcome on follow-up (Crisp, Kalucy, Lacey, & Harding, 1977; Garfinkel et al., 1977; Morgan & Russell, 1975). Bulimic anorexics experience a more chronic course to their illness than do restricters.
While the course of anorexia nervosa is influenced by different
variables (Garfinkel & Garner, 1982), the different responses of
bulimic and restricting anorexics to treatment further emphasize
their different nature.

Similarities between Restricting Anorexics and Bulimics

Although there are differences, the two groups share common features. In particular, the vigorous pursuit of a thin body, regardless
of weight, is similar in both groups. Ellen West (a bulimic) described
typical anorexic concerns: "My thoughts are exclusively concerned
with my body, my eating, my laxatives. And to be thin becomes my
life's ideal" (quoted in Lifton, 1979, p. 258). Anorexic women, like
most women in our culture, have a strong drive to appear thin;
however, the bulimic group partly because of their constitutional or
developmental predisposition to obesity and partly because of their
personality characteristics and ego deficits deal with this drive in an
extreme fashion, by alternating bouts of starvation and bulimia.
Other factors probably contribute to the presence of bulimia. Crisp
(1967) suggests bulimia often occurs first when a patient is forced to
gain weight rapidly, rather than through a process of gradual desensitization to her body size. He has suggested that the drive to
bulimia increases with the duration of carbohydrate restriction.
Similarly, Selvini-Palazzoli (1974) suggests that bulimia often may
result from iatrogenic factors, for example, force-feeding in a setting
providing inadequate psychological support. Bulimia also has been
reported as a consequence of leukotomy (Crisp, 1967) and tricyclic
antidepressant therapy (Kendler, 1978) with a small number of restricting patients.

Bulimia without Anorexia Nervosa

While our data indicate that bulimia patients with anorexia nervosa can be differentiated from restricting anorexics, not all people
with bulimia have anorexia nervosa. For example, Nogami and

Yabana (1977) described three groups of patients with what they termed Kibarashi-gui (binge eating). Only one group had anorexia nervosa. Other groups consisted of patients who were chiefly (1) neurotic and depressed and (2) borderline or actually schizophrenic. Although vomiting after overeating could be observed among members of all three groups, they felt that habitual voluntary vomiting was seen only among the anorexic group. We however, have seen self-induced vomiting in patients with somatization disorders; therefore, this criterion cannot be used to separate bulimic individuals with anorexia nervosa from others. Nogami and Yabana (1977) reported that the bulimia in the neurotic group was a transient stress-related phenomenon and in the schizophrenia group usually also transient and part of a psychotic clinical picture; only in the anorexic group did the bulimia run a chronic course. We do not agree that the duration of bulimia is a distinguishing feature; however, bulimia clearly can be a manifestation of a variety of illnesses, including many organic brain diseases.

At present the distinction between bulimia with anorexia nervosa and bulimia in the absence of anorexia nervosa is based purely on clinical descriptive criteria: (1) whether the individual's preoccupation is with body shape or not and (2) the presence of weight loss and of associated psychobiological features (Garfinkel & Garner, 1982). Palmer (1979) recently has addressed the diagnostic problem by coining the term "dietary chaos syndrome" to describe a group of individuals who may or may not have had a previous diagnosis of anorexia nervosa. According to Palmer (1979), the features of this syndrome include (1) a grossly disturbed pattern of eating (abstinence, vomiting, bulimia, etc.), (2) a preoccupation with eating and food and sometimes with weight that overrides other thoughts (the impulse to eat is experienced as out of control), and (3) a body weight that may change more than a few kilograms in hours or days in response to the balance of intake and output.

Although this syndrome may be associated with anorexia nervosa, this is not always the case. At times it may occur without a history of weight loss and amenorrhea. This description essentially corresponds to that of *DSM-III*'s definition of bulimia, with the addition of depressive moods and self-deprecating thoughts following episodes of binge eating (APA, 1980). However, *DSM-III* excludes all anorexic patients within the bulimia diagnosis, as it does when the bulimia is symptomatic of schizophrenia. Both Palmer and the authors of *DSM-III* appear to be responding to a need to describe a group of patients who do not fit previous diagnostic categories. While we agree with the need for such a diagnosis, several important questions remain unanswered. First, we need more information about how common such behavior is in a nonclinical population and how commonly bulimia is present independently of anorexia nervosa. Second, how do those bulimic patients without the core features of anorexia nervosa differ psychopathologically from those with anorexia nervosa? Are they merely individuals who never lose much weight and whose major preoccupation has shifted from body size to control of food intake but otherwise resemble anorexics, or are they fundamentally different from bulimic anorexics?

References

American Psychiatric Association. *Diagnostic and Statistical Manual of Mental Disorders,* 3rd ed. Washington, D.C.: American Psychiatric Association, 1980.

Berscheid, E., Walster, E., & Hohrnstedt, G. The happy American body: A survey report. *Psychology Today,* 1973, November, 119–131.

Beumont, P. J. V. Further categorization of patients with anorexia nervosa. *Australian and New Zealand Journal of Psychiatry,* 1977, *11,* 223–226.

Beumont, P. J. V., Abraham, S. F., & Simpson, K. G. The psychosexual histories of adolescent girls and young women with anorexia nervosa. *Psychological Medicine,* 1981, *11,* 131–140.

Beumont, P. J. V., George, G. C. W., & Smart, D. E. "Dieters" and "vomiters and purgers" in anorexia nervosa. *Psychological Medicine,* 1976, *6,* 617–622.

Binswanger, L. Der Fall Ellen West Schweiz. *Archives of Neurology and Psychiatry,* 1944, *54,* 69–117.

Boskind-Lodahl, M. Cinderella's step-sisters: A feminist perspective on anorexia nervosa and bulimia. *Signs: Journal of Women, Culture, and Society,* 1976, *2,* 342–356.

Brosin, H. W. Anorexia nervosa; case report. *Journal of Clinical Endocrinology,* 1941, *1,* 269–271.

Bruch, H. Perceptual and conceptual disturbances in anorexia nervosa. *Psychosomatic Medicine,* 1962, *24,* 187–194.

Bruch, H. Instinct and interpersonal experience. *Comparative Psychiatry,* 1970, *11,* 495–506.

Bruch, H. *Eating Disorders.* New York: Basic Books, 1973.

Button, E. J., Fransella, F., & Slade, P. D. A reappraisal of body perception disturbance in anorexia nervosa. *Psychological Medicine,* 1977, *7,* 235–243.

Casper, R. C., Eckert, E. D., Halmi, K. A., Goldberg, S. C., & Davis, J. M. Bulimia: Its incidence and clinical importance in patients with anorexia nervosa. *Archives of General Psychiatry,* 1980, *37,* 1030–1034.

Crisp, A. H. Anorexia Nervosa: *Let Me Be,* New York: Grune and Stratton, 1980.

Crisp, A. H. The possible significance of some behavioral correlates of weight and carbohydrate intake. *Journal of Psychosomatic Research,* 1967, *2,* 117–131.

Crisp, A. H., Harding, B., & McGuinness, B. Anorexia Nervosa. Psychoneurotic characteristics of parents. A qualitative study. *Journal of Psychosomatic Research,* 1974, *18,* 167–173.

Crisp, A. H., Hsu, L. K. G., & Harding, B. The starving hoarder and voracious spender: Stealing in anorexia nervosa. *Journal of Psychosomatic Research,* 1980, *24,* 225–231.

Crisp, A. H., Kalucy, R. S., Lacey, J. H., & Harding, B. The long-term prognosis in anorexia nervosa: Some factors predictive of outcome. In R. Vigersky (ed.), *Anorexia Nervosa.* New York: Raven Press, 1977.

Dally, P. *Anorexia Nervosa.* London: William Heinemann, 1969.

Derogatis, L., Lipman, R., & Rickels, D. The Hopkins Symptom Checklist (HSCL): A self-report symptom inventory. *Behavioral Science,* 1974, *19,* 1–15.

French, A. P., & Nelson, H. L. Genital self-mutilation in women. *Archives of General Psychiatry,* 1972, *27,* 618–620.

Fries, H. Studies on secondary amenorrhea, anorectic behaviour and body image perception: Importance for the early recognition of anorexia nervosa. In R. Vigersky (ed.), *Anorexia Nervosa.* New York: Raven Press, 1977.

Garfinkel, P. E. Perception of hunger and satiety in anorexia nervosa. *Psychological Medicine,* 1974, *4,* 309–315.

Garfinkel, P. E., Brown, G. M., & Darby, P. L. The psychoendocrinology of anorexia nervosa. *International Journal of Mental Health* 1981, *9,* 162–193.

Garfinkel, P. E., & Garner, D. M. *Anorexia Nervosa: A Multidimensional Perspective,* New York: Brunner/Mazel, 1982.

Garfinkel, P. E. Moldofsky, H., & Garner, D. M. The outcome of anorexia nervosa: Significance of clinical features, body image and behavior modification. In R. Vigersky (ed.), *Anorexia Nervosa.* New York: Raven Press, 1977.

Garfinkel, P. E., Moldofsky, H., & Garner, D. M. The heterogeneity of anorexia nervosa: Bulimia as a distinct subgroup. *Archives of General Psychiatry,* 1980, *37,* 1036–1040.

Garner, D. M., & Garfinkel, P. E. The Eating Attitudes Test: An index of the symptoms of anorexia nervosa. *Psychological Medicine,* 1979, *9,* 273–279.

Garner, D. M., & Garfinkel, P. E. Body image in anorexia nervosa: Measurement, theory and clinical implications. *International Journal of Psychiatry and Medicine,* 1981, *12,* 263–284.

Garner, D. M., Garfinkel, P. E., Stancer, H. C., & Moldofsky, H. Body image disturbances in anorexia nervosa and obesity. *Psychosomatic Medicine,* 1976, *58,* 317–336.

Garrow, J. S., Crisp, A. H., Jordan, H. A., Meyer, J. E., Russell, G. F. M., Silverstone, T., Stunkard, A. J., & Van Itallie, T. B. Pathology of eating, group report. In T. Silverstone (ed.), *Dahlem Konferenzen, Life Sciences Research Report 2.* Berlin: 1975.

Goldney, R. D., & Simpson, I. G. Female genital self-mutilation, dysorexia and hysterical personality: The Caenis syndrome. *Canadian Psychiatric Association Journal,* 1975, *20,* 435–441.

Gull, W. W. Anorexia nervosa. *Trans Clin Soc* (London) 1874, *7,* 22–28. Reprinted in Kaufman, R. M., & Heiman, M. (ed.), *Evolution of Psychosomatic Concepts. Anorexia Nervosa: A Paradigm.* New York: International University Press, 1964.

Halmi, K. A., Casper, R. C., Eckert, E. D., Goldberg, S. C., & Davis, J. M. Unique features associated with age of onset of anorexia nervosa. *Psychiatric Research,* 1979, *1,* 209–215.

Hsu, L. K. G., & Crisp, A. H. The Crown-Crisp Experiential Index (CCEI) profile in anorexia nervosa. *British Journal of Psychiatry,* 1980, *136,* 567–573.

Hsu, L. K. G., Crisp, A. H., & Harding, B. Outcome of anorexia nervosa. *Lancet,* 1979, *1,* 61–65.

Janis, I. L., & Field, P. B. Sex differences and personality factors related to persuasibility. In C. I. Houland, & I. L. Janis, (eds.), *Personality and Persuasibility,* New Haven: Yale University Press, 1959.

Kendler, K. S. Amitriptyline-induced obesity in anorexia nervosa: A case report. *American Journal of Psychiatry,* 1978, *135,* 1107–1108.

Lifton, R. J. *The Broken Connection.* New York: Simon & Schuster, 1979.

Meyer, J. E. The anorexia nervosa syndrome. *Catamnestic Research Archives of Psychiatria Nervenkr,* 1961, *202,* 31–59.

Morgan, H. G., & Russell, G. F. M. Value of family background and clinical features as predictors of long-term outcome in anorexia nervosa: Four-year follow-up study of 41 patients. *Psychological Medicine,* 1975, *5,* 355–372.

Nogami, Y., & Yabana, F. On Kibarashi-Gui (Binge eating). *Folia Psychiatrica et Neurologica Japonica,* 1977, *31,* 294–295.

Palmer, R. L. The dietary chaos syndrome: A useful new term? *British Journal of Medicine and Psychology,* 1979, *52,* 187–190.

Reid, D. W., & Ware, E. E. Multidimensionality of internal versus external control: Addition of a third dimension and nondistinction of self versus others. *Canadian Journal of Behavioral Science,* 1974, *6,* 131–142.

Rollins, H., & Piazza, E. Diagnosis of anorexia nervosa. A critical reappraisal. Journal of the American Academy of Child Psychiatry, 1978, *17*, 126–137.

Rosenthal, R. J., Rinzler, C., Wallsh, R., & Klausner, E. Wrist-cutting syndrome: The meaning of a gesture. *American Journal of Psychiatry*, 1972, *11*, 1363–1368.

Russell, G. Bulimia nervosa: An ominous variant of anorexia nervosa. *Psychological Medicine*, 1979, *9*, 429–448.

Selvini-Palazzoli, M. P. *Self-starvation*. London: Chaucer, 1974.

Simpson, M. A. The phenomenology of self-mutilation in a general hospital setting. *Canadian Psychiatry Association Journal*, 1975, *20*, 429–434.

Stonehill, E., & Crisp, A. H. Psychoneurotic characteristics of patients with anorexia nervosa before and after treatment and at follow-up 4–7 years later. *Journal of Psychosomatic Research*, 1977, *21*, 189–193.

Stordy, B. J., Marks, V., Kalucy, R. S., & Crisp, A. H. Weight gain, thermic effect of glucose and resting metabolic rate during recovery from anorexia nervosa. *American Journal of Clinical Nutrition*, 1977, *30*, 138–146.

Strober, M. A cross-sectional and longitudinal (post weight restoration) analysis of personality and symptomatological features in young, non-chronic anorexia nervosa patients. Personal Communication, 1982.

Strober, M. Personality and symptomatological findings in young non-chronic anorexia nervosa patients. *Journal of Psychosomatic Research*, 1980, *24*, 353–359.

Strober, M., Goldenberg, I., Green, J., & Saxon, J. Body image disturbance in anorexia nervosa during the acute and recuperative phase. *Psychological Medicine*, 1979, *9*, 695–701.

Stunkard, A. J. Presidential address—from explanation to action in psychosomatic medicine: The case of obesity. *Psychosomatic Medicine*, 1975, *37*, 195–236.

Theander, S. Anorexia nervosa. A psychiatric investigation of 94 female cases. *Acta Psychiatria Scandinavia (suppl.)*, 1970, *214*, 1–194.

3

The Obese Binge Eater: Diagnosis, Etiology, and Clinical issues

James Gormally

Introduction

No one is claiming great success in the behavioral treatment of obesity. In fact, earlier optimistic reviews (Stunkard, 1972) have been replaced by more critical appraisals of behavior therapy (Stunkard & Penick, 1979; Wilson & Brownell, 1980). The reason for this reversal is that earlier studies did not emphasize maintenance in their evaluations. Enough studies have been conducted now with long-term follow-ups to review maintenance. Wilson and Brownell (1980) concluded that most behavioral participants regain weight lossess and, more importantly, very few go on to lose additional weight to attain their goal.

When the overweight problem is complicated by binge eating, prognosis is even more dim because serious binge eating is a chronic difficulty and not easily modified. Obese binge eaters usually report histories of repeated successful diets, where significant weight loss is achieved but never maintained. Research has shown that these chronic dieters are the ones most likely to lose weight in behavioral treatment and also the ones most likely to relapse after treatment ends (Gormally, Note 1; Gormally, Rardin, & Black, 1980). At the beginning of our behavioral clinic, these chronic dieters often said, "I know I can lose the weight," and the data showed they could. However, a majority of these same persons gained back, on the average, half their weight loss by the end of the follow-up. Binge eaters with histories of prior weight loss, often by highly depriving diets, are a relapse waiting to happen.

And yet, paradoxically, binge eaters are the best-controlled eaters during the treatment program. Researchers (Herman & Polivy, 1975; Stunkard, in press) have labeled the bingers' capacity to regulate their eating on diets as "restraint." While restrained eating may produce quick weight loss, the long-range goal of learning to eat more moderately is not achieved. The eating behavior appears to be either a "feast or famine." Successful restraint of eating on a diet does not solve the binger's eating problems; in fact, restrained eating is likely to set off a binge (Gormally, Black, Daston, & Rardin, 1982). Binge eaters can fool us by their ability to diet and attain weight loss.

Some might wonder if successful weight loss will produce the needed control of eating urges. This does not seem to be the case. A participant in one of my behavioral weight control clinics, interviewed $2\frac{1}{2}$ years after treatment, reported serious and frequent problems, despite losing 30 pounds, in attaining her goal weight and staying at goal for the entire follow-up. For over 20 years previous to this, she had experienced serious eating compulsions and multiple successful diets with fairly good maintenance. Clinical records showed that she was questioning her capacity to control her eating urges at the seven-month follow-up. At the $2\frac{1}{2}$-year follow-up her sense of control was even more tenuous.

Another clinic participant with a long history of binge-eating problems successfully responded to the behavioral procedures, lost weight, and kept it off for over two years. I was consulted by her because she became a "compulsive dieter." At the time of the consultation, she was at least 10 pounds below her goal weight, very depressed, and constantly obsessed about eating.

Bruch (1974) described the negative effects of behavioral treatment for three female anorexics, whom Bruch saw subsequent to their treatment. In all three cases, the behavior therapy in a controlled hospital environment successfully produced weight gains but was followed by severe depression leading to suicidal intentions and increased binge eating. What is important about these cases is that the increased weight gain did not produce the hoped-for improvements in the women's eating behavior and overall sense of well-being. These cases raise the issue of whether or not behavior therapy aimed only at weight modification will succeed when persons also have significant eating disorders.

The obese binge eater is burdened by a double problem. Behavioral advice, like stimulus control or alternate activities, may help the binge eater lose weight; however, successful dieting and weight loss will be produced at the expense of overly restrained eating behavior. Thus, the binge eater still has not learned to eat in a moderate and well-controlled fashion. If eating compulsions are separated from weight loss issues, the clinician needs to decide on the focus of the treatment.

The current challenge is to identify criteria that will help determine which binge eaters are suitable candidates for weight reduction and which ones primarily need help in controlling their binges. It seems inappropriate to lump all obese persons together and provide treatment in a standardized fashion, which has been the typical practice. To meet this challenge of making the proper decision regarding the focus of treatment, more work is needed to delineate the nature of binge-eating problems. To this end, this chapter is divided into three sections: diagnosis, etiology, and clinical issues. The major focus of the chapter is the identification of the unique needs of the obese binge eater so that appropriate treatment can be developed.

Diagnosis

This section provides a definition for binge eating, including a consideration of the extent to which eating binges are compulsive behavior versus addictive behavior. Different kinds of assessment techniques are presented and critiqued. Finally, a typology of eating problems among obese persons is proposed to help distinguish binge eating from other overeating behavior.

Definitional Issues

The standard definition of a binge is "a period of uncontrolled eating in which a large amount of food is consumed in a short period of time." This definition is only partially adequate since only overt behavior (food amount, time spent eating) is discussed. A common problem for overweight persons is overeating, and yet not all overeating episodes qualify as binges. The reason for this claim is that obese persons do not always see overeating as a loss of control; in fact, some obese persons report that they overeat because they enjoy food and not because of poor control of eating. The importance of loss of control leads us to suggest that subjective phenomena need to be included in the definition. This is based on the premise that it is not overeating per se that characterizes a binge, but rather the meanings the person attaches to the eating episode. Thus, two other elements should be included in the definition: (1) the experience of loss of control of eating and (2) negative emotional reactions consequent to the binge.

To what extent should binge eating be called compulsive behavior? Let us first consider the essential characteristics of a compulsion. Rachman and Hodgson (1980) presented a thorough analysis of two classic compulsions—cleaning and checking. They included a definition of compulsions that will be a useful starting point for describing the compulsive character of binge eating: "A compulsion is defined as a repetitive, partly stereotyped type of behavior that is preceded or accompanied by a sense of pressure, that usually provokes internal resistance, is at least partly irrational, and often causes distress or embarrassment" (p. 110). Put simply, it is a behavior that a person has to do (not wants to do), because of some internal pressure (not external coercion), which makes little logical sense, and results in negative emotional consequences. The compulsive cleaner fears the dirt on his/her body will contaminate others. While this may be acknowledged as illogical and irrational by the cleaner, she/he nonetheless feels compelled to engage in the ritual to avoid the fear of contamination. Similarly, the binger senses that his/her behavior is irrational since the urge to eat is not based on any physical need to satisfy a hunger urge. Rachman and Hodgson (1980) also assert that compulsions are relatively unchanging and difficult to control over the long term. The implication is that a compulsive behavior represents a strong habit rather than merely a few isolated episodes of unwanted behavior.

The essence of a compulsion is the "push–pull" nature of it. The food beckons but the binger resists taking that first bite, for fear of losing total control. This is an ambivalence toward food. A good analogy to explain the ambivalence is the youngster going through the terrible twos. The child is developing enough maturity to make some definite stabs at autonomy, yet the prospect of leaving Mom on these bold ventures is utterly frightening. The child is uncertain, for a good reason, how she/he would fare without Mom. The child wants the independence and yet is afraid of giving up childhood dependencies. The binger wants to satisfy the urge to eat between meals, yet fears that taking the first bite will lead to a total unraveling of control.

Are there elements of the binge-eating syndrome that suggest an addiction? The essential quality of an addiction is the feeling that there is never enough. Bingers report constant cravings for food, but a binge never satisfies these cravings and, most important, indulging the urge to eat with a moderate amount of food is never enough. While recovering alcohol addicts control their urges by complete abstinence, binge eaters obviously cannot abstain from food, but this distinction does not disqualify binge behavior as an addiction. The abstinence for a binge eater is from unplanned eating in response to an impulse. Usually this means abstaining from between-meal eating behavior and food abuse.

In summary, an adequate definition of binge eating includes both subjective phenomena and overt behavior. It appears that eating binges can be considered compulsive behavior, in the sense that bingers are ambivalent about acting out their urges to eat. Binge eating also shares characteristics of an addiction. The inability of binge eaters to eat moderately underscores how a binger can be addicted to food.

Assessment Methods

Three assessment methods for binge eating currently are in use. Persons can (1) self-report binge eating frequency on a single scale, (2) fill out more complicated questionnaires, or (3) receive a diagnostic interview.

The simplest type of questionnaire merely asks the respondent to specify the frequency of binges in a given period of time. Usually the questionnaire includes a brief definition of a binge. Researchers have assumed that the more frequent the binge episode, the more serious the problem. While this approach is simple and straightforward, there are limitations. First, we have no idea of precisely how the person behaved during a binge. Second, the term "binge" can have a wide range of meanings to an individual, a discovery I have based on my clinical experience. Third, there is an overemphasis on eating in the assessment, to the exclusion of cognitive–emotional factors that are central to the binge-eating syndrome. Fourth, cutoffs with no conceptual or theoretical basis are used to establish who are the serious bingers. For example, a self-report of bingeing "more than once a week" is often used as the cutoff; however, binge eating is often a very episodic phenomena such that serious bingers may report two- or three-week-long periods of good control followed by constant binges followed by another bingefree period. In summary, this method is not at all discriptive of the syndrome, does not isolate more serious binge eaters in a satisfactory way, and tells us little in terms of the overt behavior of the binge eater.

A more adequate diagnostic procedure using interviewers was reported by Wermuth, Davis, Hollister, and Stunkard (1977). Persons with serious binge-eating problems were identified using three criteria: (1) reports of rapid ingestion of large quantities of food over a short period of time, (2) eating that ended only after physical discomfort or self-induced vomiting, and (3) binges that resulted in subsequent feelings of guilt and self-hate. A further criterion of at least one binge per week with no long binge-free intervals also was applied to these participants.

According to Stunkard (Note 2), these criteria later were reworked into the diagnostic system utilized in *DSM-III*. In *DSM-III*, diagnosis of bulimia (binge eating) can be made if the person reports any three of the following seven symptoms: (1) rapid consumption of food; (2) consumption of high-calorie food; (3) eating secretly during the binge; (4) binge terminated by abdominal pain, sleep, social interruption, or self-induced vomiting; (5) repeated use of severely restrictive diets or self-induced vomiting to lose weight; (6) alternating pattern of binges and fasting; (7) use of cathartics for weight control. Although no research has been conducted to detemine how many of these symptoms should be evident, three seem sufficient. This list of symptoms seems fairly complete. One qualification is that we would not expect to see extreme dieting methods among obese persons at the same frequency as binge eaters who are anorexic or bulimarexics. For example, our experience is that self-induced vomiting is rare among obese persons and is far more prevalent among bulimarexics and anorexics.

The Binge-Eating Scale. Recently, Gormally et al. (1982) developed a 16-item questionnaire that attempted to operationalize these *DSM-III* criteria. The scale has items that appraise the behaviors, emotions, and cognitions that are thought to comprise the binge-eating syndrome. To validate the measure, diagnostic interviews were conducted in which obese persons described a recent period of overeating that they considered a binge. Thoughts and emotions before and after binge episodes also were elicited. Dieting methods and weight history were determined. The interviewer determined whether the person had no binge-eating problem, a moderate one, or a serious problem. The interviewers used three dimensions to determine their rating: (1) frequency of binge episodes, (2) amount of food eaten, and (3) feelings of control before and degree of emotions after a binge. We found that the questionnaire did a good job of discriminating those judged to have no, moderate, or serious binge-eating problems. This showed that complicated interview procedures could be replaced by a self-report questionnaire. An important question remains about the scale's sensitivity to changes in binge eating over the course of treatment.

Moderate and Serious Bingers. While *DSM-III* essentially types persons as bingers or nonbingers, Gormally et al. (1982) also utilized an "in-between" category. What is the best approach? The major problem with an "either–or" approach, as in *DSM-III*, is the possibility that less serious bingers can be lumped into the same category as severe binge eaters. Our clinical and research experience indicates that moderate and serious bingers are diagnostically quite different, especially with regard to their reactions to a diet and their overall level of psychological functioning.

The groups clearly are different in their reactions when diets are broken. Moderate bingers tend to react to a slip-up on a diet by eating even more. They will say to themselves, "I've blown my diet now, so why not go all the way?" This behavior is rightly labeled a binge. However, moderate bingers are much more tolerant of their lapses in self-control. They report less guilt and self-hate when the diet is broken. Serious bingers feel a more pervasive lack of control of their eating urges and experience an almost constant preoccupation with eating or not eating. When their stuggle is lost, their overeating is much more extreme than moderate bingers. The fear of loss of control is so intense that serious bingers are unable to keep food in their homes.

Some of the differences between moderate and serious bingers are merely a matter of degree. Serious bingers will report greater amounts of food eaten, more guilt and self-hate after the binge, and more extreme dieting methods than moderates. Both moderate and serious binge eaters experience intense food cravings while on a diet, leading to mental struggles about whether to eat or not eat a forbidden food.

Serious bingers, much more than moderate bingers, present other problems besides their eating behavior. In three cases of serious bingers seen in treatment, depression was linked to the loss of a relationship in which a very deep dependency had developed. Interestingly, Rachman and Hodgson's (1980) analysis of obsessions and compulsions led them to conclude that depression, especially of a reactive type, can facilitate the occurrence of compulsions. However, the evidence they review also showed that depression was not necessarily a condition for the maintenance of compulsions.

It is certainly true that serious bingers have plenty to be depressed about, just because they feel so out of control in terms of eating. However, other problems of living also seem related to the depression. Among them are underassertiveness and extreme deference to authority figures; social anxiety; ambivalent and unsatisfying sexual involvements; negative self-image even when significant obesity is not present (Bruch's "thin-fat people," 1973); dependency on others, especially manifest in the therapy relationship when the treatment is long-term; among women, conflicts about achievement; and excessive guilt about not being an adequate caretaker, leading to a smothering of children, parents, and certain friends. All these problems can be seen as manifestations of an uncertain identity (à la Erikson) and insecure sense of autonomy.

The Indulgers. In contrast to bingers, some obese persons report significant overeating but none of the conflict and self-hate so characteristic of the binge syndrome. These obese persons report having no binges and feel quite capable of controlling eating urges. They overeat because they enjoy eating. Because eating is viewed as enjoyment rather than losing control, these nonbingers report little negative emotional response to their overeating. The indulger enjoys the gratification of a big meal. While the binger's inner voice struggles over the urge to eat, the indulger's voice proclaims, "I want what I want, when I want it." The indulger has none of the push–pull ambivalence of compulsive behavior. Indulgers find dieting extremely difficult because food is mightily satisfying. In contrast, bingers will exhibit fierce determination at controlling their intake, at least between their binges. If we focus only on the amount of food eaten, indulgers appear to be bingers. This indicates once again the importance of assessing feelings and thoughts as well as overt behavior to form an accurate diagnosis.

Summary

Binge eating is a complex syndrome characterized by both overt behavior and subjective phenomena. Assessment should include (1) behavioral descriptions of overeating episodes (amount of food eaten, frequency of binges, secret or social setting), (2) feelings of control or noncontrol over eating (manifest by impulsive, unplanned eating behavior), (3) poor response to satiety (eating that leads to physical discomfort), and (4) emotional consequences of a binge. A dieting/weight history will be useful to reveal not only the length of the problem but also periods of restraint by the use of extremely depriving diets. Self-report questionnaires and clinical interviews can be used to form a diagnosis. When a questionnaire is used, it should be suplemented with some record of actual eating behavior.

Among the population of moderately obese persons (less than 100 pounds overweight), three groups can be distinguished: moderate binge eaters, serious binge eaters, and persons with no binge-eating problems—called indulgers. While these categories need to be verified by further research, there is enough basis to expect that the obese population does not fall into an either–or dichotomy: binger or nonbinger. Further research also seems needed to establish base rates for males versus females, since most of our research has been conducted on obese women.

Etiology

The most difficult part of obesity treatment is pining down causation. What has impressed me in my clinical work is the wide variety of causes that seem linked to a person's weight problem. Almost always, poor weight control is complicated by emotional issues in the interpersonal arena, such as problems with a spouse, with self-assertion, and with self-confidence. When I probe for historical data, important problems in development also emerge. Most central are problems in attachment, for example, mother–daughter fusion, separations, and the like. Family weight problems and attitudes about eating also can be relevant causes, and eating and dieting habits, as well as activity patterns, are part of the person's weight-control problem. What this section describes are four causal models that attempt to explain binge-eating problems. Each model is presented along with a critique. The section concludes with a discussion of two important skills that appear related to weight control for persons with binge-eating problems.

The Behavioral Model

The behavioral model emphasizes the role of learning poor eating habits and, to a lesser extent, the role of social learning in terms of consequences delivered by spouses or family and models provided by spouses or family. The therapist instructs the client in new eating habits and the person self-reinforces or receives support from a spouse, family, or group to sustain motivation to stick with the new habits. Eating habits such as eating rate are identified and modified. It is the stimulus-control concept, however, that has influenced most the way behaviorists view eating habits and weight problems.

In the early 1960s, Ferster, Nurnberger, and Levitt (1962) presented a novel way to conceptualize problem eating habits. They argued that persons condition themselves to eat snacks; thus, bad eating habits are the result of pairing environmental cues with snacking. For example, a stimulus situation, such as the movie theater, comes to elicit the urge to eat popcorn. The major treatment component derived from this model focused on helping the client narrow the range of stimuli associated with eating. Dieters were encouraged to eat only in one place in the house, with a particular plate and utensils. The time of day the food was eaten could be narrowed in a similar fashion. This technique has been called stimulus control. It is a powerful way to modify between-meal snacking, since the client learns to become very conscious of exactly when and where she/he eats.

Intuitively, this model makes a lot of sense. Odysseus had himself tied to the mast to handle the beckoning of the beautiful sirens on the island. The idea is to control the environment so that the urges can be brought under control. One of my most successful clients applied the stimulus-control idea to snacking that reemerged during follow-up. As she put it, "I became like Pavlov's dog." Once she realized the association between snacking and driving the car on long-distance trips, she nicely instituted some fading procedures (decreasing the size of her packages of snack food) to reinstitute better self-control. The underlying premise is that successful weight control involves manipulation of environments to decrease the likelihood of snacking. Concepts like "strong will-power" are not necessary, since stimulus-control procedures can be viewed as learnable skills.

While controlling the external environment is crucial for bingers, understanding the internal environment is equally important to binge eating. In fact, Wilson (1976) noted that merely modifying the external environments of binge eaters was ineffective. He emphasized that negative thoughts about one's body and low self-esteem were important internal targets to modify. Unfortunately, Wilson did not present any data on the effectiveness of this alternative approach; however, what was interesting about his report was the linking of internal processes (body image, etc.), rather than external environments, to the explanation of binge eating.

Despite the inadequacies of stimulus control to explain binge eating, no new concepts have been proposed to explain it from a learning standpoint.

The Psychodynamic Model

Forever Thin (Rubin, 1970) or *The Overeaters* (Wise & Wise, 1979) are examples of the psychodynamic approach to explaining eating disorders. The model emphasizes some defect in a person's psychic structure that results in weight problems and eating disorders. Binge eating is seen as a symptom of underlying personality problems. These internal conflicts generate anxiety that gets "stuffed down" by an eating binge. This model nicely lends itself to an explanation of why binge eating is so difficult to change: To the extent that the binge successfully helps the person avoid anxiety-producing thoughts, the binge becomes highly reinforcing. The relief produced by anxiety avoidance serves as a powerful reinforcer. The therapist, therefore, engages in two strategies: first, probing for historical data to produce insight into the unfortunate developmental experience that is influential upon eating behavior and second, evoking the trapped emotion attached to these experiences.

Bruch (1973) also places the focus on the past to explain eating disorders; however, she emphasizes the role of the caregiver (primarily the mother) in training the child to confuse hunger with eating urges. For example, when the child feels disappointed the caregiver provides a cookie to cheer up the child. While one such experience is unlikely to have lasting impact, when eating is repeatedly paired with emotion, and when appropriate emotional expression is not encouraged in the child, eating disorders will result, according to Bruch.

The major problem is that insight and emotional acceptance do not necessarily translate into behavior that leads to weight reduction. In fact, Stunkard (1975) published an account of obese persons in psychoanalysis and found that their weight remained unchanged. This is not surprising, since dynamic therapies are quite successful at producing self-acceptance, which may undermine a person's motivation to lose weight. Overweight persons come to peace with their past and start to like themselves the way they are, which indeed may be indication of improvement. However, insight may not lead to successful control of binge eating. My clinical experience is that insight, at best, serves to explain why binges occur and, at worst, serves as a rationalization for not controlling binge behavior. What is lacking in the model is a focus on coping skills that can be to deal with the inevitable urges to eat on impulse. Because binge eating is an addictive behavior, successful treatment involves supports for not continuing the addiction.

The Social Model

The focus in the social model is upon the persistent emphasis in contemporary Western society for women to be thin. Orbach (1978) presents an explanation for binge eating based on the ambivalence binge eaters feel toward these social standards. The binge is taken to symbolize the resentment and rage for adopting such standards as a way of defining oneself. In effect, the binge represents a willful rebellion against the standard, which ultimately only hurts the individual. The therapy is highly evocative and has a consciousness-raising quality. Insight also is promoted by probing into current emotions about social standards and past development. The real advantage of this method is that it focuses nicely on the unfair and inhumane quality of a society that trains its members to define people in terms of body fat. The drawback is similar to the dynamic model, in that weight control is unaddressed. Also, no explanation is offered for binge-eating problems in men.

Even normal-weight women can be susceptible to binge-eating problems. When social conditioning has eroded a woman's self-esteem and body image, having a socially acceptable body weight does not produce bodily satisfaction. In fact, these women become obsessed by slight weight gains and engage in depriving diets that ultimately lead to a binge, which can lead to purging.

There are indications that this social perspective is needed to complement other models of causation and treatment. For example, over 90 percent of our samples in behavioral studies have been women, most of whom have been treated by male therapists (Stuart, Mitchell, & Jensen, 1981). One might speculate that this is related to Orbach's social discrimination assertion, particularly since epidemiological studies show that an equal number of men and women are between 10 and 20 percent overweight. Further, there is ambiguity as to what goal weights should be for our behavioral participants. In particular, the possibility that goal weights are too low has not been considered. This is curious, since the benchmark of behaviorism is setting realistic goals. Perhaps a person who is 50 pounds overweight by the charts and loses 30 pounds could be helped to be happy at that weight, rather than going for the extra 20 pounds.

The Physiological Model

This fourth model includes genetic endowment, body frame, food allergies, fat-cell count and size, metabolism and caloric imbalance, and experience of hunger. I will not comment generally on these elements except on two specific points.

First, physiology and nutrition have been neglected, inappropriately, by most clinical behavior therapists. Because behavior therapists are good at modifying behavior, the alteration of eating habits fits nicely into their treatment model. How does one modify a fat cell or frame size? Yet, these matters seem crucial to understanding weight problems.

Second, Wooley, Wooley and Dyrenforth (1979) have speculated recently that different persons experience hunger produced by dieting in different ways. They discuss specific emotional reactions to hunger at moderate levels of deprivation as compared to fasting. For example, they speculate that for some persons the deprivation produced by a fast is easier to handle emotionally than the typical moderate calorically balanced diet. It is too early to tell how these speculations will hold up under empirical study, but their ideas are interesting, make sense, and have clinical implications.

All four of the preceding models are useful in understanding eating binges. Table 3–1 summarizes some of the major concepts of the causal models as they apply to binge eating. The roles of reinforcement (learning model), poor emotional awareness (psychodynamic model), socially induced evaluations of self-esteem based on body size (social model), and differences in the experience of hunger (physiological model) seem crucial to explain binge eating. However, the theories do not discriminate carefully between weight-control problems and binge-eating problems, which are two separable problems with different causes. While learning to control eating compulsions does not necessarily generalize to successful weight loss, I assert that control of eating binges is a prerequisite

Table 3-1. Assertions about Binge Eating Based on Four Theories of Eating Disorders

---

Learning Model

Binge-eating problems can be understood as skill deficits. New skills can be learned to gain control of compulsive urges to eat.

Avoidance of problem emotions by going on eating binges provides a sense of relief that serves as a negative reinforcer; this explains the maintenance of eating compulsions.

Excessively harsh diets are a positive event for the binger because they provide short-term improvements in mood and self-esteem. Since these diets follow a binge, these events serve as positive reinforcers of a binge.

Psychodynamic

The binge eater has learned to confuse hunger urges with urges to eat. This learning has been produced by faulty developmental experiences.

Not engaging in eating binges is highly threatening to persons because the habit is central to a person's psychic structure. Supportive treatment environments are needed to offset this threat.

Social

Weight loss per se does not necessarily produce improvements in self-esteem and negative evaluations of one's body for the obese binge eater. This is one reason why weight modification does not produce durable changes in eating compulsions.

Physiological

The experience of hunger is unique. Individuals will vary on how they experience their urges to eat. Learning to eat when hungry requires careful attention to these individual differences.

---

to successful weight-loss maintenance. Without this sense of control over eating urges, weight losses that are attained ultimately will be regained and thus are of questionable benefit to the obese binge eater.

Skills Deficits of the Obese Binge Eater

The binge eater confronts two skills problems that occur frequently enough to be commonplace. One of these is coping with stressful emotions. Although these are a normal part of life, the binger has learned to respond to stressful emotions by eating. A second problem is cognitive in nature and involves the binger's standards of control. Slip-ups in control are inevitable, especially since regulation of food intake must occur daily; however, binge eaters appear to overcompensate for this sense of weakness by attempting excessively harsh and depriving diets. These two problems can be translated into two skills that relate to successful control of eating urges: appropriate restraint and good emotional coping.

Appropriate Restraint. Binge eaters appear to react to a binge by being even more harsh with themseves in terms of what they should not eat. It is as if a critical voice is scolding the bingers for showing personal weakness. While no rational person would expect perfect control of an addiction, binge eaters place such standards on themselves. Slip-ups in control seem inevitable, especially since food cannot be excluded from a person's life. These typical reactions to slip-ups by bingers seem mediated by two cognitive factors: standards for control and efficacy expectations. When standards are impossibly high and efficacy is low, bingers are very susceptible to a binge following a slip-up.

Let us examine how efficacy expectation and standards are involved in binge-eating problems. Binge eaters attempt to maintain a very high standard of control while on a diet, perhaps to compensate for overeating. The harshness of such depriving diets ultimately is self-defeating, because a person who promises that "This is going to be a perfect dieting day" is only one bite away from violating the standard. So, in a paradoxical way, binge eaters not only are capable of eating to excess, they also are prone to dieting to excess. The unique feature of the obese binge eater, compared to the underweight model or actor who uses harsh diets, is that the binge eater's track record for sustaining the diet is poor. Obese binge eaters break their promises to be perfect so often that they feel desperately unsure of their ability to restrain themselves. Thus, the self-defeating nature of high standards is heightened when a person feels little sense of personal efficacy in following them.

Gormally et al. (1982) constructed a scale they called the Cognitive Factors Scale, which contained two factors: strict dieting standards and self-efficacy expectations to sustain a diet. The Cognitive Factors Scale correlated at about $r = .50$ $(p < .001)$ with their Binge Eating Scale for two independent samples. We propose the following model to explain binge eating after diet breaking:

High dieting standards accompanied by low personal efficacy tend to increase the likelihood of a slip in control when a person confronts a "high-risk" situation. Instead of coping with a dieting slip-up with a problem-solving attitude, the binge eater attributes the lapse of control to a lack of willpower. This leads to a complete unraveling of control from there and to a binge. High standards and low efficacy not only increase the likelihood of a binge but can reinforce the belief that even stricter controls are needed.

Obese binge eaters need to be able to diet to lose weight; however, bingers readily transform the diet into a rigid set of rules that must be followed perfectly. There is no sense of the futility of expecting to be perfectly in control. These dieting practices are well-ingrained habits, extending over many years. My clinical observation is that such depriving diets are highly reinforcing. There is a self-righteous feeling of control, even if it is short-term, which seems to offset the tremendous feelings of shame and personal weakness for binge eating.

What is it that seems to cause bingers' tendency to see harsh and depriving diets as the solution to their problem of control? The attribution process is central to understanding the answer. Give bingers a choice, and they will attribute their problem to personal failings or weaknesses. Social modeling teaches these attributional tendencies. In the same way that society judges drunk or fat people as weak and unable to control themselves, they themselves learn to internalize these explanations for their problems.

The key to learning a sense of appropriate restraint lies in correcting the attributional errors of a binger. Marlatt (1979) linked these weak willpower attributions to the relapses in self-control for alcoholics and drug addicts. What Marlatt encouraged was a more rational, problem-solving attitude about a slip-up; for example, a binger could be trained to find out what was taxing about a particular situation. In fact, Marlatt encourages persons to have a relapse to practice this new way of reacting to a slip-up.

Overeaters Anonymous (OA) provides further examples of correcting the attribution process of bingers. The emphasis in OA is upon recovering from a disease, which allows bingers to take themselves off the "weak willpower hook" that society uses to explain addictions. The attribution training is most evident in what is called the spiritual part of the OA program. Members are taught to use attendance at meetings, telephoning a fellow member, and faith in God to maintain abstinence. In effect, the spirituality fostered by these suggestions is a form of cognitive modification. OA'ers with "good spirituality," as they like to call it, adopt a belief that, on their own, control of binges is not possible, but, with the help of others, control is attainable. The attributions that are reinforced all center upon one important point, the bingers' self-admissions that they lack power to control binges *on their own*. The first step of their 12-step program states, "We admitted we were powerless over food—that our lives had become unmanageable."

Serious bingers are afraid of learning new attributions for their lapses for fear of losing total control. The kind of treatment environment that is created, in terms of relationship factors, should attend to this fear. My hypothesis is that binge eaters will be helped by treatment environments that provide supports in the form of personal sharing, reinforcement for successful control of binges, and encouragement for avoiding labeling the cause of slip-ups in terms of personal weakness. This supportive environment will spell out clearly the limits of acceptable behavior (e.g., in OA, abstinence from binges means no between-meal eating) and confront any deviations from these limits. It acts much the same as a parent who has limits for a child but who also provides adequate freedom for self-determination within the limits. The effect of a firm but forgiving environment is that bingers can give up their chronic and lonely attempts to solve their problem of control through futile attempts to be more restrictive.

Good Emotional Coping. In Gormally and Rardin's (1981) study of behavioral obesity treatment, some attempt was made to identify a profile of successful weight-loss maintainers. Among the participants who lost at least 15 pounds during treatment, those who maintained the loss were compared to those who relapsed during follow-up. Results showed that relapsers were much more likely that maintainers to report overeating in response to emotional cues. For example, a maintainer told us about an instance of being angry with her husband where, instead of eating as was her habit, she assertively expressed her feelings. Relapsers seemed to deal with day-to-day emotions by eating them away. Even during times of more serious life stress in the follow-up (e.g., a promotion, or major setback), relapsers reported a complete breakdown on their diet while maintainers appeared to cope more effectively. Thus, good emotional coping seems crucial to weight-loss maintenance. For the obese binger, it is important to recognize both the emotional antecedents of a binge and the emotional consequences of a binge.

One way to keep track of emotions antecedent to eating is to keep a food diary. My clinical observation is that few persons at the outset of treatment seem capable of accurately reporting their mood after they have had a binge, because eating serves to "stuff down" the feeling. This use of eating to avoid problem emotions can provide a powerful reinforcer.

The long-range goal would be to have the person talk out the feeling rather than stuff it down; however, there are key skills that must be learned to accomplish this goal. First, labels for emotions must be learned and substituted for what previously was labeled hunger. Persons must disconnect the emotional arousal from the arousal produced by hunger. Second, an increased tolerance for anxiety must be encouraged, because, once the person has labeled the hunger as an emotion, there will be an increased anxiety level as the binger refrains from eating. Coping with emotional cues by not eating provides none of the powerful visceral reinforcement following the act of eating, and the heightened anxiety will be additionally distressing. Third, emotions produced by the act of dieting must be targeted. Most commonly, persons can report irritability when on moderate diets. For some persons, a moderately controlled eating day is more difficult than being on a complete fast or a low-calorie structured food plan (i.e., diets that completely specify meals). Needing to exercise some restraint on a moderate diet and to tolerate some hunger produced by not eating between meals is likely to cause additional emotional reactions, at least for some bingers. Fourth, emotional control also involves a willingness to delay the impulse to eat. In effect, bingers need to reverse completely their typical impulsive style of eating.

Overweight bingers, like all obese persons, deal with the emotional consequences of their problem in several ways. Some totally deny the obesity, refusing to weigh themselves for months, not looking at a mirror, and so on. Others become obsessively preoccupied by their body weight, weighing many times each day. Still others accept the reality of their weight and swear that this has to end, forever—tomorrow. Obese bingers react by pounding themselves for being so weak and out of control. They "own up" to the reality of their problem but in a way that is punitive and productive of harmful negative emotions. This emotional overreaction to overweight has the same qualities as the private contempt that many others feel toward the overweight person.

Transactional Analysis theory of personality provides a way of understanding what causes the self-punitive emotions of bingers. The TA conceptualization consists of three basic entities, a Parent, a Child, and an Adult. Each of these structures can be divided further. The Parent can be either Nurturing or Controlling, and the child is either Rebellious, Adapted, or Natural.

The Controlling Parent is concerned with conditions and domination. It is within this part of our personalities that absolutes and perfection are internalized into shoulds, oughts, musts, and nevers. In contrast, the Nurturing Parent is viewed as having the instinct to take care of and protect self and others. Nurturers give people permission to love and to care for others; compassion, comfort, and encouragement are the strengths of the Nurturant Parent.

The Natural Child is a source of spontaneity, sexuality, joy, and autonomy, while both the Adapted Child and the Rebellious Child states are nonautonomous. The Adapted Child follows parental directives and feels he/she must please the parents, whereas the Rebellious Child reacts against parental directives yet without awareness of his/her own spontaneous feelings. The Adapted Child and Rebellious Child are combined to represent the "pig parent," which contains all of the hidden conditions and expectations of the parent.

One can view each structure as a system of cognitions. For example, the Controlling Parent contains self-statements that predict failure and prevent action, such as, "You should become perfect at everything you try," or "Fat people are terrible because they have no willpower," or "You should be able to solve all of your problems, on your own."

The personality deficits of binge eaters become evident through some of their self-statements. In the binge eater there are deficits in both the compassionate self-talk from a Nurturing Parent and from the mature, reality oriented observations/cognitions of the Adult. The absence of statements that are supportive, encouraging, hopeful, forgiving, and accepting are detrimental to anyone working on a long-range goal.

Not only do the rigid parental injunctions from the Controlling Parent contaminate the Adult by inhibiting more reality oriented thoughts, these "parent tapes" also produce feelings of guilt and shame and, most important, agitate a desire to rebel against their internalized impossible standards. Binge eating functions to release the increasing internal pressure to maintain perfect self-control resulting from a constant awareness of restraint. A person, while bingeing, is in a feeling state (as opposed to a thinking state) and is acting out against these internal parental injunctions from a powerless position. Notice that the directives still remain after the binge; they are neither challenged nor changed by bingeing. The binge is an ineffective protest against an oppressive situation, much like the temper tantrums of a disappointed child. The binge eater is experiencing the Rebellious Child state at the time of a binge.

One of my colleagues described her successful therapy with a serious binge eater as a paradox. She helped her client become more accepting and tolerant; once she felt this sense of compassion, she could stop her binges. What is interesting is my estimate of my colleague as very nurturing. An explanation of the therapy in TA terms is that the therapist modeled a nurturing parent that her client later internalized. Interestingly, one way her client became more understanding of herself was to write a cookbook. She meets her needs about liking food but in a way that is helpful for others and not harmful to herself.

In sum, then, binge eating has little to do with eating and everything to do with effective living. The powerful reinforcement provided by eating in response to emotional cues makes it difficult to stop and presents a challenging coping task. Coping with emotions involves accurate emotional labeling, tolerating anxiety, delaying impulses to eat, and appropriate expression of emotion.

Clinical Issues

In this section, quotations from a diary task given to a serious binge eater in treatment with the author will be used to highlight the clinical issues presented by binge eating. The client ("Ann") was single and in her early 40s. She reported a long history of battling her urges to eat and yet was able to maintain a normal weight throughout her life. This weight control was impressive, given the extent of her regular binges on calorically dense, high-carbohydrate foods (e.g., whole boxes of sweetened natural cereals). Nonetheless, Ann felt excessive negative reactions to her body size and, in particular, a tremendous concern about being sexually unattractive. Ann's major complaint at the beginning of treatment was her binges, but it quickly became apparent that she also lacked a secure sense of autonomy. This was manifested by her dependency on her parents and an ambivalence about being successful in her career. I asked her to keep a diary at the beginning of treatment, recording her "food thoughts" and "self-controlling thoughts." The task was highly revealing, in part because of Ann's skill, willingness, and courage in reporting a thorough account of her behavior and inner thoughts. Each of the following sections reveals a particular deficit in Ann's life.

Disruption of Lifestyle

Ann: I'm not stuffed so I *want to eat,* want to fill myself up, want to do away with the space between my inner and outer stomach walls; am *aware always* of food and my resisting, but am pretty sure that I'll continue resisting—because not resisting means remaining a child, and I'm sunk that way. [Ann's emphasis]

It's a terrible battle tonight, but I *have* to win it because there's absolutely nothing in the house to binge on, and at night I don't go out for food. Nonetheless—I'm giving myself a headache, this is such a tough one!

Comment: Rachman and Hodgson (1980) noted that obsessive–compulsive behavior (O–C) is sometimes encapsulated but more often affects a person's whole lifestyle, causing great burdens to relatives as well. Ann's whole life seemed to center on thoughts about eating or not eating; however, it was a much more private struggle. In fact, a key characteristic of binge eating is secret eating. So, O–C seems to cause much more outer disruption in a client's life and the family; for the binge eater, costs seem much more internal—Ann is in a constant, lonely struggle over food. In contrast to other addictive behaviors, like alcoholism, the binge eater may never "bottom-out." The binge eating causes a significant amount of misery, but never the broken marriages or lost jobs that finally lead the alcoholic to control his/her drinking. Even when health concerns are present, obese binge eaters can resist accepting their need to change.

Sense of Powerlessness

Ann: It's a struggle each time, to avoid the restaurant's mints and my own cake—and even now my impulses are pulling me toward the kitchen—but there is, though, a slight, very slight, sense of *bodily* comfort with the resisting, a sense of physical freedom (just the way the binges give me a sense of physically being hampered and smothered and tied down like Gulliver by the Lilliputians).

Comment: The key feature of binge eating that qualifies it as a compulsion is the sense of being helplessly unable to control urges to eat. Here we see Ann's image of being helpless. Some physical—perhaps external—force ties down the rational, less-impulsive side of her. One way Ann coped with this lack of power, which is common among serious bingers, was to remove all tempting foods from the house. The more typical stimulus-control procedure of keeping food out of sight (but present in the house) is far too dangerous for serious bingers.

Emotional Coping

Ann: Tonight I'm in a little danger: it was a good day, I felt thin and liked feeling thin—but tonight I called the man I'd met at the singles dance to say I was having some friends in to dinner next Wednesday and could he come; his response was that no he didn't think he could. . . . Later I did go eat (bran flakes). Feel very angry and very blocked up. It is as if my sexual feelings are *bad* (for he rejected me) and so where can I put them, what can I do with them, except by eating, turning *inward*. Must remember this: *my* sexual feelings too easily seem *bad* to me.

What else that has resulted is that there's more "space" between me and panic—i.e., when something difficult or upsetting happens (e.g., the phone call to my parents), I don't panic right away and dig into food, but instead have more psychological "leeway" in my head to deal with the feelings before reaching the point when panic smothers me and food is all I can let into my head.

Comment: Sexual assertiveness caused considerable anxiety and conflict for Ann. She regularly binged before going out on a date, almost as if she dealt with predate anxiety by eating. This interpretation is clearly psychodynamic since it presumes the compulsive behavior serves as a defense against anxiety. An alternative view, based on Mowrer (1950), is that anxiety is a causal factor and motivates avoidance behaviors. In this context, binge eating helps the person avoid, at least temporarily, the anxiety associated with sexual assertiveness. Furthermore, the compulsive behavior is highly reinforcing because it results in immediate relief from anxiety and discomfort. This analysis is also used to explain the extreme persistence of such unwanted and self-defeating behavior. Both theoretical models emphasize the role of coping with anxiety in compulsive behavior. Whatever model is used, we can see the tremendous reinforcement, provided by eating, for the avoidance of stressful emotion.

In a more positive light, the second paragraph of this quote describes the emotional coping process. The important feeling for Ann is not being overwhelmed by the emotion so that the only response is to panic and binge. Poor emotional coping for the binge eater involves the experience of emotion that is overwhelming. The last passage nicely conveys how *not* eating impulsively can be achieved by gaining some psychological distance between the anxiety and the urge to eat.

Reactions to a Binge

Ann: Brought my coffee cake to brunch this morning and ate about six pieces: was dying to have some of *my* cake, and also knew that because everyone else was around I couldn't (wouldn't) go really overboard (ate two of the six pieces in the kitchen, hidden from everyone else); so I let go—but was also restrained . . . and on the way home from school imagined buying foods in the grocery store—nuts, cookies, etc.—partly as if I'd already stepped beyond the pale then there was the urge to *keep going,* to "ratify" what I'd already done; what stopped me was partly the memory of having refrained yesterday. . . .

[After eating a batch of cookies] I didn't go *right* into the bedroom and hide in the dark, stayed in the living room at first, doing some junk reading—but felt as if I really had thrown myself down some drain and so retreated after a while into the bedroom, my cave for hiding, for cowering, for being unconscious and paralyzed and licking my wounds (although what wounds?).

Comment: The psychological reactions of a binge eater after a binge are crucial in understanding the syndrome. The first quote shows Ann rationalizing her continued eating. As she puts it, she *ratifies* her slip in control by eating even more. It is common for binge eaters, as well as dieters in general, to view a slip-up as an excuse to eat even more. The self-statement that often is given is, "I've blown my diet now, so why not go all the way?" What the person lacks is a more realistic, problem-solving approach to the slip-up; however, it is difficult to have an objective, rational approach to a slip-up if the binge eater reacts in an overly negative emotional fashion.

Ann's second paragraph conveys a regressed, sulky, "I'm-a-bad-little-girl" reaction to a binge. Depression is common following a binge, in part because of the meaning a person attaches to the binge. When the binge is attributed to a personal weakness, self-pounding and depression are likely to follow because of the binge eater's contempt for her/himself for failing to show better control. Learning to modify such maladaptive appraisals of a binge actually comes down to helping the binge eaters give up their solutions to improving their weak willpower. As they see it, the way to solve a personal failing is to get tougher with oneself; slip-ups deserve punishment. This, in part, is the cause of overly harsh diets or fasting after a binge. Such excessive restraint, of course, is self-defeating, but in the short run it does solve the problem of feeling weak and unable to control eating urges. Initially, the binge eater will respond to suggestions of giving up his/her solution by expressing fears of going totally out of control. Learning to become more tolerant and compassionate of slip-ups is a difficult lesson, particularly because binge eaters often have had overly harsh, critical, and controlling parents as models.

Awareness

Ann: A fight was going on outside my study window, an argument between father and son—it triggers a lot; I thought about eating some brown sugar, but didn't; I already *know* how bad I'll feel afterwards. (This *also* is a first, to experience vicariously what the stuffed and sluggish feeling, bodily, *will* be, and to resist on the basis of that anticipation of the known)—a version of *not* going unconscious.

Comment: As one binge eater put it, going on a binge was like "flying on automatic pilot." "Not going unconscious" goes against the very nature of a binge as an impulsive act and requires achieving the ability to process or think about the urge to eat, to delay gratification of that urge (by substituting an alternate activity as a distraction or waiting to eat), and to gain an awareness of the long-term negative consequences (despite the highly reinforcing short-term consequences) of eating.

Impact of Success

Ann: Each day when I control my eating, really control it by eating only after a period of being hungry, I feel almost confident about being able to manage the stay at my brother's (the site of many binges); each day of feeling in control gives me the sense that I *can* do it, gives me the precedent to look back to, in the future.

Comment: It is my clinical experience that pure insight into the roots of one's behavior, produced by an understanding and supportive therapist, is not sufficient to produce durable changes in binge eating. Because binge eating is an addictive behavior, treatment ultimately must reinforce abstinence from food abuse. Rachman and Hodgson (1980) emphasize the use of response-prevention methods in the modification of O–C. Essentially, the technique involves support and reinforcement to not act out the compulsive urge. The successful control of an urge provided Ann with a powerful incentive to be successful in the future. A reservoir of self-efficacy information is built up with each experience of success. Treatment ultimately must focus on techniques to produce control over eating urges—insight without behavior change adds up to little relief for the client.

Summary

These diary entries illustrate several important issues discussed in this chapter: (1) the independence of weight-control problems and eating compulsions (Ann was not overweight), (2) the features of binge eating that qualify it as a compulsion and an addiction, (3) the powerful stimulus values of stressful emotions as cues for binges, and (4) the tendency to view a binge as a personal weakness, prompting highly depriving and rigid diets. The diary approach seems well suited to uncovering the complex emotional and cognitive causes of binge eating.

Reference Notes

1. Gormally, J. Factors associated with maintenance of weight loss. Paper presented at Johns Hopkins Hospital, Conference on the Treatment of Obesity, March 1981.
2. Stunkard, A. Personal communication, June 1981.

References

Bruch, H. *Eating Disorders*. New York: Basic Books, 1973.
Bruch, H. Perils of behavior modification in treatment of anorexia nervosa. *Journal of the American Medical Association*, 1974, *230*, 1419–1422.

Ferster, C. B., Nurnberger, J. I., & Levitt, E. The control of eating. *Journal of Mathetics*, 1962, *1*, 87–109.

Gormally, J., Black, S., Daston, S., & Rardin, D. The assessment of binge eating severity among obese persons. *Addictive Behaviors*, 1982, *7*, 47–55.

Gormally, J., & Rardin, D. Weight loss and maintenance, changes in diet and exercise for behavioral counseling and nutrition education. *Journal of Counseling Psychology*, 1981, *28*, 295–304.

Gormally, J., Rardin, D., & Black, S. Correlates of successful response to a behavioral weight control clinic. *Journal of Counseling Psychology*, 1980, *27*, 179–191.

Herman, C. P., & Polivy, J. Anxiety, restraint, and eating behavior. *Journal of Abnormal Psychology*, 1975, *84*, 666–672.

Marlatt, G. A. A cognitive–behavioral model of the relapse process. In N. A. Krasnegor (ed.), *Behavioral Analysis and Treatment of Substance Abuse*. NIDA Research Monograph 25. Washington, D. C.: Department of Health, Education and Welfare, 1979.

Mowrer. O. *Learning Theory and Personality Dynamics*. New York: Ronald Press, 1950.

Orbach, S. Social dimensions in compulsive eating in women. *Psychotherapy: Theory, Research and Practice*, 1978, *15*, 180–189.

Rachman, S., & Hodgson, R. *Obsessions and Compulsions*. Englewood Cliffs, N. J.: Prentice-Hall, 1980.

Rubin, D. *Forever Thin*. New York: Grammercy, 1970.

Stuart, R., Mitchell, C., & Jensen, J. Therapeutic options in the management of obesity. In C. Prokop & L. A. Bradley (eds.), *Medical Psychology: Contributions to Behavioral Medicine*. New York: Academic Press, 1981.

Stunkard, A. J. New therapies for the eating disorders. *Archives of General Psychiatry*, 1972, *20*, 391–398.

Stunkard, A. J. Presidential address—from explanation to action in psychosomatic medicine: The case of obesity. *Psychosomatic Medicine*, 1975, *37*, 195–236.

Stunkard, A. "Restrained Eating": What it is and a new scale to measure it. In L. A. Cloffl, T. B. Van Itallie, & N. M. James (eds.), *The Body Weight Regulatory System: Normal and Disturbed Mechanisms*. New York: Raven Press, in press.

Stunkard, A., & Penick, S. Behavior modification in the treatment of obesity. *Archives of General Psychiatry*, 1979, *36*, 801–806.

Wermuth, B., Davis, F., Hollister, L., & Stunkard, A. Phenytoin treatment of the binge-eating syndrome. *American Journal of Psychiatry*, 1977, *134*, 1249–1253.

Wilson, G. T. Obesity, binge eating, and behavior therapy: Some clinical observations. *Behavior Therapy*, 1976, *7*, 700–701.

Wilson, G. T., & Brownell, K. D. Behavior therapy for obesity: An evaluation of treatment outcome. *Advances in Behavioral Research and Therapy,* 1980, *3,* 49–85.

Wooley, S., Wooley, O., & Dyrenforth, S. Theoretical, practical and social issues in behavioral treatments of obesity. *Journal of Applied Behavior Analysis,* 1979, *12,* 3–25.

II

Assessment and Treatment

4

Experiential–Behavioral Treatment Program for Bulimarexic Women

William C. White, Jr.
Marlene Boskind-White

Knowledge is not enough; we must apply
Willing is not enough; we must do.
                                        —*Goethe*

If we were to ask most women what it would take to make them happier, the vast majority no doubt would indicate that they would prefer to be 10 pounds thinner. There is little doubt that most middle-class American women wholeheartedly accept reducing as a way of life, its value unquestioned. To be thin is equated with being attractive and successful. To look one's best has become a precursor to feeling one's best. To this end, no price is too dear. If it means a lifetime of counting calories and agonizing over another few pounds, so be it!

The women to whom this chapter is addressed, however, have gone a step further. They are the victims of societal overkill, for they have overinternalized society's definition of attractiveness, love, and the importance of approval. Caricatures of sweetness, submissiveness, and dependency, these women represent the media's feminine ideal. For some, food bingeing and purging has become a temporary means of escaping a world of proscriptions and pain. Many use it to withdraw, thereby punishing significant others whom they hold responsible for their unhappiness. Unlike alcohol and drugs, which are more popular means of achieving the same end, food bingeing is far less overt and antisocial; in fact, it is rarely detectable and therefore often continues for years.

This chapter will be devoted exclusively to a description of over five years of applied clinical research that has been devoted to understanding and treating a large contingent of these bulimarexic women. The reader is referred to our recent book (Boskind-White & White, 1983) for a complete exploration of the family dynamics, socialization rituals, and physiological implications of gorging and purging.

In the fall of 1975, while interning at Cornell, Marlene encountered Suzanne, a petite nutrition major whose initial complaint centered around loneliness and depression. It was during their second session that she revealed her major problem. In order to maintan her ideal weight and still consume what she wanted, Suzanne had resorted to vomiting. Purging was initiated at the age of 16 when she chanced upon an especially gifted girlfriend throwing up after a gymnastics class. Caught in the act, this young woman revealed that she had been purging for some time in order to sustain her weight. For several months thereafter, Suzanne purged only upon overeating. Soon, however, her bingeing intensified such that, when confronted by moderate anxiety, she began to binge uncontrollably. Within weeks, each binge was followed by self-induced vomiting. Suzanne reported engaging in such behavior at least twice a day during the previous two years. She had revealed her "secret" to no one during the first year; however, as the frequency of these binge–purge episodes increased, she became frightened and sought professional help. In the process, however, she did not inform her therapist of the frequency, intensity, and duration of her binge–purge cycle, which had been consuming an inordinate amount of time and energy. Six months of therapy was therefore devoted almost exclusively to an exploration of her past. As might be anticipated, her therapist was reassuring, indicating that since she was so thin there was no need to worry about overeating. Thus, by the time she came to the clinic, Suzanne was quite disillusioned.

We soon began to discover others within our student population who had similar problems. Some binged and instead of vomiting relied heavily upon emetics, laxatives, rigorous fasting, or compulsive exercise to rid themselves of dreaded calories. All were women. Marlene felt she was onto something!

After an extensive review of the literature on eating disorders, she began working individually with these women, as did Bill. Concurrently, Marlene committed herself to an applied dissertation in this area. Follow-up surveys, conducted over the next few months were quite disappointing, however, in that the vast majority of these coeds, despite initial strides, had reverted to their old, familiar eating patterns within three months after one-to-one treatment. Extensive interviews with these women suggested that therapy had failed to emphasize the development of critical coping strategies necessary to sustain them in the face of anxiety. They still reported feeling very much alone and out of control. Considerable probing and reevaluation of therapy was therefore undertaken in a group context. These exploratory sessions progressed extremely well, serving to reveal that many of these women had developed very little in the way of support upon leaving therapy. Furthermore, those with viable support systems failed to utilize them. Because the group sessions had been so productive and, as such, represented precisely what many felt they needed, we began group therapy programs that were offered over a two-year period to those who were interested. In the meantime, we continued individual therapy with those who were uncomfortable with the group format.

During the next several months, we learned more and more about this maladaptive behavior and decided to share our findings by publishing an article in *Psychology Today* (Boskind-Lodahl & Sirlin, 1977). The response was overwhelming. Scores of letters arrived daily, each pouring forth a similar, tragic story. Some were from women in their forties who had been bingeing and purging for 15 years. At the other end of the spectrum were those in their late teens and early twenties who had adopted the behavior only a short time before encountering the article. Most were amazed and relieved to learn that they were not alone. All of them were eager to learn more. Our first survey of demographic and dynamic issues surrounding the problem therefore was accomplished easily. Upon mailing 300 detailed questionnaires to women who had written us, our return rate was well over 70 percent within one month!

Popular articles regarding our work soon began to emerge, thereby stimulating inquiries from women across the United States and Canada. In fact, *Glamour* magazine devoted their December 1979 editorial to a discussion of the enormous response they had received as a result of their article describing our early exploration and treatment of the binge–purge syndrome. This response served to dispel any doubt that the syndrome was quite prevalent and that no effective treatment program had been developed yet.

What Is Bulimarexia?

Eating disorders have received substantial attention in both professional and public arenas, particularly during the past few decades. In fact, research on obesity and anorexia has consumed volumes. The women we are addressing, however, do not fit neatly into either of these categories, despite intriguing similarities, particularly with anorexia (White & Boskind-White, 1982). In fact, about 15 percent of the women we have experienced were diagnosed as anorexic at an earlier point in time. Furthermore, those salient behaviors associated with anorexia, such as abnormally low self-esteem, a paralyzing sense of ineffectiveness, distorted body image, obsessive thinking about food, a history of being a "good girl," and bingeing and purging in solitude, are quite apparent among some of the women we view as bulimarexic. It is the binge–purge behavior, however, that represents an important point of departure between the women we see and those who are suffering from anorexia nervosa. For anorexics, such eating rampages are typically erratic, if they occur at all; in fact, most anorexics are close to starvation level much of the time. In contrast, the hallmark of the women we have observed is their commitment to the cyclic *ritual* of binges and purges. Thus, in moments of stress, these women turn *toward* food, not away from it. Furthermore, during interim periods they typically are capable of regulating their consummatory patterns, often eating nutritious meals. In addition, these women characteristically are able to handle most aspects of daily living, despite bingeing and purging. Anorexics typically are not. Finally, anorexics are usually younger, more isolated, and far more dependent upon their families than the women we have studied.

Despite these apparent differences, hundreds of the women we encountered had been labeled anorexic. Most found the clinical description of the emaciated adolescent foreign and frightening. We, too, had great difficulty "categorizing" these women whose weight was within normal limits and who were not intent upon starving themselves. On the contrary, most of them appeared to be desperately searching for ways of coping with their seemingly uncontrollable binge-eating and purging behaviors. On the other hand, the diagnostic category of *bulimia* was devoid of any reference to purging at the time of our initial research in 1975. We therefore felt compelled to distinguish this binge–purge syndrome from both anorexia and bulimia; hence the term *bulimarexia* was introduced to the professional literature in 1976 (Boskind-Lodahl, 1976). We had grave reservations about assigning a label to the problem, primarily because by so doing we ran the risk that bulimarexia would be considered a disease. In order to avoid this, we chose to define bulimarexia operationally in terms of specific primary and secondary behaviors (Boskind-Lodahl & White, 1978) and were opposed emphatically to including this term in the soon-to-be-revised *DSM-III*.

Bulimarexia is, from our perspective, a habit. It is a learned response, not a disease process. As such, it can be unlearned. It is important, however, that we take care not to underestimate the impact of this habitual response pattern. Cigarette smoking and alcohol consumption are also habits which, over time, have proven quite resistant to treatment. The first step in altering a specific behavior should involve an accurate description of its basic components. Let us therefore begin with a review of our definition of bulimarexia.

Bulimarexia is a recurrent eating pattern exhibited almost exclusively by women who alternately engage in food binges and then purge, usually by self-induced vomiting or laxative abuse. Although severe fasting is utilized as an alternative to purging, it is far less prevalent and should not be confused with classic anorexia in which the major emphasis is on starvation.

Furthermore, bulimarexia entails an obsession with body image. The concern is not so much with body weight as with body proportions; the crucial fact is that these women distort their body image.

In addition to these primary characteristics, secondary aspects include abnormally low self-esteem, perfectionism, isolationism, and a strong commitment toward pleasing others, often at the bulimarexic's expense.

With these characteristics in mind, it is our contention that such women subscribe to a belief system that nullifies the development of a healthy self-concept. Furthermore, our pilot research suggests that little correlation exists between the frequency, intensity, and duration of the purging and the prognosis. Far more relevant prognostically is the bulimarexic's *level of commitment* and the *precise strategies* she employs when confronted by discriminative stimuli. Thus, the woman who is committed to *risk taking* in order to initiate and maintain growth through alternative behaviors appears to be an excellent candidate for therapy. In our experience, this is a tall order. Nevertheless, we have known scores of women who have given up bingeing and purging without therapy. Our book (Boskind-White & White, 1983) is directed primarily toward these women and those who would like to emulate them. These remarkable women have played a large part in the development of the treatment program we will discuss in this chapter. It represents a *beginning*. We hope that it will stimulate professional interest and growth in this embryonic area, which has fascinated us for over five years. Finally, we are particularly indebted to Ellis, Berne, Perls, Glasser, and Adler, from whose therapies we have borrowed significantly in order to design our own flexible program of therapy.

Myths Associated with Bulimarexia

In the process of therapy, we have become painfully aware of six major propositions that the vast majority of bulimarexics adhere to tenaciously. Each of these is based upon an irrational premise that has proven elusive. Thus, once we have defined our treatment population so as to include bulimarexic women exclusively, we then focus upon helping each individual within the group to identify those irrational beliefs that are serving to initiate and maintain her binge–purge behavior. They are as follows:

1. Primary among these beliefs is the view that *bulimarexia is a disease, a mental illness*. The danger underlying such a subscription is the inherent implication that someone else must either do "it" to her or for her. Thus, the client is conveniently "off the hook," surrendering her power to someone else. Under such circumstances, little progress can be expected.
2. In this same vein, the unwarranted assumption that, *because it has taken years to become bulimarexic, it will take years to stop* also must be confronted directly. This irrational belief is easily dispelled by sharing feedback from other women who once were extremely entrenched bulimarexics. Because these women are

quite eager to share their successes, we often ask them to address our groups as well as other self-help groups in areas where therapists are not available.

3. One of the most frustrating beliefs requiring careful reflection involves the view that, *unless it is possible for the bulimarexic to discover why she binges, she will never prove capable of eliminating the behavior.* Taking care to point out that behavior is purposive, we emphasize that one does not maintain a particular response pattern unless there is a reward. Shifting the emphasis from *why* to *what* avails women of the opportunity to determine *how* bingeing and purging are serving them. In fact, when these payoffs are clearly delineated, the selection of appropriate alternatives is thereby enhanced.

4. Another myth involves the contemporary assertion that, *if the bulimarexic is to stop bingeing, she must do so on her own.* Admirable as it may seem, this is grandiose. It makes little sense that someone, confronted by an exceedingly difficult habit, should be left exclusively on her own. In fact, in the vast majority of cases, the bulimarexic will not engage in bingeing or purging in the presence of someone else unless that person is a party to the process. Thus, carefully designed goal contracts with significant others should not be ruled out; however, such contracts should be specific, easily evaluated, and renegotiable, if the client is to derive precisely what she needs from those capable of rendering support. It is unfair to expect someone to know precisely what to do unless the bulimarexic has been specific in her requests. This is the primary reason that so few bingers have been successful in their attempts to establish a viable support network.

5. To accept the philosophy that *bulimarexics are powerless in the face of food* may prove advantageous initially; however, in the final analysis, such an expectation is not only unwarranted but often highly demotivating. Once again, showing beats telling: We have found this premise most easily dispelled by relying upon former clients. Women who, within a few months, reestablished control over food are often eager to share their success experiences directly or indirectly. Providing the group with the opportunity to experience chronic bingers who have taught themselves to enjoy a meal is, in our experience, quite effective.

6. Finally, those who maintain that *everything will be fine when they stop bingeing and purging* are holding the syndrome accountable rather than directly accepting responsibility for their maladaptive behavior. Furthermore, such a naive viewpoint typi-

cally insures that bingeing will continue—after all, who among us is capable of controlling life so as to completely avoid discomfort? In addition, this role orientation exudes perfectionism by virtue of the fact that it will not allow even one mistake. Thus, even when she has been strong enough to avoid bingeing for months, as many of those with whom we have worked have done, *one* episode of overeating characteristically elicits a return to extreme binge–purge behavior. Such setbacks, although frequently demotivating, provide excellent opportunities to "own" such sabotage maneuvers. Unless this is accomplished, the bulimarexic is likely to continue making the same self-defeating mistakes over and over again.

Common Evasive Maneuvers

Upon direct confrontation of the preceding six myths, most women are eager to begin formulating new strategies. This is premature, however, since a number of misconceptions common to the over-whelming majority of bulimarexics first must be addressed. In fact, such well-intentioned bursts of enthusiasm often precipitate major setbacks, which prove difficult to counteract. Although determination and commitment are necessary, they are rarely sufficient to maintain change. In fact, most women with whom we have worked have been able to eliminate bingeing and purging for a period of weeks or even months, primarily because of strenuous commit-ment. Although admirable and encouraging, the ultimate impact is typically transient and demotivating. Such ill-conceived strategy is comparable to confronting a marauding beast with a B-B gun. At this crucial point in therapy, it is therefore important to help the bulimarexic fortify herself. Before effective alternatives can be ini-tiated, she must become cognizant of a myriad of evasive ma-neuvers that serve to reinforce bingeing behavior. Let us now exam-ine these.

Irreversibility

Emphasizing the dysfunctional nature of old response patterns, we rely upon the Adlerian technique (Ansbacher & Ansbacher, 1956) of inviting each member of the group to develop *new responses to old problems*. In order to facilitate risk taking, we are careful to stress that new behaviors are rarely irreversible and therefore can be abandoned if unproductive. At the same time, special attention is devoted to experiential work that illustrates that anything new is typically unfamiliar and therefore often uncomfortable. Role-plays offer an excellent means of eliciting such feeling states, thereby allowing the group a valuable opportunity to experience uncomfortable situations that, in the past, characteristically have led to abandonment of potentially therapeutic strategies.

Pain As a Precursor to Change

In general, bulimarexics capitulate and withdraw in the face of stress, conflict, and confrontation. On the surface, this appears reasonable; however, close examination of the consequences of these common avoidance patterns within the context of the group reveals an exceedingly important means of sabotage. For in withdrawing, the bulimarexic often denies herself invaluable opportunities for growth. This is so because, whether we like it or not, pain serves as a common precursor to change for most of us; thus, to avoid painful experiences is to avoid major opportunities to learn and grow. That is precisely what the bulimarexic does when she resorts to bingeing in the face of threat. Beginning with moderately uncomfortable stimuli, such avoidance patterns soon generalize so that, with time, even the mildest challenge serves to elicit that old, familiar binge-purge repertoire. The goal obviously isn't to court pain; however, risk taking insures discomfort. Thus, the bulimarexic needs to learn to use such painful moments to initiate new alternatives.

Living in the Present

Most bulimarexics are unaware that they tend to live in either the past or the future. Thus, upon being confronted by stress, they turn to past experiences for old, familiar coping strategies, or they rehearse for tragedy by living in the future. In either case, bingeing is the number-one response in their hierarchy. Part of our therapy is for each woman in the group to learn to pose the question, "What tense am I in?" especially when confronted by stress. She then is availed of the opportunity to invest energy in the present, for it is here and now that the battle is raging. Heavy reliance upon double-chair, top-dog–underdog, and similar here-and-now techniques often serves to facilitate a present-tense, action-oriented role orientation, more commensurate with responsible problem solving.

Self-Stroking

Another problem prominent among women we have treated involves an inability or unwillingness to reward themselves for success experiences. This can be demonstrated quite readily by reinforcing one or several group members in a genuine manner. Invariably, they will prove incapable of acknowledging such strokes at first. Until they begin to accept reinforcement and enhance their limited self-stroking skills, we have found that bulimarexics consistently deny themselves relevant opportunities to enhance their sense of self-worth. We therefore rely heavily upon "homework assignments" undertaken within and outside the group in order to facilitate the development of these skills.

Toxic Words

Inherent in the vocabulary of most bulimarexics are a number of words that render them particularly vulnerable. Primary among these are "can't," "never," and "forever." In most cases, "can't," is spelled "won't" (Krausz, 1959). Acknowledging this often allows the bulimarexics to identify precisely what they are attempting to avoid. This can be invaluable as a precursor to goal contracting.

Statements involving the words "never" and "forever" are not only unwarranted but smack of sabotage. Implicit in the statement, "I'm quitting bingeing *forever*" is the commitment to continue bingeing upon making even a slight error, regardless of the circumstances. It is not a goal; it is an *expectation* that, if not fulfilled entirely, points directly to a binge. "I'll *never* binge again," is of course a variation on the same theme. Such words are best stricken from the vocabulary of therapy if progress is to be maximized.

Finally, a word that is underutilized consistently by bulimarexics in general is "no." Because of their pernicious adherence to people-pleasing, these women often will say "yes" when they sincerely mean "no." Such a response style, in addition to being deceptive, creates innumerable opportunities to "brown stamp" (Berne, 1964). Thus upon feeling sufficiently put-upon, bulimarexics may "reimburse" themselves with a binge. To be nice and accommodating at their own expense then, has become equated with being appropriate, well-socialized women. To be honest and straightforward under pressure is foreign and frightening. Inhibited women are not likely to do what they dread without considerable stimulation. It is at this point that we turn to the structured milieu of a women's group.

Role Redefinition

Bulimarexic women rarely experience intimacy, primarily because of their basically inhibited lifestyle. One of the fundamental goals of the all-women's segment of our treatment program therefore, is to facilitate open, honest communication among group members, something we have found next to impossible to accomplish in the presence of a male therapist. This important point is illustrated easily by drawing attention to earlier transactions between Bill and several group participants. Invariably, these women vie for his attention, often attributing change to his intervention. Such a response style, especially when contrasted with the ways that Marlene relates to him, serve as excellent illustrations of how bulimarexics tend to relinquish their power to men. By so doing, they are undermining their credibility and endorsing the need to be rescued.

The basic tenet that "oneness must precede twoness," therefore, is emphasized strenuously throughout this segment of therapy. Adhering to a framework that stresses societal precursors to bulimarexia while at the same time confronting the tendency to embrace the role of "tragic victim," Marlene models her own struggles with similar issues involving body image, acceptability to others, and self-worth. Because most bulimarexics have experienced an absence of positive role models, they have been denied exposure to alternative behaviors. Furthermore, such self-disclosure often serves to penetrate, perhaps for the first time, a number of formidable barriers to psychological growth (Mosak, 1967). Thus, many of the women with whom we have worked begin to feel a sense of connectedness, camaraderie, and sisterhood, which in turn facilitates breaking through the isolation, guilt, and shame that has held them in check for years. In the process of removing these barriers, many begin to like and respect one another, subverting notions of individual inadequacy and psychopathology. Anecdotal input from scores of women over the past five years suggests that such feelings may serve to motivate them to initiate risk-taking behaviors commensurate with their immediate needs.

Participant Modeling

Treatment programs consisting primarily of modeling and guided participation have been quite effective as a means of curtailing defensive behavior (Bandura, 1975). Rather than attempting to attenuate aberrant behavior by eliminating anxiety, the participant modeling paradigm utilizes success experiences as a means of eliciting change (Bandura, Jeffery, & Gajdos, 1975). A technique that facilitates rapid reality testing by structuring the environment so as to maximize success seemed ideally suited to bulimarexics who are intent on avoiding painful situations. Maintaining that cultural factors reinforce their pathognomonic pursuit of thinness, we rely upon a clinical variation of this participant modeling paradigm. Initially, Marlene models specific strategies for overcoming passivity, dependency, and accommodation. Most bulimarexics require the support of the therapist from the onset. Later, with self-directed practice outside the group, many are able to continue these strides. Such guided explorations often serve to expose the myopia that accompanies the endorsement of their limited definition of womanhood. Invaluable opportunities to enhance attempts at being honest, intimate, and assertive thereby are created and can be enhanced selectively by the group.

Bulimarexics often have difficulty proceeding from awareness into action. As prime examples of Bem's (1976) "feminine women," they seem paralyzed under conditions that might serve to embarrass them or result in negative evaluation. Relying upon such experiential exercises such as role-reversal, fish-bowling, and guided imagery as means of confronting situation-specific anxieties, group members are helped to explore alternatives to passivity and irresponsibility. This individual work within a group context provides each woman opportunities to experience, directly or vicariously, painful feedback. By observing others coping, initially with the help of the therapist and the group and later on their own, women discover that criticism can initiate *risk taking* rather than retreat.

As an example, let us consider one of the major means by which bulimarexics tend to surrender their power to men. As relatively naive, "good girls" whose limited sexual experiences typically have led to deriving pleasure primarily from giving, they often have subverted their own sexual desires. Since it is not uncommon among women in general, Marlene often initiates scenarios that facilitate the expression of such needs by *asking* for what she needs rather than *interpreting* or *submitting* to the needs of significant others. Hand in hand with this basic issue is the inordinate self-loathing bulimarexics characteristically feel toward their bodies. Thus, women who, at 115 pounds, consider themselves overweight, quickly perceive the irrationality of their viewpoint upon experiencing exceedingly slim and attractive group members who feel and act just as unlovable.

The emphasis is therefore upon creating guided modeling experiences that are relevant to each woman's specific needs. Mother–child dialogues, parent–daughter dilemmas, and husband–wife transactions therefore consume much of the women's group session and serve to *show* women how to encounter pain while at the same time accepting the validity of their own emotions. Few will need to binge any longer upon discovering more effective ways of identifying and satisfying these specific needs.

All of this is in preparation for relationship training. At this point, the male therapist rejoins the group, thereby providing opportunities for continued exploration and resolution of new ways of encountering men. In this same vein, Marlene and Bill's relationship often serves as a focal point for group interaction. Over the years, we have chosen to reveal our struggles and deficiencies as a couple, modeling alternatives, some of which we have learned from our work with other groups. Spontaneous feedback from scores of former clients indicates that such behavior serves at least two purposes. It exposes the myths of the perfect partner as well as the all-knowing therapist and at the same time provides the opportunity to assure members that issues specific to each group will not go unexplored.

Behavior Contracting and Rehearsal

By now, the group should be prepared to establish goals. Each woman therefore is encouraged to articulate clearly and then explicate her goals as specific "how," "when," and "where" behaviors. By so doing, she makes an overt commitment that others are aware of and can reinforce. Already sensitive to the not-so-subtle difference between goals and expectations, bulimarexics now can practice what they preach. By consistently reminding themselves and each other of toxic words and myths outlined previously, they can avoid important pitfalls inherent to behavior contracting. Furthermore, they can be mindful of the fact that several alternatives to bingeing will be necessary since their histories indicate that no single behavior is strong enough to displace consistently this well-nurtured habit. These alternatives, although sometimes elusive, usually are transferable, since bulimarexics frequently engage in comparable avoidance patterns. Problem solving in this manner also serves to emphasize the basic premise of reality therapy (Glasser, 1961) that we wholeheartedly endorse: *Your are what you do.* What remains then, is to actualize specific goal contracts by engaging in certain behaviors more consistently, more effectively, and, on occasion, for the first time.

New Responses to Old Problems

Let us now examine those behaviors that the majority of these women must adopt if they are to eliminate or curtail their binge–purge behavior. First, bulimarexics are more vulnerable to bingeing when they are alone. It is crucial, therefore, that they avoid being alone, particularly when confronted by stimuli strongly associated with bingeing. Because they are frequently isolationists, contracts involving the initiation of social contacts are common. Furthermore, it is impossible to binge if there is nothing available to consume. At a minimum, therefore, women who are truly committed to exploring alternatives will enhance their social repertoires and get rid of their secret stashes. Should they choose to binge at a later time, they at least have demonstrated their ability to stop bingeing under circumstances that previously had resulted in failure.

Such success experiences create valuable opportunities to reinforce another common behavior that is critical to eliminating bingeing. As pointed out previously, bulimarexics are inept at self-stroking. We therefore find it therapeutic to confront the group with the following paradox: "On the one hand, you are obsessed with your body, yet on the other you do little to take care of it." Part of any good strategy, therefore, will involve finding ways to reward oneself so as to insure success experiences and, ultimately, a better self-concept.

Often, other therapists with whom we have worked ask what we do with a client who, despite conscientiously adhering to these basic principles of behavior contracting, succumbs to a binge. Such a quesion is answered best by the group, because, in the final analysis, they, not we, must decide. Drawing upon their knowledge of previous "rackets" (Berne, 1964) most group members are now in a position to acknowledge that they made a mistake. That mistake must be scrutinized *immediately,* for unless a *prompt* reassessment is accomplished it is quite likely that a similar series of events will elicit additional binges. Thus, rather than return to cyclic bingeing and purging immediately, well-educated bulimarexics are committed to identifying those discriminative stimuli they missed or ignored. After all, what have they to lose by reversing the response hierarchy so that trouble-shooting precedes purging? Furthermore, since they now are committed to taking better care of themselves, they have at their disposal a number of alternatives to purging. Our files are bursting with mail vividly describing alternatives that served to weaken and ultimately break the strong association between the binge and the purge. These important strategies, although individualized and situation-specific, are also quite generalizable.

At this point, group members are encouraged to rehearse for tragedy in preparation for "Monday morning," when they will be on their own. This is a major part of leave-taking, during which we reinforce additional strategies as they spontaneously emerge, relying heavily upon a successive approximation technique with those who require it. Special emphasis also is given to what we refer to as "looking at the bottom line," a technique based on rational–emotive therapy (Ellis, 1973). In other words, we examine what is the worst that could happen should they engage in a particular alternative to bingeing. If the outcome is catastrophic, then the proposed strategy is in need of considerable revision. However, if it is not, as is typically the case, then we focus upon how one can attenuate or harness such discomfort and grow in the process. Through considerable experiential work, each woman elicits honest feedback so that, over time, the intensity that has characterized her response to threat gives way to humor. Lightening the situation in such a manner is a technique upon which Adlerians rely (Way, 1962). Learning *how to laugh* once more is often quite therapeutic in that a great part of their difficulty stems from the debilitating intensity which is elicited when they are confronted by precursors to bingeing. Upon learning to use humor in the face of challenge, bulimarexics often are able to deal more effectively with those stimulus antecedents that characteristically had proven devastating. The ease with which the group is able thereby to persuade and advise each other often seems contagious. As Strupp (1972) points out, giving advice is inherent to all forms of therapy and often serves to generate an atmosphere of hopefulness and redirection. Care must be taken, however, to insure that group participants assume responsibility for much of their own problem solving, for in their enthusiasm, the more articulate and socially bold often are inclined to "do it for" others. Such intervention, although well intentioned, can rob others of invaluable opportunities to experience directly their own capacity to troubleshoot and act accordingly.

Case Example

In order to illustrate further the methods by which we work, let us examine a day in the life of Jenny, a college sophomore, who offered the following scenario for group processing:

> Upon awakening, Jenny reeled off to herself a series of commitments that she intended to fulfill that day. She would complete a term paper, attend all of her classes, go to the library and the gym, and meet some friends for dinner.
>
> Upon arriving at the university, that old, familiar panic ensued. In order to curb her need to eat, Jenny detoured to the mini-deli to buy some gum. She intended to fast all day, particularly since she was running out of money and felt she just couldn't ask her parents for more. She felt like such a burden.
>
> Once in the deli, her panic intensified. One candy bar won't hurt! Besides, there was a restroom next to her first class. If she ate quickly she could get there in time to purge. While plotting her strategy, Jenny purchased a packet of six candy bars. Streaking to class, she ate the candy while praying for an empty bathroom. Upon arriving, Jenny gulped copious amounts of water and vomited.
>
> Sitting in class, she was unable to concentrate. She wrote hourly, daily, weekly plans regarding what to do between classes, after classes, and at night. Quite discouraged, Jenny thought about cutting her next class and going back to her apartment. Supermarket sale signs flooded her mind. She could get loads of food, cheap! Today was already ruined anyway. Rushing around the store while thinking about what she could buy with limited funds, Jenny stole four small packets of cheese, which fit easily into her pockets. Upon leaving, disgust and self-loathing ensued. Before reaching her apartment, she stopped at a fast-food chain to purchase burgers, fries, and soda. Driving in a hazardous fashion while inhaling food, Jenny recalled the two speeding tickets she recently received under similar circumstances. Once home her mind continued to race while preparing more binge food, always with lots of liquids. This way she could eat, throw up, eat again, throw up, and on and on.

At 3:30 P.M., Jenny had been bingeing and purging continually since morning. Today the food had been difficult to expel, hurting like mad each time! In desperation she punched her stomach, screamed, and cried as she examined her profile in the ever-present mirror. There was little time and energy left to do anything productive now. She was too tired and sick.

Someone was at the door but she wouldn't answer. Friends called but she felt tired and unworthy of their attention. She decided to sleep. Upon awakening around 11:00 P.M., her first thought centered upon food. She immediately reinitiated the cycle by calling the pizza parlor. In the process of picking up the pizza, a guy from school, whom she had been very interested in, spotted her. Much to her dismay, he asked her to dinner and a movie the following evening. Fleeing the pizza parlor, elated by the invitation, Jenny came to her senses. She returned home and slipped the pizzas into her refrigerator with a new resolve.

Morning came early and the strains of the previous day made awakening especially unpleasant. Reality struck—a paper due tomorrow! Panic, hunger pangs; then the phone rang. It was Mom and Dad with questions as to her well-being. The lying began. Everything's fine, great date again tonight, weight is no longer a problem, eating *very* well, paper due soon, unexpected expenses necessitate another "loan" but she will do better in the future. Hanging up the phone, Jenny jumped out of bed, determined to make good on her promises to them.

After skipping breakfast, she went to her classes and the morning passed quickly. Jenny then returned to her apartment to begin writing her paper. About midafternoon, after having gotten a good start, she took her first break. Wandering through her past, she focused on her early morning phone conversation and the deceit inherent therein. In an attempt to regain her positive orientation, she returned to her work. Upon rereading the paper, she judged it grossly inadequate and began to panic. Jenny then streaked to the fridge, inhaled the cold pizzas, thereby reinitiating the gorge–purge ritual. By 4:00 P.M. she looked and felt so hideous that she had no recourse but to call and cancel her date due to an "unexpected illness."

As Jenny outlined her dilemma, group members were encouraged to make careful notes and to focus specifically upon precursors to bingeing. Several members of the group, including Jenny, agreed that a major deterrent to psychological growth involved her obvious commitment to isolationism. Jenny then placed herself on the "hot seat of responsibility" (Perls, 1969) and began enumerating alternatives to withdrawal. The first of these included the possibility of finding a roommate to share her apartment or moving into a dorm suite. Since these alternatives were commensurate with the needs of others within the group, the therapists suggested that everyone examine the bottom line by considering the worst that might happen if they embraced one of these alternatives. Several women pointed to an incompatibility problem that facilitated careful delineation of those qualities that Jenny and others might require in a roommate. Jenny proposed screening applicants, pointing to the desirability of her location and the fact that she had a car with which to shop. In the past, her strenuous adherence to people-pleasing had denied her the opportunity to evaluate and choose. Furthermore, if she agreed to joint shopping ventures, bingeing might be curtailed since she would be less likely to purchase those junk foods that typically lined her shelves. Another group member aksed Jenny if she would feel compelled to reveal her problem to a roommate. The group was eager to process this issue, since most of them had struggled with that same question with regard to friends, husbands, or parents. Before proceeding, the therapists requested that each woman answer the question, "How will telling this person help me?" Jenny decided that she would prefer not to reveal her behavior initially but would rather try to find a roommate who was interested in structuring time each day to study and who also might enjoy swimming or jogging with her. In time, if she felt the need to become more intimate with her partner, she might then reveal her problem and ask specifically for the support she might need.

Another member of the group was skeptical, suggesting that, despite such planning, the roommate still might prove aversive. Jenny quickly pointed out the worst that could happen. She might experience discomfort yet learn something useful from the experience. Addressing the concept of irreversibility, Jenny indicated that at least she would have an opportunity to examine those aspects of her living situation with which she did not feel comfortable. At the same time, she was able to recognize that past attempts at living with others no doubt had proven disastrous because she had become defensive and never addressed these important issues.

Upon establishing new goals that involved pursuing a roommate and a more social orientation, Jenny and the group addressed another stimulus for bingeing—her habit of driving by "irresistible" stores on her way to and from the university. At this point, nervous laughter served to reveal that this was a pervasive tendency. Several others spontaneously confessed to inordinate food stashes locked in cars and office drawers. Such behaviors were labeled appropriately as rackets designed to temporarily satiate yet, in the long run, undermine each woman who continued to rely upon them.

Alternative strategies were outlined quickly and trouble-shot by the group. Some of these included driving alternate routes, avoiding the sabotage inherent in stashes, and rewarding oneself for a good morning by eating lunch with friends. Jenny came up with an even better alternative, however. She had always wanted a tape deck in her car, but due to financial constraints and the fact that she squandered so much money on food, she had never seriously considered buying one. Such a strategy might help her accomplish several goals. First, it might render her car a discriminative stimulus for pleasure rather than painful bingeing. In addition, she could use the stereo as a way of relaxing to and from school, thereby rewarding herself for attending class regularly, something she had been failing to do. Her contract, therefore, involved saving $5 each day that she did not binge. Since she had been spending anywhere from $10 to $20 each day on binge food, she reasoned that the stereo was an incredible bargain.

Throughout this problem-solving experience, Jenny was animated, enthusiastic, and irresistible to all of us as the architect of her own goal contracting. Genuine strokes were elicited easily under such circumstances, and Jenny, perhaps for the first time, accepted such compliments readily. As a result, she fell back on an old, familiar, yet detrimental behavior pattern that had remained elusive for some time: In her eagerness to excel, Jenny often became overextended. By establishing too many goals, she often set herself up for failure. Reflecting upon how she began her monologue, Jenny agreed. Lying in bed each morning she often would give herself daily "assignments" that she rarely completed. Thus, although well intentioned and action oriented, such grandiose expectations had been subtracting immeasurably from her effectiveness. As a result of this feedback, Jenny decided to be nice to herself and scale down such plans. As success experiences gradually accrued, they might serve to motivate new, more challenging goal contracts on a day-to-day basis.

At this point, Jenny reached out to the group for feedback regarding her interactions with her parents. Based upon feedback during the group as well as discussions with other group members outside of our formal sessions, several women helped Jenny to see how her relationship with her parents was predicated on dishonesty and childish manipulation. In addition, she came to understand how *she* often created situations that elicited parental overprotection and intrusion into her life. Although she abhorred their interference, for years she had been embracing the role of "helpless child," asking them to rescue her from each and every difficulty she encountered. In a series of role-plays, initially with the therapists and later with selected group members, she practiced a new repertoire of risk-taking behaviors that were much more honest and confrontative. Marlene often served as a model by role-playing and coaching Jenny and others regarding the ways they related to Bill.

One of Jenny's goals involved developing an honest relationship with her father. As a result of these role-plays, she formulated new strategies. From now on she would initiate and respond to telephone calls from her father at times when she felt well fortified. Heretofore, Jenny often delayed calling her family for weeks. This merely engendered concern on their part and a defensive posture on hers. Furthermore, her father often called quite early in the morning or late at night. Because she felt vulnerable and was often deceptive at such times, Jenny decided to ask her father to phone at more appropriate times. In so doing, she would have to accept responsibility for being available during times of her own choosing.

In order to foster this role orientation, Jenny accepted two homework assignments. Since the group had intended to socialize that evening, Jenny was asked to encounter men honestly and to note their responses. In addition, she was to determine how she would respond to her father's questions regarding the value of the group experience upon returning home the next afternoon. That evening, Jenny initiated a new, more assertive stance with men. Much to her delight, such behavior was referred to as "refreshing" by the most interesting man she had encountered. As a result, Jenny and others began delineating additional behavioral contracts. At this point, the atmosphere of the group was notably different in one regard—the therapists had very little to say. Group members were demonstrating their newly developed coping strategies with considerable zeal.

Follow-up Considerations

As indicated previously, we routinely inform those women with whom we work of our commitment to evaluating the outcome of our treatment programs. In order to maximize input, we offered each participant the option of remaining anonymous, despite the limitations inherent in such a research design. As a result, follow-up questionnaires have elicited excellent return rates ranging from 71 to 89 percent.

Initially, our groups were composed of college women treated exclusively by women therapists (Boskind-Lodahl & White, 1978). Twenty-six women, who had been bingeing and purging daily for at least three years, were assigned to a treatment or control (waiting-list) condition in the order that they entered the clinic. Dependent measures included pre-, post- and three-month-follow-up scores on the Sixteen Personality-Factor Questionnaire (16PF) (Cattell, 1972), a modified Body Cathexis Test (BCT) (Secord & Jourard, 1953), and an extensive behavioral questionnaire that we designed based upon pilot work with over 100 bulimarexics (Boskind-Lodahl, 1976). Both groups met weekly with a female cotherapist team for 11 two-hour sessions. In addition, a six-hour marathon session was held midway during therapy in order to ascertain better what group members felt they needed during the last half of their treatment program.

Issues addressed under the treatment condition included a sense of personal isolation, shame and guilt surrounding the syndrome, parental problems, social competence, sex-role stereotypes, and the development of more effective coping strategies within each of these areas. Behavioral techniques consistently employed included keeping daily food intake charts, examining precipitating factors associated with bingeing and purging, and initiating short-term (weekly) goal contracts based upon specific troublesome situations.

Control-group members were offered guided discussion of readings on feminist issues and food-related problems. All of these waiting-list controls were availed of our group therapy program four months after the study was completed.

Following the suggestions of Overall and Woodward (1977) for analysis of data when nonrandom assignment is used to form groups, an analysis of covariance was applied to the data. Pretest scores on the 16PF and the BCT served as covariates, with group assignment and time intervals representing two factors.

Although few of our results in this pilot reached acceptable levels of statistical significance, we were encouraged by a number of consistent trends that suggested that our treatment efforts had impacted measures of self-assurance positively. Such trends were in line with significant changes on the BCT. Additional changes on the 16PF reflecting self-sufficiency and self-control factors were evident immediately after treatment but regressed toward initial levels upon follow-up. Nevertheless, these changes suggested that the group experience per se was an important component of such positive posttest scores.

One of our primary treatment goals involved facilitating awareness and acceptance of one's body image. We were therefore quite pleased that 82 percent of the treatment group as opposed to 32 percent of our controls were involved in activities (e.g. sports, health clubs, activity groups) that they initiated and truly enjoyed. This differed dramatically from previous inactivity or compulsive exercise focused upon burning dreaded calories. Significant increases in their BCT scores seemed to reflect such attitude changes.

At three-month follow-up, four members of the treatment group had stopped bingeing and purging, while six others reported binges that were less frequent and of shorter duration. In contrast, only one of the control-group members had curtailed her bingeing behavior to any extent. Although initially encouraged by these reports, follow-up over the next several months revealed that five of these 10 women had reverted to extreme binge–purge behaviors once again. Strides obviously were not being maintained over time.

For the next two years we revised our treatment program and modified our research design. Major changes were based primarily upon hours of discussion and reevaluation of the life scripts of those women who responded to our questionnaires, as well as those with whom we continued to work. Therapists from across the USA and Canada who came to work with us also wrote regarding their experiences with bulimarexic women. In the final analysis, one overriding prognostic indicator emerged: Sustained progress appeared to be contingent upon initiating, maintaining, and enhancing the quality of their interpersonal relationships, particularly with men. Those who were engaged in fulfilling relationships with others consistently spoke of risk taking and ensuing growth experiences. Pain was an integral part of their lives—something they had reluctantly accepted as inherent to psychosocial growth and development. Bingeing was tertiary, if present at all, because their lives were filled with relevant pursuits. Most had learned to reinforce themselves, noting that significant others had seemed unwilling or unable to stroke them as consistently as they had needed. All lived mainly in the present and were quite action-oriented in their responses to life. On the other hand, those whose lives were devoid of intimacy and meaningful interpersonal interactions inevitably returned to bingeing and purging despite intermittent success experiences in a variety of personal and professional endeavors.

In light of this consistent feedback and the transient impact of our early efforts at treating bulimarexic women, we decided to revise our therapy once again. Following suggestions from these exceptional women, we initiated more experiential exercises that highlighted interpersonal communicative skills. By introducing a male cotherapist we were able to underscore the importance of interpersonal risk taking in a heterosexual context—something that we had not emphasized previously due to our myopic adherence to separatist philosophy. This new emphasis did not subtract from the impact of an all-women's group; in fact, it enriched it by providing innumerable opportunities for women to evaluate their new skills and risk-taking behaviors. Thus, opportunities for goal contracting, behavior rehearsal, relationship training, and assertiveness were broadened to include *in vivo* transactions with the male therapist, who could play the roles of father, husband, male boss, or boyfriend. Furthermore, honest feedback could be elicited directly, thereby helping to dispel paralyzing misconceptions inherent in the bulimarexic's "male script."

In order to evaluate empirically the revised treatment program presented in this chapter, we began a series of studies. The first of these involved administering the California Psychological Inventory (CPI) (Gough, 1957), a modified Body Cathexis Test (BCT) (Secord & Jourard, 1953), and a behavioral questionnaire to 14 bulimarexic women who ranged in age from 14 to 45 years (White & Boskind-White, 1982). These dependent measures were used prior to therapy, immediately thereafter, and at one-year follow-up in order to assess stability of change. This group was quite committed to bulimarexia in that, despite the fact that they all had been in therapy for at least two consecutive years prior to being referred to our group, they were continuing to binge and purge at least twice daily. They were, in fact, the most severely impacted group we had ever treated.

Repeated measures of analysis of variance were performed on each of the 18 CPI scales, as well as on the BCT data. Sources of variation for these analyses included the three time intervals, the 14 group members, and the interactions among these variables. Our primary interest centered upon the main effect of time intervals. The F statistic was computed using the interaction mean square for test intervals times the number of subjects as the error term. For each scale that yielded a significant F value, multiple comparisons utilizing Tukey's pairwise procedure were performed in order to determine: (1) whether significant changes were evident during treatment, (2) whether these changes were maintained at one-year follow-up, (3) whether group participants improved or deteriorated on follow-up, or (4) whether some combination of treatment effects and any significant events, subsequent to therapy or prior to follow, altered responses to the CPI or BCT.

We were aware of a potential threat to the internal validity of our experimental design—a design in which subjects were assessed repeatedly in the absence of a no-treatment control group, which would serve to control for the possibility that some other event, occurring during the period between measures, might have contributed to any change noted on our dependent measures. However, we were committed to this "intractable" group and wanted to avoid a waiting-list control condition. Furthermore, Sellitz, Wrightsman, and Cook (1976, pp. 149) have pointed out that whatever effect past experience or enduring characteristics have on a particular measure, such influence would tend to impact measurement at *each* of the three test intervals. In addition, we were aware that confounding maturational or developmental changes characteristically are manifest in a gradual, not abrupt, shift in scores.

Analysis of the CPI data revealed that group members who initially had described themselves as dependent, helpless, inadequate, and myopic viewed themselves as significantly more independent, progressive, responsible, and versatile as reflected by scores attained on the CPI one year after treatment. Furthermore, consistent trends toward feeling more assertive, self-reliant, and capable of thinking and planning more clearly and accurately were noted. Such attitude changes were commensurate with previous research (Boskind-Lodahl & White, 1978) and, more important, also were consistent with changes in overt behavior reported on questionnaires administered at one-year follow-up. These questionnaires revealed that three of the 14 women had stopped bingeing completely one year after treatment. This change had not occurred abruptly, however. In each case, at least five separate bingeing episodes had occurred during the initial six months following therapy. None of these binges had led to purging, however.

Of the remaining 11 women, seven had attenuated their bingeing frequency to less than five times a month during the last six months. Again, purging had been curtailed even more in that all of them had engaged in self-induced vomiting less than five times during that same six-month interval.

The four remaining women reported little change in their binge–purge cycles on follow-up. All continued some form of psychotherapy but still described themselves as desperate and unhappy. Thus, the treatment rendered was not effective for all those involved. Those who failed possessed one major commonality—they were committed to creating a favorable impression, to being seen as "good girls." All of these women required further therapy. All but one are currently in treatment. In fact, five of those who curtailed their bingeing significantly were referred to therapists in their locales because of their obvious need for professional help in other aspects of their lives. This is as it should be, for our treatment program is quite specific in focus. It is not a panacea but a means of overcoming the habitual urge to binge and purge. Once that is accomplished, women will choose to fill the resultant time void with other pursuits. Some of these, no doubt, will elicit new challenges and occasional setbacks that might require professional consultation. We therefore feel compelled to help educate clients in this regard and, whenever feasible, recommend therapy to those in need.

Future Directions

Although we are encouraged by our recent research results, it is obvious that a plethora of questions remain unanswered; however, questions of fact will not be resolved by rhetoric and debate. They will require experimental and empirical scrutiny. Primary among these questions are evaluations as to optimal group size; sex of therapists; and duration, composition, and outcome of specific treatment programs. We are continuing to address such issues and are hopeful that by introducing this syndrome to the professional community we will stimulate further research.

Until the deeper problems of the society which has spawned such a behavioral pattern are addressed directly, however, it is apparent that we will continue to see more and more bulimarexics. We are hopeful that consciousness raising will continue to have a positive influence upon women's attitudes toward their bodies by providing a more balanced perspective on the narrow and limited feminine role definitions promulgated by society, modeled by mothers, endorsed by fathers, and expected by prospective mates. Our work with bulimarexics painfully reminds us how sex-role stereotyping has served to deter women from actualizing their full human potential and denied them opportunities to develop competence and intimacy. It is therefore crucial that today's parents be made aware of the contemporary pressures that impinge on their daughters. Only then will they prove capable of offering support. Well-informed fathers then can encourage their daughters to achieve and develop a passion for success and accomplishment—rather than protect them from challenge and responsibility—in spite of their helpless protestations, tears, and charming, manipulative ploys. Studies of famous women consistently have revealed unusually strong childhood relationships with fathers (Henning, 1970). Mothers too, must become more aware of the enormous impact they have as role-models for their daughters. Children, in general, need sources of identification. It is therefore particularly important that women continue to broaden their interests and activities in ways that engender self-respect. The parent who *shows,* rather than tells, offers an invaluable legacy.

This is not enough, however, for no matter how fortified she may be, the young woman will encounter significant pressure to embrace "feminine" behaviors outside her immediate family. The media have attained enormous power in this regard. By consistently bombarding us with unrealistic and unhealthy models of womanhood, millions of young women are continuing to embrace a "feminine ideal" that is practically impossible to emulate. The ramifications are horrifying! Who decides how slim a woman should be? The responsibility in part, rests with the media. If a concerted effort were made to introduce models whose torsos were not emaciated, what would be the outcome? In our estimation, the impact would be quite positive. Until then, however, we must rely heavily upon those who refuse to conform to such rigid, restrictive definitions of womanhood.

References

Ansbacher, H. L., & Ansbacher, R. (eds.). *The Individual Psychology of Alfred Adler.* New York: Basic Books, 1956.

Bandura, A. Effecting change through participant modeling. In J. D. Krumboltz & C. E. Thoresen (eds.), *Counseling Methods.* New York: Holt, Rinehart and Winston, 1975.

Bandura, A., Jeffery, R. W., & Gajdos, E. Generalizing change through participant modeling with self-directed mastery. *Behavior Research and Therapy,* 1975, *13,* 144–152.

Bem, S. Probing the promise of androgyny. In A. G. Kaplan & J. P. Bean (eds.), *Beyond Sex-Role Stereotypes*. Boston: Little, Brown, 1976.

Berne, E. *Games People Play*. New York: Grove Press, 1964.

Boskind-Lodahl, M. Cinderella's Stepsisters: A Feminist Perspective on Anorexia Nervosa and Bulimia. *Signs: The Journal of Women in Culture and Society, 2,* (2), 1976, 342–356.

Boskind-Lodahl, M., & Sirlin, J. The gorging–purging syndrome. *Psychology Today,* March 1977, Vol. II, 50.

Boskind-Lodahl, M, & White, W. C. The definition and treatment of bulimarexia in college women—A pilot study. *Journal of American College Health Association, 2,* October 1978, 27.

Boskind-White, M., & White, W. C. Bulimarexia: The Binge/Purge Cycle. New York: W.W. Norton, 1983.

Cattell, R. B. The 16PF and basic personality structure: A reply to Eysenck. *Journal of Behavioral Science,* 1972, *4,* 169–187.

Ellis, A. Rational–emotive therapy. In R. Corsini (ed.), *Current Psychotherapies*. Itasca, Ill.: F. E. Peacock, 1973.

Glasser, W. *Reality Therapy*. New York: Harper & Row, 1961.

Gough, H. *Manual for the California Psychological Inventory*. Palo Alto, Calif.: Counseling Psychologists Press, 1957.

Henning, M. *Career Development for Women Executives*. Unpublished doctoral dissertation. Cambridge, Mass.: Harvard University, 1970.

Krausz, E. O. The commonest neurosis. In K. A. Alder & D. Deutsch (eds.), *Essays on Individual Psychology*. New York: Grove Press, 1959.

Mosak, H. H. Subjective criteria of normality. *Psychotherapy,* 1967, *4,* 159–161.

Overall, J. & Woodward, F. Nonrandom assignment and the analysis of covariance, *Psychological Bulletin,* 1977, *84*(3), 588–594.

Perls, F. *Gestalt Therapy Verbatim*. Lafayette, Calif.: Real People Press, 1969.

Secord, P., & Jourard, S. The appraisal of body cathexis and the self. *Journal of Consulting Psychology,* 1953, *17,* 343–347.

Sellitz, C., Wrightsman, L. S., & Cook, S. W. *Research Methods in Social Relations*. New York: Holt, Rinehart and Winston, 1976.

Strupp, H. H. Freudian analysis today. *Psychology Today, 2*(6), 1972, 33–40.

Way, L. *Adler's Place in Psychology*. New York: Collier Books, 1962.

White, W. C., & Boskind-White, M. An experiential–behavioral approach to the treatment of bulimarexia. *Psychotherapy: Theory, Research and Practice,* 1983 (in press).

5

Restraint and Binge Eating

Janet Polivy
C. Peter Herman
Marion P. Olmsted
Carol Jazwinski

Our work on the correlates of dieting (Herman & Polivy, 1980) has relied on the use of a self-report scale (the Restraint Scale, Herman & Mack, 1975) to identify dieters. This scale has proven successful in discriminating among normal-weight subjects in that high scorers on the scale have been shown to differ markedly from low scorers in eating style, emotionality, and physiological characteristics. One notable feature of this scale, confirmed by repeated psychometric analyses, is its internal reliability despite the presence of seemingly incongruous items. Specifically, while a number of items concern dieting as ordinarily conceived (e.g., How often are you dieting? What is the maximum amount of weight that you have lost within one month?), other items seem inherently *un*characteristic of someone dieting to lose weight (e.g., Do you eat sensibly in front of others and splurge alone? What is your maximum weight gain within a week?). Still, the scale as a whole has been demonstrably successful at discriminating among similar (to all overt appearances) normal-weight college students, predicting, most notably, radically different eating patterns in response to identical stimuli or situations. The success of the scale in predicting individual differences in behavior, combined with its psychometric integrity, inclines us to accept the notion that dieting and overeating[1] co-occur with surprising frequency in the same individuals. What are we to make of the presence of contradictory or mutually exclusive behaviors within individuals?

Naturally, we must recognize that such contradictory behaviors cannot occur simultaneously. Our restrained eaters, apparently, engage in cycles—or at least irregular alternations—of dieting and overeating. It takes not much more psychological acumen to recognize that dieters who indulge in bouts of overeating are almost *compelled* (by the laws of caloric arithmetic) to compensate for these splurges by subsequent atonement in the form of more dieting. For these people, dieting follows overeating as inexorably as Monday follows the weekend. The typical dieter, then, may be seen as bouncing between the extremes of consummatory abandon and compensatory inhibition, with overeating creating the need for dieting, and dieting periodically undone by further bouts of overeating. This model corresponds to the descriptive scheme that most dieters apply to their own behavior. Moreover, not only does it describe their behavior, but it explains it; as far as the dieter is concerned, it is the "disease" of overeating that requires the "cure" of dieting.

One of the interesting questions raised by this model concerns the origin of the "disease" of overeating. From a clinical perspective, "curing" the "disease" (by eliminating its cause) would be preferable to merely "treating" it (by correcting its effects). Dieting is a classic treatment, not a cure. Also, from a theoretical perspective, we naturally are curious as to the processes that underlie the problematic overeating. The cause–effect relationship between overeating and dieting does not seem to present any great scientific or intellectual challenge. The *cause* of overeating, though, is at present obscured in the mists of psychodynamic, sensory–perceptual, and physiological theorizing.

[1] It is perhaps worthwhile to discriminate between bingeing and overeating at the outset. Although the distinction is imprecise—and occasionally ignored altogether in the research literature—we suggest that bingeing differs from "mere" overeating in that (1) it involves a truly prodigious consumption of food, in terms of total consumption of a particular food (relative to the norm for its consumption) and (2) it goes beyond the needs ordinarily signaled by hunger and satiety, presumably because it serves a more compulsive psychodynamic purpose. Overeating, by contrast, does not appear to be as forcefully "driven"; neither does it exceed the possible range of "normal" consumption.

Dieting and Bingeing: Another
Chicken-and-Egg Story

The co-occurrence of overeating and dieting in the same individuals ordinarily is understood in terms of the overeating-demands-dieting model just discussed. While overeating and dieting *alternate* in real-life eaters—at least, in dieters—it is assumed that the overeating comes first (in some abstract conceptual sense). However, Boskind-Lodahl's examination of more than 100 binge-eating patients suffering from what she called "bulimarexia" showed dieting to have preceded the binges in almost every case (Boskind-Lodahl, 1976; Boskind-Lodahl & Sirlin, 1977). Likewise, Bruch's "thin–fat" patients, formerly overweight people who have dieted successfully, becoming and staying thin, often report that they "either diet or go hog wild on sweets and all that stuff" (Bruch, 1973, p. 200). Such clinical observations clearly support the notion that rigid dieting and weight loss are frequently followed by bouts of overeating or bingeing.

The Restraint Scale, however, was designed primarily for use with normal populations, not for clinically pathological samples. If the evidence that bingeing follows dieting came only from clinical samples, it might seem illegitimate to conclude that normal groups follow the same "backwards" pattern; but there is ample evidence that even among "normal," nonclinical dieters, overeating often follows attempts at self-denial. One of the earliest reports of diet-induced bingeing appears in the work by Keys and his colleagues (Franklin, Schiele, Brozek, & Keys, 1948). They had a group of normal young men (conscientious objectors to World War II) self-starve until they weighed approximately 74 percent of normal. After refeeding and returning to their prior normal weight, these subjects exhibited a tendency to gorge, eating at meals as much food as they could hold, despite the unlimited availability of food. Wardle (1980) examined the relation between more common, fashion-inspired dieting and disordered eating, particularly binges, in 68 normal subjects. She found that restrained subjects were more likely than were unrestrained ones both to crave food and to go on eating binges, regardless of their degree of overweight. Hawkins and Clement (1980) also found "more severe binge eating problems coincident with more stringent attempts at restraining eating behavior" (page 225) in a normal population. Their binge-eating measure correlated significantly with the Restraint Scale, with or without body weight partialled out. Furthermore, the amount eaten during a particular binge was correlated with the reported precipitant of "going off a strict diet." This finding in particular suggests that the association between binge-eating and dieting, though circularly self-perpetuating, may originate with dieting rather than with bingeing. Olmsted (1981) also found powerful correlations between restraint and bingeing and between "pursuit of thinness" and bingeing in a normal college-student sample.

The inclusion of items related to periodic overeating in a dieting or "restraint" scale is thus not anomalous, despite first appearances. Observations of clinical populations and self-reports by normal dieters indicate a striking relationship between dieting and eating binges. While the data are largely correlational and cross-sectional, what little evidence there is on the issue of causal precedence suggests that binges are more likely to follow than to precede dieting. Dieting, it seems, usually is undertaken (initially) to achieve weight loss, not to combat binge eating per se. Eventually, of course, dieting becomes required, to counteract the binges that dieting itself somehow produces.

Experimental Evidence of Overeating Episodes of Dieters

Laboratory investigations of "normal" restrained eaters have demonstrated repeatedly the association between dieting and overeating. The earliest studies of restrained eaters (Herman & Mack, 1975; Herman & Polivy, 1975) were attempts to extend Schachter's externality theory (cf. Schachter, 1971) of obesity to normal-weight dieters. Schachter's work (Schachter, 1971; Schachter & Rodin, 1974) had indicated that overweight people are hyperresponsive to external, environmental events and underresponsive to internal regulators of behavior. Herman and Mack (1975) attempted to show that, like overweight people, normal-weight dieters are not responsive to the internal cues of hunger and satiety but instead eat when food is present and eat the same amount whether they are hungry or sated (cf. Schachter, Goldman, & Gordon, 1968). Herman and Mack (1975) manipulated their subjects' degree of hunger by preloading them with zero, one, or two milkshakes (rather than food like sandwiches as in Schachter et al., 1968). Unrestrained eaters behaved just like Schachter and colleagues' (1968) normal-weight subjects, eating a substantial amount (of icecream) when given no preload, decreasing their consumption after one milkshake, and eating least after two milkshakes. Restrained eaters, however, were not simply unresponsive to their hunger (or, conversely, preload) level; they did not merely eat equally in all three conditions, the way Schachter's obese subjects did; neither did they regulate their intake normally by decreasing consumption according to the amount of preload they were given. Restrained eaters, in fact, appeared to *counter*regulate, eating *more* ice cream after one or two milkshakes than after none at all.

Similarly, restrained eaters who were made to feel anxious (Herman & Polivy, 1975) did not simply fail to reduce their intake from their nonanxious level, as did unrestrained eaters and Schachter and colleagues' (1968) normal-weight subjects, but they actually ate somewhat *more* when anxious than when calm. Herman and Polivy (1975; Polivy & Herman, 1976a, 1976b, 1976c) accordingly proposed that disinhibition of any sort disrupts the dieter's restraint and unleashes "deprivation-motivated eating behavior" (Herman & Polivy, 1975, p. 672). Indeed, other disinhibitors, such as alcohol (Polivy & Herman, 1976a, 1976b) and distressing emotional states (e.g., depression, Polivy & Herman, 1976c), were found to increase eating in restrained eaters (rather than decreasing consumption, as was the case for unrestrained eaters in these studies).

Fattening Preloads and the Disinhibitions of Restrained Eating

The disinhibiting or restraint-releasing effects of a high-calorie preload have been investigated in some depth. Polivy (1976) showed that, regardless of the actual number of calories in the preload, restrained eaters ate more following a preload that they *believed* to be high in calories, while unrestrained eaters ate relatively little after the preload, whatever its actual or perceived caloris value. Spencer & Fremouw (1979) and Woody, Costanzo, Leifer, & Conger (1980) gave a single preload, simply labeled either high-calorie or low-calorie. Both groups of investigators again found that, while unrestrained eaters responded minimally to such a cognitive manipulation, reducing their intake slightly after a preload that they were told was high calorie (as compared to one that they thought to be low calorie), restrained eaters ate *more* when they thought they had consumed a high-calorie drink than after one they thought to be low-calorie. Thus, the counterregulation of restrained eaters seems to be mediated by cognitions. Regardless of the actual number of calories consumed, restrained eaters eat little as long as they believe they have not already eaten very much, but eat a lot when they *believe* they have already eaten a high number of calories. It seems, then, that restrained eaters are able to maintain their restraint as long as they believe their diet (or self-imposed caloric limit) to be unviolated, but become disinhibited when they think that they already have "blown" their diet.

Overeating by restrained eaters who have consumed a fattening preload (usually milkshakes) has been demonstrated with male as well as with female subjects (e.g., Hibscher & Herman, 1977; Polivy, 1976). Disinhibition seems to be comparable for both sexes, except that females are more likely than males to be dieters and generally score higher on the restraint scale (Herman & Polivy, 1980).

The use of a preload and/or a test food that is at least perceived as being (qualitatively) fattening seems to be one major factor that distinguishes between the previously reported "nonregulation" of obese subjects (e.g., Schachter et al., 1968) and the counterregulation of restrained dieters. Schachter and colleagues' (1968) subjects were preloaded on roast beef sandwiches. Since they had been asked to skip a meal, subjects may well have seen the preload as a substitute for a regular meal, and thus felt that their diets were still intact. In support of this, we point to the subsequent cracker consumption of low-fear full and empty obese subjects, which was as low as that of the full normal-weight subjects. Obese subjects thus seemed to be behaving the way restrained eaters whose diets are intact do; that is, they ate minimally (cf. Polivy, Herman, Younger, & Erskine, 1979). The "fattening," frequently gratuitous (i.e., not substituting for a meal) nature of the preloads, and even test foods, typically employed in restraint studies may account for the excessive eating by restrained subjects of all weight levels (e.g., Hibscher & Herman, 1977; Spencer & Fremouw, 1979).[2] The "test"

---

[2]Ruderman & Wilson (1979) have argued that restrained obese actually don't seem to counterregulate the way normal-weight restrained eaters do. On the other hand, the restrained obese also don't regulate normally. Since the three studies (Hibscher & Herman, 1977; Ruderman & Wilson, 1979; Spencer & Fremouw, 1979) that measured both obesity and restraint all have used ice cream as the test food, it is possible that obese subjects have a lower threshold for disinhibition and are "overeating" (rather than maintaining restraint and "dieting") in all conditions. Certainly they all are eating moderately (as opposed to minimally), and in all three studies, any eating was outside the bounds of normal mealtimes, and so any intake beyond the minimum necessary for taste ratings was thus "excess" or "overeating" in some sense.

food also must meet at least minimal palatability criteria in order to be overeaten by counterregulating restrained eaters. Polivy (1976) was still able to find overeating after a perceived high-calorie preload using sandwiches, but Woody et al. (1980) found that bad-tasting (adulterated) ice cream was *not* overeaten by preload-disinhibited dieters (though good-tasting ice cream was).

Restrained eaters thus have been shown repeatedly to be susceptible to bouts of overeating. Such eating may be triggered by the perception that one's restrictions already have been violated or by simple disinhibitors like stress or alcohol. It should be noted that, when not provoked by such disinhibitors, restrained eaters eat less than normal subjects. That is, subjects with no or low preload, low anxiety, no alcohol, and so on, and all restrained subjects in Polivy et al. (1979) ate less than unrestrained eaters in the comparable experimental conditions, as well as less than disinhibited dieters. It is only under the imposition of the various experimental manipulations deliberately designed to interfere with restraint that counterregulation or overeating appears. Unfortunately, this does not bode well for the eating behavior of such chronic dieters outside the laboratory. We often are put into situations where caloric limitations are "unavoidably" exceeded (e.g., at dinner parties, weddings, and other celebrations; at restaurants; in situations where we are made anxious or upset or where we drink alcohol), so we—if we are restrained eaters—are likely to overeat frequently. As Polivy and Herman (1976c) demonstrated, chronic events of this sort (clinical depression, in that case) do result in weight gain for restrained eaters.

Determinants of Bingeing

The clinical evidence, as we have seen, has suggested that bingeing may be preceded by dieting. The experimental evidence, as we have seen, has demonstrated that dieters, at least in the laboratory, are prone to binges, if the circumstances are right. These data, however, do not explain precisely what it is about dieting that predisposes its practitioners to binges. While it is useful to know that dieters are predisposed to binge, and perhaps even more useful to know when, most interesting (and ultimately, useful) would be to know why.

There are features of dieting that suggest themselves as possible causes of subsequent binges (when combined with the "right" situational triggers). It may be, for instance, that dieters, by virtue of their successes, have lowered their weight significantly below some set-point level and are therefore chronically hungry. Bingeing, then, might be the body's attempt to restore a more biologically appropriate weight. Such was the interpretation that we favored when we proposed that "disinhibition of any sort disrupts the dieter's restraint and unleashes 'deprivation-motivated eating behavior' " (Herman & Polivy, 1975, p. 672). Alternatively, as is evident by now, many if not most dieters are not especially successful at maintaining their diets and actually may not lower their body weights significantly; it may be the case, for them, that bingeing represents less an attempt to "correct" their body weights than the disengagement of normal regulatory processes and influences, with a corresponding overresponsiveness to short-term "appetitive" cues. We have begun recently to research the physiological correlates of dieting, specifically with a view to testing the notion that dieters' cephalic phase (anticipatory digestive) responses (e.g., salivation, insulin release) may predispose them to overrespond to palatable food cues. Powley's (1977) cephalic phase hypothesis suggests that the overeating and subsequent obesity of organisms such as ventro-medial hypothalamically lesioned rats results from excessive physiological, predigestive response to the sensory qualities of palatable food; this response, in turn, causes the animal to "feel hungrier" and overeat. One might argue that overeating in dieting and self-starving humans is driven similarly by such physiological pressures and hypersecretions. Klajner, Herman, Polivy, & Chhabra (1981) found that restrained eaters do indeed salivate more than do unrestrained eaters when confronted with attractive food cues (in this case the sight and smell of fresh-baked pizza or chocolate chip cookies). (Unpalatable food cues, in this case cookies adulterated with green food coloring, elicited very little salivation from either group of subjects.) Despite their heightened salivary response to the food, however, restrained eaters did not overeat either pizza or cookies.

Further studies measuring cephalic phase responses more directly through blood sampling indicated an elevated response by restrained eaters for some hormones (e.g., motilin) and a depressed response for others (e.g., insulin and pancreatic polypetide) (Klajner, Herman, Polivy, Marliss, & Greenberg, 1981). The upshot of these studies seems to be that restrained eaters have a reduced hormonal satiety response to food, although, as with the salivation studies, the amount they eat apparently is unaffected by this deficit in satiety. Thus, although the evidence at this time is far from complete or conclusive, it seems that, while there are physiological correlates of chronic dieting, they do not necessarily determine the amount of food ingested on any given occasion. At the very least, it seems to be the case that hormonal changes are not capable, *on their own,* of producing the sort of differential eating observed in our dieters and nondieters in response to our standard laboratory situations. It may be that the "special" hormonal status of dieters (i.e., suppressed satiety mechanisms) contributes in some way to the behavior released by, say, fattening preloads; however, in the absence of such cognitive disinhibition, hormonal influences are not manifested in behavior. Accordingly, we are reluctant to give the dieter's hormonal state full recognition as a *cause* of binge eating. Indeed, the nature of the observed hormonal differences between restrained and unrestrained eaters perhaps may be interpreted more readily as governing the *disposition* of whatever food is ingested than as the determinant of how much is consumed. Although most physiological theories, such as Powley's (1977) cephalic phase hypothesis, focus on physiological factors as determinants of hunger and food intake in obese or starving (e.g., Nisbett, 1972) organisms, it may be that physiological changes in response to food deprivation are designed for a completely different function. Such hormonal responses probably were evolved to help the organism survive in times of food scarcity. Despite the voluntary nature of dieting and the usual availability of sufficient food, the body may well respond to the well-intentioned self-starvation that we call dieting as if it were a signal of impending famine. If so, increasing hunger signals to induce the organism to eat more hardly would be a successful strategy for preventing starvation; greater hunger does not alter the fact of environmental famine. If food is (presumably) unavailable, as in a famine, a more effective means of preserving the organism's viability would be to alter its metabolic disposition of whatever food *is* available, so that such food provides a maximal amount of energy. Thus, our findings that restrained eaters secrete less insulin than do unrestrained eaters, despite eating the same amount of food, and that they achieve *the same* blood glucose levels with this decreased insulin, suggests that the insulin of restrained eaters is acting more efficiently than that of unrestrained eaters (i.e., only half as much is needed to get the same metabolic result). This accords well with work by Coscina and Dixon (1981), which showed that rats that had been starved for one to three days (and lost weight accordingly) were able to achieve normal weights within a short time by eating the same amount of food as nonstarved rats who simply were maintaining their weights. In other words, the starved rats were using their food more efficiently than were the nonstarved rats. Similarly, patients with anorexia nervosa who are refed in hospital treatment programs don't necessarily gain weight at the rate of one pound per 3500 calories in excess of daily needs. Some patients gain weight much faster than expected, on a much lower daily intake (e.g., Stordy, Marks, Kalucy, & Crisp, 1977), and, even under carefully controlled conditions, the measured correlation between caloric intake and weight gain in such patients was extremely low (Pertschuk, Crosby, & Mullen, 1981). Finally, recent work on diet-induced thermogenesis shows that formerly overweight people who have dieted and attained normal weight have a postmeal thermogenic (heat-producing) response only *half* that of nondieting normal-weight individuals (Shetty, Jung, James, Barrand, & Callingham, 1982). Thus, while there do appear to be physiological changes in food-related systems in response to chronic dieting or starvation, they may not be responsible for the tendency to binge or eat excessively in such deprived (or previously deprived) organisms.

While we can't yet rule out a physiological basis for overeating in dieters, it does seem at this point as if cognitive factors may play a greater role than physiological ones in determining intake on a given occasion. The evidence we have reviewed above concerning the tendency of dieters to overeat involved manipulations of cognitive factors. For the most part (with the possible exception of obese dieters given ice cream), restrained eaters who were asked simply to "taste and rate" various foods, most of them highly palatable (e.g., ice cream), ate less than their unrestrained counterparts, as well as eating less than other "disinhibited" restrained eaters. As long as they were not convinced that they had overeaten already, *not* made anxious or upset, or *not* rendered intoxicated, restrained eaters seemed to be relatively successful at restricting their intake, at least in a laboratory setting (e.g., the "control" or "low/no manipulation" groups in Herman & Mack, 1975; Herman & Polivy, 1975; Herman, Polivy, & Silver, 1979; Hibscher & Herman, 1977; Polivy, 1976; Polivy & Herman, 1976a, 1976b; Spencer & Fremouw, 1979; and Woody et al., 1980; as well as all restrained subjects in Polivy et al., 1979). The disinhibition that results in overeating seems to be cognitive in nature, as is the inhibition represented by the diet. Even the gluttony noted in refed conscientious objectors (who had starved themselves to 74 percent of their normal weight) seems to be cognitively mediated. Franklin et al.

(1948) described the behavior of these refed (i.e., returned to normal weight) volunteers as follows: "attempts to avoid wasting even a particle (of food) continued in the face of unlimited supplies of immediately available food. An irrational fear that food would not be available or that the opportunity to eat would somehow be taken away from them was present in some of the men. This may have motivated their (observed behavior of) eating as much as they could hold at any given time" (p. 38, parenthetical material inserted by the present authors). Even when they were no longer underweight or deprived in any way, the men seemed to feel afraid that they might not get enough food and consequently "ate more food than they were prepared to cope with," making themselves sick. Whether there is some as yet undiscovered physiological basis for such binge eating is unknown, but the cognitive elements of such behavior are apparent.

A Proposal

We would like to propose a model for the occurrence of bingeing in dieters that combines cognitive and physiological parameters in a way that may illuminate the apparent conflict between the cognitive "triggering" of binge eating and the physiological mechanisms presumably activated in the organism by deprivation (be it chronic or intermittent, current or historic). We propose that food restriction and/or starvation cause a physiological imbalance plus a psychological deprivation which, singly or together, create a potential for binge eating. Actual bingeing then is triggered and/or prevented primarily by cognitive events.

The physiological potential may consist simply of a chronic, heightened "hunger," reflected in the hypersalivation of restrained eaters confronted with palatable food, or it may be a more complex (as yet largely unexplored) phenomenon. It is not likely, in either case, to be the body's primary means of compensating for the initial deficit or protecting itself against hypothetical future shortages. That role probably is fulfilled by changes in the metabolism and disposition of food, rather than by alternations in quantity consumed (or even hungered after).

The cognitive factors have been investigated more fully and thus can be described in more detail. For the voluntary dieter, the initial cognitive factor is dissatisfaction with one's self or body that results in the decision to attempt to lose weight. Olmsted (1981) has shown that body size dissatisfaction is the best predictor of both restraint and pursuit of thinness in normal female university students, better even than body weight or percent of average weight. (Correspondingly, Hawkins & Clement will show in Chapter 10 that they found body image dissatisfaction to predict Binge Scale scores.) This decision to lose weight results in the initiation of dieting or restrained eating, which causes a sense of psychological (if not physiological) deprivation that presumably increases as a function of the rigidity of the diet. As has been documented with anorexia nervosa patients (Bruch, 1978) and starving conscientious objectors (Franklin et al., 1948) food and weight begin to take on a major role in the psychic economy of the "dieter." This may contribute to the establishment of dichotomous thinking of the sort previously identified in anorexia nervosa patients (Garner, Garfinkel, & Bemis, 1981) and probably characteristic of most dieters. This dichotomous thinking involves the perception of "good" diet foods versus "bad" fattening foods, and "good," small, dietetic amounts versus large "binge" or "break-the-diet" quantities. These polarized cognitions may well develop over a short time, setting the stage for the dieter's ensuing struggles with food. The dieter must rely increasingly on cognition to control intake, since the rebellious body sends signals of hunger that are not placated with restricted amounts of "diet" food. Thus, although restrained eaters salivate more, they do not respond to their bodies' signals by eating more.[3] Cognitive regulation of intake, combined with a tendency toward dichotomous thinking, could account easily for the pattern of restricting and overeating that seems to characterize the eating behavior of restrained eaters and other self-starvers. Under normal circumstances, the dieter eats small (diet-enhancing or at least diet-preserving) amounts, the less-than-normal consumption described earlier. Under conditions of disinhibition, however, the preoccupation with food and the dichotomous thinking pattern make the dieter especially prone to overeat, particularly if there is palatable food available. Once any such "bad" food has been eaten, the disruption of usual restraints and the dichotomous thinking that allows only for "good dieting" or "splurging" leaves the restrained eater virtually no recourse but to overeat.

---

[3]Even nondieters use cognitive eating cues to some extent, as their responsiveness to the eating behavior of "models," for example, attests (Conger, Conger, Costanzo, Wright, & Matter, 1980; Nisbett & Storms, 1974; Polivy et al., 1979); hence, cognitive regulation of intake in dieters is probably more a difference of degree than a total aberration from normal regulation.

Determinants of Amount Eaten

We have seen that it is not necessary to posit a physiological impetus for the initiation of bingeing. The model we have presented thus far attempts to explain who "binges," when (under what conditions), and, to some extent, why. But we have not yet discussed what determines *how much* is eaten during a "binge" or what terminates such eating. Normal eating in nondieters presumably is controlled by a combination of cognitive and physiological signals. Basically though, the normal person is assumed to eat when hungry, usually as indicated by internal signals, and to stop when sated, again as determined by internal cues (e.g., Schachter, 1971). In our restrained eating experiments, such eating is thought to be characteristic of unrestrained eaters. We assume that they eat more when not preloaded than after a preload, or when calm rather than anxious, because in the former conditions they are hungrier than in the latter ones. Unrestrained eaters' consumption is thus determined by their physiological state of hunger or satiety (which itself may be influenced by psychological factors, as when anxiety reduces hunger by causing sugar to be released into the bloodstream). For restrained eaters though, the parameters of consumption are more complex. Under normal circumstances, their intake is cognitively controlled to conform to caloric restrictions imposed by their dieting. Thus, they would be expected to eat within a more limited range up to but not beyond the "upper boundary" on consumption dictated by their diet calculations; that is, they should eat *less than* unrestrained eaters under normal (nondisinhibited) conditions. As we have pointed out already, this is just what they do. If what unrestrained eaters do is called regulation, this "good dieting" behavior of restrained eaters could be called cognitive regulation, the upper boundary of consumption being presumably "lower" than for normal regulation. The upper boundary of such cognitive regulation is the maximum amount "allowed" by the restrained eater's diet. But this cognitive upper boundary limits consumption only as long as the diet is intact. If the diet is disrupted, either because this boundary is perceived to be surpassed already, or because cognitive inhibitions have been overcome by stress, alcohol, or some other mechanism, the restrained eater eats more. No longer is eating constrained by the artificial "diet boundary"; the effective upper boundary on consumption is that of true satiety, which occurs much later, calorically, than the diet quota. The upper boundary of this new, expanded range of consumption probably is determined by physiological satiety factors, just as the unrestrained eater's upper limit is (see Figure 5–1 for a depiction of this "boundary model"). Since the restrained eater seems to have weaker than normal satiety signals (i.e., less pancreatic polypetide, a presumed satiety hormone; more motilin, a gastric activator; and less insulin, proposed by Woods to be a satiety hormone [e.g., Porte & Woods, 1981; Klajner et al., 1981], this upper boundary is probably much higher in dieters than in nondieters. Thus, when the restrained eater is "disinhibited" and eats to the physiological upper boundary rather than the cognitive one, the result would be greater-than-normal consumption, or what we have been calling "counterregulation." Since the eating of disinhibited restrained eaters has been shown to be greater than normal yet not unlimited (i.e., they do not eat all the food available to them, or even half of it), the data seem to fit this model, thus providing us a mechanism for explaining not only what starts a binge (the disruption of the cognitive boundary) but what stops it (satiety). What we have been calling counterregulatory behavior by restrained eaters, then, is actually normal regulation, albeit within a larger-than-normal range. We have not yet finished collecting the data to prove that this is the case (e.g., do restrained eaters eat less after four milkshakes than after two, as the preload approaches the limits of the physiological satiety boundary?), but the concept of such bilevel regulation for restrained eaters seems more parsimonious and more in keeping with the data than does the crude notion of counterregulation (which would seem to call for continuous eating by disinhibited dieters).

Figure 5-1. Boundary Model of Consumption.

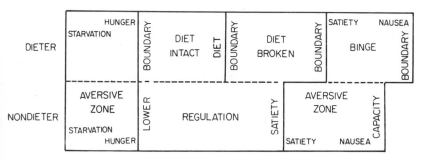

LEVEL / RATE OF CONSUMPTION ⟶

Overeating and Bingeing

Although we at times have referred to overeating by disinhibited restrained eaters in the laboratory as "bingeing" (e.g., Polivy, 1976; Herman & Polivy, 1980), the model we propose here implies that such overeating is not really pathological binge eating or bulimia. The *DSM-III* (APA, 1980) defines bulimia as uncontrolled eating terminated by sickness (vomiting), physical pain, or loss of consciousness. The overeating of restrained eaters in the laboratory does not seem to fit such criteria. Such true binge eating suggests a third boundary for our model, though. Binge eating, according to our model, is eating that surpasses the bounds of physiological *satiety* and is terminated by the limits of physical *capacity*. The model we are proposing, then, posits a continuum of termination points for eating. The first (and lowest) is the cognitive boundary imposed by a restrained eater's diet; next is the physiological satiety level for unrestrained eaters, followed by the satiety level for disinhibited restrained eaters; and, finally, the limits of physical space—the binger is literally full of food. Unrestrained eaters regulate within the range determined by the second of these boundary points; restrained eaters, normal and pathological (i.e., bulimic), stay within the confined limits imposed by their cognitive boundaries until these are breached. Then, normal restrained eaters regulate their consumption within the limits posed by the third boundary (their physiological satiety level), while true bulimic restrained eaters binge until they are physically unable to eat any more (or all the food it gone). So, while physiological factors may not be responsible for initiating a binge, we believe they may determine how much is eaten during the binge and when the binger will stop eating.

Ways to Discourage Overeating

While most restrained eating studies thus far have concentrated on the disruption of restraint (and production of overeating), a few studies have attempted to maintain or strengthen restraint. Since the trigger for overeating seems to be cognitive, the manipulations designed to prevent it have thus far been cognitive in nature. Herman, Polivy, and Silver (1979) theorized that the self-consciousness induced by the presence of an observer while the subject was eating would prevent preload-induced disinhibition and force dieters to maintain their diets. Unrestrained eaters, as expected, were unaffected by the experimenter's presence. Restrained eaters, on the other hand, did not show their usual "counterregulation" in the experimenter's presence; nor, however, did they simply eat minimally. Instead, they behaved like unrestrained eaters, eating more after a small preload and less after a large one, i.e., they regulated normally (and within the "normal boundary range"). Unfortunately, this "socially-induced" normal eating pattern lasted only as long as did the experimenter's presence in the room. When left alone for further "tasting," the restrained eaters reverted to their usual pattern and, since they had exceeded their cognitive limit, overate until (presumably) sated.

In a similar study, a social stimulus was supplied by a confederate posing as a fellow (eating) subject, instead of the experimenter as a noneating observer (Polivy, Herman, Younger, & Erskine, 1979). The confederate ate either a small or a large amount and indirectly identified herself as a dieter or a nondieter. While the confederate was present, restrained eaters ate less than unrestrained eaters. All subjects were influenced by the behavior of the confederate, eating more when she did and suppressing their intake when she claimed to be a dieter. Thus, not only the mere presence of another person, but the amount she eats and her "identity" can inhibit eating in restrained eaters. Although the effect, again, lasted only until the confederate left the room, less eating had occurred in the initial phase of the experiment, so only one group of restrained eaters (those exposed to the nondieter who ate a lot) had apparently exceeded their cognitive quota and subsequently overate.

A more direct attempt to prevent the breakdown of restraint involved the induction of self-awareness, or awareness, plus self-consciousness (Polivy, Herman, & Hackett, 1980). Subjects were preloaded, and then made aware of how much they were eating by giving them candy in wrappers and having them keep the wrappers on the table in front of them. The control subjects simply threw the wrappers in a half-filled garbage can next to them as they "tasted and rated." Subjects who were self-conscious as well as self-aware were not given any place to throw their wrappers (so the experimenter was sure to see them), while self-aware subjects threw away their wrappers after they ate and before the experimenter returned. "Control" restrained eaters ate the most, while both experimental groups ate about the same as nonpreloaded subjects (i.e., did not overeat). Unrestrained eaters ate very little in all three preloaded conditions, but they too suppressed their intake even further under the double inhibition of self-consciousness and awareness of how much they were eating.

Cognitive manipulations do seem capable of curtailing the usual overeating or disinhibited restrained eaters, at least in the short run. A possibly more effective technique is suggested by our model. If the cognitive (diet quota) boundary could be made more flexible, so that it bends rather than breaks under caloric pressure, it could prevent further consumption following lapses. One way to do this might be to encourage dieters to eat small amounts of "forbidden" foods and to accept occasional "splurges" as treats instead of unforgivable (no turning back now) disasters. This approach sometimes is included in the treatment of individuals with clinical eating disorders (e.g., Garner & Bemis, 1982; Garner et al., 1981; Orbach, 1978). This restructuring of both cognitive and eating patterns would allow the cognitive diet boundary to remain more often unbreached and also would serve to reduce the dichotomy inherent in "diet" thinking. By attacking the problem on this level, it may be possible for dieters to escape the apparently natural consequences of dieting—overeating—and, in time, for us to no longer be able to claim that dieting is counterproductive to weight loss.

References

American Psychiatric Association. *Diagnostic and Statistical Manual of Mental Disorders,* 3rd ed. Washington, D.C.: American Psychiatric Association, 1980.

Boskind-Lodahl, M. Cinderella's stepsisters: A feminist perspective on anorexia nervosa and bulimia. *Signs: Journal of Women in Culture and Society,* 1976, *2,* 342–356.

Boskind-Lodahl, M., & Sirlin, J. The gorging–purging syndrome. *Psychology Today,* March 1977, 50–52, 82, 85.

Bruch, H. *Eating Disorders.* New York: Basic Books, 1973.

Conger, J. C., Conger, A. J., Costanzo, P. R., Wright, K. L., & Matter, J. A. The effect of social cues on the eating behavior of obese and normal subjects. *Journal of Personality,* 1980, *48,* 258–271.

Coscina, D. V., & Dixon, L. Body weight regulation in starving females: Insights from an animal model. Paper presented at the Anorexia Nervosa Conference, Toronto, Canada, September 12–13, 1981.

Franklin, J. S., Schiele, B. C., Brozek, J., & Keys, A. Observations on human behavior in experimental starvation and rehabilitation. *Journal of Clinical Psychology,* 1948, *4,* 28–45.

Garner, D. M., & Bemis, K. M. A cognitive–behavior approach to anorexia nervosa. *Cognitive Therapy & Research,* 1982, *6,* 123–150.

Garner, D. M., Garfinkel, P. E., & Bemis, K. M. A multidimensional psychotherapy for anorexia nervosa. *International Journal of Eating Disorders,* 1981, *2,* 3–46.

Hawkins, R. C., II, & Clement, P. F. Development and construct validation of a self-report measure of binge eating tendencies. *Addictive Behaviors,* 1980, *5,* 219–226.

Herman, C. P., & Mack, D. Restrained and unrestrained eating. *Journal of Personality,* 1975, *43,* 647–660.

Herman, C. P., & Polivy, J. Anxiety, restraint, and eating behavior. *Journal of Abnormal Psychology,* 1975, *84,* 666–672.

Herman, C. P., & Polivy, J. Restrained eating. In A. Stunkard (ed.), *Obesity.* Philadelphia: W. B. Saunders, 1980.

Herman, C. P., Polivy, J., & Silver, R. Effects of an observer on eating behavior: The induction of sensible eating. *Journal of Personality,* 1979, *47,* 85–99.

Hibscher, J. A., & Herman, C. P. Obesity, dieting, and the expression of obese characteristics. *Journal of Comparative and Physiological Psychology,* 1977, *91,* 374–380.

Klajner, F., Herman, C. P., Polivy, J., & Chhabra, R. Human obesity, dieting, and anticipatory salivation to food. *Physiology & Behavior,* 1981, *27,* 195–198.

Klajner, F., Herman, C. P., Polivy, J., Marliss, E. B., & Greenberg, G. R. Elevated post-prandial motilin secretion in normal weight and obese dieters, and elevated post-prandial insulin response after exposure to food. Paper presented a the International Symposium on the Brain-Gut Axis: The New Frontier, Florence, Italy, 1981.

Nisbett, R. E. Hunger, obesity and the ventro-medial hypothalamus. *Psychological Review,* 1972, *79,* 433–453.

Nisbett, R. E., & Storms, M. D. Cognitive, social and physiological determinants of food intake. In H. London & R. E. Nisbett (eds.), *Cognitive Modification of Emotional Behavior.* Chicago: Aldine, 1974.

Olmsted, M. P. Anorexic normal differences and predictors of concern with dieting and ideal body image in college women. Unpublished master's thesis, University of Guelph, Ontario, Canada, 1981.

Orbach, S. *Fat is a Feminist Issue: The Anti-diet Guide to Permanent Weight Loss.* New York: Paddington Press, 1978.

Pertschuk, M. J., Crosby, L. O., & Mullen, J. L. Non-linearity of weight gain and nutrition intake in anorexia nervosa. Paper presented at the Anorexia Nervosa Conference, Toronto, Canada, September 12–13, 1981.

Polivy, J. Perception of calories and regulation of intake in restrained and unrestrained subjects. *Addictive Behaviors,* 1976, *1,* 237–243.

Polivy, J., & Herman, C. P. Clinical depression and weight change: A complex relation. *Journal of Abnormal Psychology,* 1976, *85,* 338–340. (a)

Polivy, J., & Herman, C. P. The effects of alcohol of eating behavior: Disinhibition or sedation? *Addictive Behaviors,* 1976, *1,* 121–125. (b)

Polivy, J., & Herman, C. P. Effects of alcohol on eating behavior: Influences of mood and perceived intoxication. *Journal of Abnormal Psychology,* 1976, *85,* 601–606. (c)

Polivy, J., Herman, C. P., & Hackett, R. Self-awareness, self-consciousness, and the inhibition of eating. Unpublished manuscript, University of Toronto, 1980.

Polivy, J., Herman, C. P., Younger, J. C., & Erskine, B. Effects of a model on eating behavior: The induction of a restrained eating style. *Journal of Personality,* 1979, *47,* 100–114.

Porte, D., & Woods, S. C. Regulation of food intake and body weight by insulin. *Diabetologia,* 1981, *20,* 274–280.

Powley, T. L. The ventromedial hypothalamic syndrome, satiety, and a cephalic phase hypothesis. *Psychological Review,* 1977, *84,* 89–126.

Ruderman, A., & Wilson, G. T. Weight, restraint, cognitions and counter-regulation. *Behavior Research and Therapy,* 1979, *17,* 581–590.

Schachter, S. Some extraordinary facts about obese humans and rats. *American Psychologist,* 1971, *26,* 129–144.

Schachter, S., Goldman, R., & Gordon, A. Effects of fear, food deprivation, and obesity on eating. *Journal of Personality & Social Psychology,* 1968, *10,* 98–106.

Schachter, S., & Rodin, J. *Obese Humans and Rats.* Potomac, Md.: Erlbaum Associates, 1974.

Shetty, P. S., Jung, R. T., James, W. P. T., Barrand, M. A., & Callingham, B. A. Post-prandial thermogenesis in obesity. *Clinical Science,* 1982, *60,* 519–525.

Spencer, J. A., & Fremouw, W. J. Binge eating as a function of restraint and weight classification. *Journal of Abnormal Psychology,* 1979, *88,* 262–267.

Stordy, B. J., Marks, V., Kalucy, R. S., & Crisp, A. H. Weight gain, thermic effect of glucose and resting metabolic rate during recovery from anorexia nervosa. *America Journal of Clinical Nutrition,* 1977, *30,* 138–146.

Wardle, J. Dietary restraint and binge eating. *Behavioral Analysis and Modification,* 1980, *4,* 201–209.

Woody, E. Z., Costanzo, P. R., Leifer, H., & Conger, J. The effects of taste and caloric perceptions on the eating behavior of restrained and unrestrained subjects. Unpublished manuscript, Duke University, 1980.

6

Neurological Factors Affecting Binge Eating: Body over Mind*

John H. Rau
Richard S. Green

*Can we be sure . . . that we are seeing the patient as he
really is, knowing him in his own reality: or are we seeing
merely a projection of our own theories about him? . . . May
not this particular person require another system, another
quite different frame of reference? And does not this
patient . . . evade our investigations, slip through our scientific fingers like seafoam, precisely to the extent that we rely
on the logical consistency of our own system?*
(May, Angel, & Ellenberger, 1958)

So far in this book, contributors have focused on binge eating as a
functional phenomenon. While there is little question that for
many patients emotional and psychological factors are frequently
responsible for disturbances in eating behavior, organic or neurological factors always should be considered and may be the most
significant determinant of eating dysfunction in some patients. Although binge eaters may be of varying weight, from emaciated to

*This work was supported in part by Long Island Jewish-Hillside Medical Center
internal grant funds.

obese, they share a number of similarities. Their behavior is frequently characterized by excessive intake of food, usually gulped or eaten quickly, in private, to the point of satiation, with feelings of guilt and shame consequent to the binges and anticipatory anxiety preceding them. These similarities have tended to obscure the fact that some of these patients binge for psychological reasons while others—a minority—binge because they are driven by a neurologically based disorder of impulse control. Attempts to treat bulimia with a single therapy, therefore, will be unsuccessful to a greater or lesser extent; that is, psychogenic binge eaters will not respond to medication but may to psychotherapy; and neurologically driven binge eaters will not respond to psychological treatment, but may to medication. In these latter patients, all psychological forms of treatment are ineffective and probably in addition produce iatrogenic low self-esteem as patients experience failure after failure in their attempts to control their eating.

It is the principal function of this chapter to alert the reader to the existence of these two different binge eaters and to provide a method for differential assessment for both the clinicians and the researchers. If this distinction between the two classes of bulimic patients is not made, then investigators will make the mistake of trying to treat all patients similarly and thus will report no statistically significant results: while in truth they will fail to delineate the person who could benefit from a proper and specific treatment for neurologically based bulimia.

We initially will define and classify neurologically based disordered binge eating, since careful phenomenological observation is necessary to differentiate it from functional bulimia. A reanalysis of Robert Lindner's (1954) case of a woman called Laura will be presented to illustrate how a mind-over-body set interferes with therapists' considering a neurological etiology. We then shall review some of the literature showing that there is a substantial though scattered collection of reports supporting the possibility of organic etiology to eating disorders in some patients. This review will include a brief summary of our own work, which we believe lends strong support to a neurological etiology for a minority of binge eaters. Replication studies by others will be discussed briefly, along with methodological issues that require further clarification. Brief vignettes will be presented throughout to illustrate major points to be made. Finally, we shall present a theoretical explanation of the results so as to form a base from which further exploration of these problems can take place.

Assessment, Evaluation and
Differential Diagnosis

The *DSM-III* (1980) sets forth the basic criteria for classification of patients with bulimia. Excluded from the definition are persons with known physical disorders. For differential diagnostic purposes it is stated that "in certain neurological diseases, such as epileptic equivalent seizures, . . . there are abnormal eating patterns but the diagnosis is rarely warranted; where it is both diagnoses should be given." This makes it unclear whether a person with abnormal electroencephalographs (EEGs) of the epileptic equivalent type whose eating behavior meets the other criteria for bulimia ought to receive the diagnosis of bulimia. Although ostensibly a pheno-menologically based, rather than etiologically based, diagnostic system, "bulimia" seems to be conceptualized erroneously in *DSM-III* solely as a functional disorder.

The clinician should be alerted to the fact that many bingers are poor self-reporters and in general do not like to talk about their eating, as this behavior elicits uncomfortable feelings. In addition, they tend to block out their feelings surrounding the eating binges. It is thus essential that adequate rapport between the therapist and the patient be established in order to explore the differential criteria that we are suggesting, as many patients will not report these phenomena spontaneously. The remainder of this section is devoted to a discussion of the objective criteria that have been suggested for use in distinguishing between the two groups of patients.

Aura

The classic neurogenic binge eater often will report that just prior to a binge she experiences an unusual sensation or aura. This sometimes is experienced in the stomach or in other parts of the body. At times, patients report sensations very similar to auras experienced by epileptics, such as flashes of light, unusual smells, a sense of increasing tension with the fear that they are about to explode unless they indulge in their compulsive behavior.

A 23-year-old female with anorexia and bulimia reported that she had a very poor memory for each episode but she did recall feeling a sense of "strangeness" prior to their occurrence. While the patient was in the office she complained of similar feelings of "strangeness." An EEG taken at that time showed high-voltage negative spike discharges in the right temporal and occipital areas during drowsiness.

Ego-Alien Nature of Episodes

Neurogenic binge eaters describe their binges as "coming out of the blue," "unpredictable," "weird," and the like. The patients usually ascribe it to forces external to the self, forces perceived as disassociated. These patients, when questioned carefully, describe the feeling that not only is the binge eating ego-dystonic, by which we mean that it is not constant with their sense of themselves, but it is also ego-alien. Ego-alien refers to the phenomenon that the body or the self is acting in a way that is really not perceived as part of the person's true self. It is similar to depersonalization in that many patients describe themselves as standing outside of themselves observing their behavior and feeling that "the true me" is not really gorging in this manner. A strong sense that bingeing is ego-alien has been one of the more reliable objective diagnostic signs of a neurological etiology.

> A young, slim, attractive nurse in her twenties worked on an infectious disease ward in a voluntary hospital in New York. At times, she would have compulsive eating episodes while on duty, and she reported that on occasion she would eat food left over from her patients—food she knew to be contaminated. She stated that an overwhelming urge overcame her. She related this story with horror and felt that in no way was she responsible for doing something so dangerous and yet she felt compelled to do it. While bingeing she felt that she was observing some stranger doing the eating.

Lack of Psychological Pattern

In related fashion, neurogenic binge eaters usually do not indicate any psychological pattern to their bingeing. Most do not see any pattern; some claim a pattern exists but more frequently than not the patient has engaged in retrospective rationalization. This is especially true for binge eaters with extensive past histories of psychodynamically oriented therapy. The failure to find a psychogenic precipitant does not rule out the presence of a latent functional cause; however, it does increase the possibility of a neurological etiology.

A young woman reported that she frequently fought with her boyfriend when at parties or in other public places. She felt her binge eating was a response to her anger and upset in her relationship with him. In fact, however, she would experience the urge to binge as an aura-like phenomenon and "arranged" the fight so as to be able to go home and binge in private. In this instance, cause was effect and effect was cause.

Post-ictal Phenomena

While many bulimic patients report that after a binge they fall asleep satiated, some patients, if questioned closely, will report post-ictal symptoms such as an extended period of sleep or loss of consciousness, confusion, memory loss or disruption, headaches, or loss of bladder control on or after awakening. This finding often is associated with patients who report an aura-like experience, but is uncommon even among neurogenic binge eaters.

Neurological Signs

Neurologically determined bingeing is often associated with the presence of certain diffuse, not focal, neurological soft signs (Rau & Green, 1978). The more signs, the more likely that the patient has a neurological substrate as a basis for her bingeing. These signs are as follows.

Rage Attacks and/or Temper Tantrums. These behaviors are usually more violent than the ordinary angry outburst. They occur episodically and usually without a psychological pattern or precipitant. Sometimes patients do not recall them. This sign correlated most highly with findings of abnormal EEG ($r = +.24$) (Rau & Green, 1978).

An 18-year-old bingeing female with anorexia nervosa was referred to the hospital because of episodes of severe temper tantrums and rage attacks. Her EEG showed "small sharp spikes;" she was placed on 300 mg Dilantin, which resulted in cessation of her rage attacks and temper tantrums as well as her binges. This serendipitous finding was one of several that led to development of our own research project (Green & Rau, 1974).

Headaches. While many patients with headaches describe them as no different from ordinary headaches, some patients describe migrainelike headaches, or headaches of such severity and/or frequency as to be exceptional. The latter usually are not relieved by an ordinary dose of aspirin or its equivalent, and they often render the patient nonfunctional during their course.

> A 23-year-old bingeing male college student weighed 307 pounds and had been grossly overweight for many years; as an adolescent he had a complete evaluation for endocrine dysfunction, which was negative. He reported frequent paresthesias of his hands and/or arms and rare, long-lasting headaches. His EEG showed marked diffuse paroxysmal slowing and minimally express 14 + 6 per-second positive spikes in the right midtemporal-posterior temporal occipital area. He was treated with 100 mg Dilantin, t.i.d. After eight weeks, he had lost 22 pounds without attempting to diet and experienced remission of the paresthesias and headaches. He stopped the medication for psychological reasons and reported the return of binge eating and the paresthesias and headaches.

Dizziness.   Patients sometimes report episodes of dizziness not otherwise explained by physical disorders. This soft sign has one of the highest correlations with improvement when anticonvulsants are used ($r = +.30$) (Rau & Green, 1978).

Stomachaches, Nausea.   When these soft signs are reported as frequently following rapid ingestion of food or satiation, they are not relevant to differentiating binge eaters. If, however, these symptoms are reported at other times, occurring episodically and in an otherwise physically healthy person, they may be related to a neurological etiology.

Paresthesias.   This soft sign has especially predictive value, since it is unlikely to be affected by the act of eating itself. Numbness and/or tingling or the hands, arms, feet, or legs should raise the index of suspicion of neurogenic bingeing.

> A psychiatrist referred a personal friend to us, a middle-aged woman who had been bingeing secretly for many years. Among other signs, she reported parethesias. These remitted with Dilantin, along with the bingeing. This patient, after a year of taking medication, wanted to know whether the relief was truly the result of medication. A four-month double-blind Dilantin–placebo study was initiated with four, month-long, randomly selected trials with either medication or placebo. This patient's records and reports were entirely consistent with a drug response.

Perceptual Disturbances. Many nonpsychotic bingeing patients report some experiences of depersonalization, derealization, déjà vu, or hypnogogic or hynopompic sleep experiences. Psychotic patients also may report auditory, visual, or other hallucinations. Neurogenic binge eaters may be medicated if the frequency, intensity, and psychological unrelatedness of the symptoms is especially severe. However, these signs do not appear to be powerful predictors.

An 11-year-old premenarchial bingeing female reported "being able to see through people," a very bizarre and poorly articulated perceptual anomaly. With 300 mg Dilantin, she showed remission from bingeing and disappearance of this particular disturbed perception. She was followed through puberty until the age of 15, when she moved to another state. A double-blind study was initiated with her to assess the effect of the medication. Her records and those of her mother clearly revealed a drug response; that is, five to seven days following a change in medication from placebo, bingeing and the perceptual anomaly ceased; in contrast, within a week following a change to placebo from medication, bingeing and the anomaly recurred.

Other Compulsions. Compulsive stealing is a fairly common symptom associated with anorexia nervosa and bulimia (Pyle, Mitchell, & Eckert, 1981). It may be functionally related or secondarily related (stealing food to eat), or, if episodic and described as ego-alien, may point toward a neurological etiology.

A 25-year-old, 5'3'' female college graduate weighed 79 pounds and was emaciated. She had been in intensive psychoanalytically oriented psychotherapy for five years because of family difficulties. She and her therapist understood that her compulsive eating, her throwing up afterward, and her use of laxatives were symptoms of an underlying problem. When this problem was "worked out" the expectation was that her eating problems would subside. She was referred by a colleague who was aware of our previous research.
She described her eating episodes as follows: "I feel suddenly that my head is going to split open. . . . I feel I may go crazy unless I get something to eat. . . . I will eat anything I can find. If I am on the street, I will go to the nearest food store and buy crackers or candy, open the box and drop it into my handbag and start eating. . . . As soon as that is finished, I must have something else." She would consume enormous quantities of food, feel terribly bloated and satiated; finally she would vomit and then sleep.
Talking about this evoked tremendous feelings of shame and guilt. She described her need to be thin as a way of putting money in the

bank. Her compulsive eating started at age 15½. Since then she periodically decreased her weight in order to ensure herself that she would not become obese. She felt completely ineffective in controlling her eating. She was obsessed by thoughts about food. She also had been a compulsive stealer who had been apprehended frequently in major department stores. She was bright, articulate, and in touch with her feelings. Her EEG revealed 14 + 6 per-second positive spikes in the right temporal occipital area. She was placed on 100 mg Dilantin, t.i.d. Two weeks later she reported a "miracle." She had no further compulsive eating episodes; she no longer compulsively stole, and she was less obsessed by thoughts of food. After four years she remains symptom free and is approaching normal weight.

Abnormal EEG. An abnormal EEG is the most clinically significant objective sign of an underlying neurological etiology. In a recent paper, Rau and Green (1978) studied 59 binge eaters, of whom 38 (64.4%) had abnormal EEGs. Of these, 30 were treated with Dilantin, while 17 of 21 patients with normal EEGs also were treated. Seventy percent of the patients with abnormal EEGs improved, as contrasted with 35 percent of those with normal EEGs. This was highly significant ($p < .001$).

There are two important points that should be recognized in evaluating the significance of the EEG data. First, and by far the most common pattern associated with binge eating, is the controversial 14 + 6 positive spike pattern. This occurred in 37 percent of the total patient sample and 58 percent of the patients with abnormal EEGs. While we believe this pattern to be abnormal, it is obviously not necessary to so regard it, provided one is aware that the pattern is associated with improvement with Dilantin in 89 percent of patients having it. Thus, this pattern is the single most reliable predictor of a neurological substrate and of a positive prognosis with medication. Unfortunately, other researchers do not regard the pattern as abnormal, do not report it in their data, (e.g., Wermuth, Davis, Hollister, & Stunkard, 1977), and may not even provide the necessary conditions for it to be recorded. This latter is because the pattern almost always appears during drowsy and sleep states (Gibbs & Gibbs, 1965). Those researchers giving awake-only EEGs often will miss it entirely. If further research is to continue on the validity of this association between 14 + 6 positive spikes and positive medication treatment response, researchers and clinicians will have to secure full EEG tracings and report data by EEG patterns rather than by dichotomizing patterns into "normal" and "abnormal."

The second point concerns the fact that there is 40- to 50-percent false negative probability in known grand mal epileptics (Gibbs & Gibbs, 1965); therefore, a normal EEG does not necessarily signify the absence of an abnormal EEG. That this is so is indicated by the fact that over one-third of all binge eaters with normal EEGs responded to Dilantin.

A 23-year-old, 5'4'' female weighed 81 pounds. She presented a history of episodic aggressive behavior, depression, and wrist cutting. She was diagnosed initially with chronic undifferentiated schizophrenia and anorexia nervosa. She was hospitalized for six months, after which she was seen twice a week for outpatient psychotherapy and treated with moderate doses of phenothiazines, which finally were discontinued because of their ineffectiveness. In therapy she revealed that she was a compulsive eater and that, after eating, she would vomit; in this way she maintained her low weight. This had been her practice since the age of 14, when she had had a bout of whooping cough and started throwing up after eating.

The compulsive aspect of eating had assumed such proportions that her family had locked the refrigerator and the pantry to prevent her from eating everything available. During the second year of treatment, the patient was admitted to the emergency service of several psychiatric hospitals and on one occasion was detained by the police, all because of violent behavior. She had a very poor memory for each episode, but she did recall "feelings of strangeness" before each one. After the fourth such occurrence, an EEG was taken. The EEG record showed no abnormality; however, a subsequent EEG showed an unequivocally abnormal spike pattern.

In light of this abnormality, 100 mg of phenytoin (Dilantin) four times a day was prescribed in hopes of eliminating the episodic aggressive behavior. Very shortly thereafter, however, the patient reported that her compulsive desire to eat had stopped. The need to vomit disappeared soon after. She was no longer preoccupied with food, and her weight returned to normal. Ten months later, the patient discontinued the medication on her own and the entire syndrome recurred within a few days. The medication was restarted and she again showed remission of symptoms. She has remained asymtomatic for four years, currently leads a productive life, working and socializing, and shows no signs of being schizophrenic. Five years ago she married and gave birth to a baby girl, without sequelae. It was this patient's response that stimulated our further search for patients with a compulsive eating syndrome.

Soft-Sign Scale.   It is possible to construct a scale of these soft signs such that each sign constitutes one point. Such a scale has been shown to be correlated significantly with improvement with Dilantin (Rau & Green, 1978). With large numbers of patients, our experience would suggest a weighted scale most likely would yield even better results, although this was not the case in a sample of 30 patients.

Deviant Weight. In our prior studies there was some suggestion in the data (Rau & Green, 1978) that improvement with Dilantin was more likely to occur among deviant-weight subjects (25% variation over or under normal weight) than for those of normal weight. This was especially true for those patients whose EEGs were abnormal and who were of deviant weight. The factor of weight had not been included in the soft-sign scale, since, at that time, the authors felt that weight deviation was a secondary psychopathological reaction to the primary neurological disorder. Thus, some people, it was felt, chose to be fat and "gave in" to their condition, while others, using reaction formation, were emaciated. The latter results call for a more careful examination of weight deviation, as it may be a primary factor reflecting indirectly a high drive for eating due to excessive neuronal discharges.

Summary

The assessment of patients for an underlying neurological etiology for their bingeing requires a sensitive, thorough exploration of ego states, defenses, and neurological soft signs, as well as the securing of a complete awake, drowsy, and sleep EEG, and its reading by an electroencephalographer familiar with all the controversial epileptic-equivalent patterns. The rewards of such an expenditure of time and effort can be substantial, especially to the patient who may be spared an unnecessary course of psychotherapy and further devaluation in self-esteem attendant upon failure.

When taken together, the preceding factors can be used to generate a description of the typical neurologically determined bulimic. She is female and of good, sound general physical health. She may be emaciated, obese, or of normal weight. She is loath to discuss her bingeing, as it generates intense feelings of guilt and shame. When described, her binges are perceived as due to an external force impinging on her own free will, ego-alien and disassociated from herself. She is bewildered by them, as they are episodic, unpredictable, ego-dystonic, and not psychogenically patterned. Psychological causation, if volunteered, usually is found among patients who are or have been in psychodynamically oriented therapy, but more often than not the causes consist of retrospective rationalizations rather than true causal relationships. Sometimes, upon careful examination, patients will reveal a pre-ictal auralike sensation prior to their binges and a post-ictal epilepticlike somnolence with transient confusion and memory deficits, along with several of the previously described neurological soft signs. An awake, drowsy, and sleep EEG often will reveal one of several paroxysmal dysrhythmias. It is unusual to find focal asymmetrical abnormalities or slow tracings. Of the various patterns, the most likely are the 14 + 6 positive spike pattern, mitten patterns, and the small sharp spike pattern. These patients are not responsive to psychotherapy but do respond to 300 mg Dilantin daily with a variation in dosage in most patients ranging from 200 to 400 mg. Response and adequate blood levels usually are achieved within two weeks. Some patients require a supportive psychotherapy to help them deal with the radical adjustments that improvement causes. Obese patients, in particular, show difficult postmedication adjustments, since they have other psychogenic reasons for their excessive weight gain that are attributable directly to bulimia. The same is true for those few patients with primary anorexia nervosa.

Prognosis for cessation of binges is excellent for patients who fit this description who are weight deviant and show the 14 + 6 spike pattern.

Mind-over-Body Set:
The Case of Laura Reanalyzed

As the earlier chapters in this book indicate, and as the prior literature reflects, there is a trend to view binge eating as primarily a functional, psychogenically determined disorder. The phenomenon of the illusory correlation (Chapman & Chapman, 1969) would appear to be operative here as well; that is, the tendency for clinicians to develop a belief system from preliminary observations or findings that remains resistant to change, even in the presence of later conflicting data. It would seem that there is a need for premature closure to relieve cognitive dissonance and feelings of inadequacy due to the lack of sufficient certain knowledge. For bulimia then, there is a mind-over-body set that predisposes many to see bingeing patients as functionally disturbed and precludes observations that are at variance with preexisting beliefs.

That the mindset of a clinician may influence his/her observations is a well-known phenomenon. As regards bulimia, there exists no more well-known example of this than the case of "Laura," called "Solitaire" in Robert Lindner's book, *The Fifty-Minute Hour* (1954). Lindner reported on his psychoanalytic treatment of a young woman with bulimia. Her primary symptoms consisted of "episodes of depression during which she would be seized by an overwhelming compulsion to gorge herself." After more than two years of intensive psychoanalysis, four times a week, the patient became aware of her Oedipal conflicts and their relation to her eating. More specifically, her eating was viewed as a substitute for her sexual hunger for her father and for her wish to be impregnated by him. There was no report, however, that her episodic compulsion to eat was affected by this insight, and no follow-up data were presented.

Since Lindner and his patient were excellent observers and he presented an articulate description of her symptoms, treatment, and some history, it is possible to reanalyze the data to assess whether a neurological etiology could be supported. The following summarizes the pertinent information about Laura.

Her age was not disclosed. She apparently was a young woman, most likely in her twenties. The episodic nature of her symptoms was described as follows: "It seems to come out of nowhere. I've tried to discover what touches it off, what leads up to it, but I can't. Suddenly, it hits me. . . . It seems I can be doing anything at the time, painting, working at the Gallery, cleaning the apartment, reading or talking to someone" (p. 81). She referred to these episodes as "fits" and felt she was a "victim of forces beyond her ken or control" (p. 81). As she put it, "It's a frenzy, a fit, something automatic and uncontrollable. I want to stop it, but I can't" (p. 81). The ego-alien nature of these episodes thus was described clearly. Lindner stated that he was unable to ascertain any pattern to her eating or any relationship between these episodes and other current events in her life.

In her words, her eating episodes began as follows: "Something, I don't know what to call it, starts to ache; something right in the center of me feels as if it's opening up, spreading apart maybe. . . . Then the emptiness starts to throb—at first softly like a fluttering pulse. . . . But then the pulsing turns into a regular beat, and the beat gets stronger and stronger" (p. 81–82). The moment she became aware of the "hole opening inside" she became "terrified" and began to eat compulsively: "I eat and eat—

everything, anything I can find to put in my mouth. I eat until my jaws get numb with chewing. I get sick with eating and still eat—fighting the sickness with swallowing, retching, vomiting— but always eating more and more" (p. 92). Thus a possible pre-ictal stage seems to be followed by the onset of what Lindner himself refers to as "seizures of uncontrollable hunger, the furious eating" (p. 81).

The episode ends with the patient usually losing consciousness, suggesting a post-ictal phenomenon. As she describes it, "Most of the time I eat myself into unconsciousness. I think I reach a state of drunkenness, or something very like it. Anyhow, I pass out. . . . No matter how the 'fit' ends, it's followed by a long sleep, sometimes for as much as two whole days and nights" (p. 83). At a later point, Lindner describes her as not recalling the episodes: "As always, she had only a vague, confused memory of events during her seizure, recollecting them hazily through a fog of total intoxication. Until I recounted the episode, she had no clear remembrance of my visit and thought she had dreamed my presence in her room. Of the portion that concerned her pitiful imitation of pregnancy, not the slightest memorial trace remained" (p. 117). Laura describes awakening as "coming out of a fog" (p. 118).

In between episodes she imposed an ascetic regime on herself that "kept her fashionably thin." She had repetitive dreams nightly, but did not recall much of their content. She had difficulty in controlling her impulses, once grabbing the analyst physically and at another time cutting her wrists. She was described as having a "histrionic talent and used the therapy sessions as means of venting her enormous rage and anger at her parents" (p. 84). Her interpersonal relationships were poor and characterized by impermanence, bitchiness, and variation. Her father had deserted her mother when Laura was in the sixth grade. Her mother was a cripple, paralyzed from some unknown illness after having three children.

The salient characteristics, then, of Laura's syndrome consisted of an episodic, ego-alien, nonpredictable, irregular "seizure" involving binge eating preceded by an apparent aura and followed by a probable post-ictal phase involving loss of consciousness, amnesia, and confusion. That these episodes may have been an epileptic equivalent thus is a viable hypothesis, judging from the data. Interestingly, both Lindner and Laura unconsciously may have viewed her problems in this vein, since the words "fit" and "seizure" appear frequently throughout the report.

Review of the Literature

In contrast with Laura's highly publicized dramatic case history, there is a little-read, rather mundane literature reporting on an organic etiology to eating disorders. Thus, Bruch (1973) mentions a case of a man (also treated by Stunkard) whose eating episodes clearly were related to demonstrable organic brain syndrome following encephalitis when he was 12 years old (Stunkard, 1961). Terzian & Ore, (1955) report a case of the Klüver-Bucy syndrome in a man who also suffered from episodic excessive eating. Bulimia and obesity have been reported following temporal lobectomies (Alajouanine, Villey, and Nehlil, 1957; Grosman, 1972; Sawa, Ueki, Arita, and Hurada 1954) and following frontal lobotomy or accidental damage to the frontal neocortex (Hercaen, 1964; Hofstatter, Smolik, & Busch, 1945; Kirschbaum, 1951). Goor (1954) reported four anorexic patients with abnormal EEGs indicating diencephalic dysfunction with similar findings observed in 11 of 15 relatives, suggesting a genetic neurologic defect.

Balagura (1972) has suggested that recent animal research implicates hypothalamic factors in human eating disturbances. Similarly, Schachter's research (1971a, 1971b, 1974) presents evidence that obese persons behave like hyperphagic rats with lesions in the ventromedial nuclei of the hypothalamus. Hyperphagic rats eat fewer meals, eat more per meal, and eat at faster speeds than do normal rats (Teitelbaum & Campbell 1958), findings not inconsistent with the concept of compulsive eating. Reeves and Plum (1969) reported an obese patient with a neoplasm that precisely destroyed the ventromedial hypothalamus. She consumed up to 10,000 calories daily in a series of uncontrolled eating episodes. Other authors (Heron & Johnston, 1976; King, 1963; Lundberg & Wolinder, 1967; Templar, 1971) present data suggesting the possibility that some anorexic patients suffer from hypothalamic dysregulation. Stunkard (1959, 1961) and Stunkard, Grace, and Wolff (1955) also have suggested this for obese patients in some of their papers. They classified obese persons into two main groups: night eaters and binge eaters. The night eaters' behavior was considered to be consistent with a disturbance in the satiation center of the hypothalamus, while the binge eaters' behavior was suggestive of a disturbance in the appetitive hypothalamic center.

Crisp (1967) found that 10 percent of his anorexic patients had had epileptic seizures, while Dally (1969) found a history of epilepsy in 9 percent of his patients. Crisp, Fenton, and Strotton

(1968) found that 15 percent of hospitalized anorexic patients had severely abnormal EEGs.

Whittier (1976) reported episodes of bulimia in patients with Huntington's chorea, and Rosenberg, Herishanu, and Bellin (1977) reported bulimia as a symptom in Parkinson's disease, both of which further suggest that bulimia may have a neurophysiological substrate. Liebowitz and Klein (1979) suggested that bulimia may be found among hysteroid dysphorics who binge on chocolate and suggest a neuroendocrine etiology. Moskovitz and Lingao (1979) reported binge eating associated with oral contraceptives and abnormal EEGs. This article takes on special significance in view of Struve, Saraf, Arko, Klein, and Becka's (1976) paper on the correlates between abnormal EEGs and oral contraceptive use.

Remick, Jones, and Campos (1980) reported episodes of bulimia post-ictally in patients with temporal lobe EEG abnormalities and suggest that cognitive and memory dysfunctions in the post-ictal state may be reasons for the infrequent report of bulimia by patients. They suggest that in-depth EEG investigation may be a fruitful area of research into abnormal eating behavior. Finally, Pyle et al. (1981) describe bulimia associated with kleptomania and chemical abuse and suggest that these are indications of loss of generalized impulse control in these patients, with a possible neurological etiology.

Since 1974, we ourselves have worked with bulimic patients with a focus on differentiating the neurologically determined binge eater from the functional binge eater. Published reports on our results with a series of patients totaling 59 are available (Green & Rau, 1974, 1977; Rau & Green, 1975, 1978). These data will not be repeated here in detail. Some of the results were used to provide the criteria suggested for differential diagnosis, delineated earlier in this chapter.

In summary, we found that phenytoin (Dilantin) effects a complete remission in binge eating in a substantial number of patients (27 out of 59) and a partial remission in a smaller group (8 out of 59). Some of these patients have been followed up for as long as five years, with continued good response. Several patients were given placebos, serving as their own controls; the results were entirely concordant with drug response. Invariably, those patients switching to either placebo or Dilantin altered their bingeing behavior in a predictable fashion, five to seven days after the drug change. This is an unlikely result to have occurred as a placebo response but is consistent with the average time for blood levels to increase or decrease sufficiently to affect response.

In addition, Wermuth et al. (1977) found a phenytoin response in a controlled study, despite the confusion by their failure to report the 14 + 6 positive spike pattern. Davis, Quallis, Hollister and Stunkard (1974) reported favorable results in an uncontrolled study. In contrast, two uncontrolled studies (Greenway, Dahms, & Brag, 1977; Weiss & Levitz, 1976) involving eight bingers found phenytoin to be ineffective, although these results are inconclusive since there was no report of the nature and type of EEG tracing and recording.

Given the present level of research data, a trial with phenytoin may be an effective way of ascertaining whether or not patients have a neurologically based eating disorder. There has been increasing attention given to using response to medication for classification of patients (see Klein & Davis, 1969). Results can be obtained within a short time (usually within two weeks) with little risk to the patient. For those patients achieving a complete remission, a prolonged, expensive, ineffective course of psychotherapy can be avoided.

Theoretical Discussion

The basic principle underlying this chapter is that similar behaviors often are elicited by a diversity of etiologies. The history of bulimia suggests, however, a decided preference to regard the excessive gorging associated with it as strictly psychogenic. We have presented contrary evidence from a variety of sources so that readers may be more likely to consider alternative etiologies. Assuming that bulimic behavior can be accounted for by a neurophysiological mechanism, how might one conceptualize it? In the absence of specific experimental data, we have considered a number of theoretical models as an aid to understanding.

It has been fairly well established that almost all patients with bulimic behavior are female. Why? Lindner's (1954) hypothesis was that the act of gorging and vomiting was a symbolic acting out of unconscious impregnation and abortion. Since pregnancy is obviously restricted to females, such an hypothesis accounts rather nicely for the difference in occurrence between men and women. In the neurophysiological sphere there is less theoretical clarity. Moskovitz and Lingao's (1979) paper on the association between bulimia and oral contraceptive use leads inevitably to the suspicion that female hormone dysregulation may be an important factor. All but one of our 59 patients were postpubertal and premenopausal. Further, as far as we have been able to ascertain from the literature, no child or postmenopausal person has bulimia. This restriction in age range corresponds to the age distribution of the 14 + 6 positive spike EEG dysrhythmia. This pattern is rarely found in children, increases in frequency after puberty to the early twenties, then declines until it is uncommon in persons over 35 (e.g., Wegner & Struve, 1977). These observations take on heightened salience from Struve et al.'s (1976) paper linking EEG dysrhythmias and oral contraceptive use in psychiatric patients. A theoretical model is suggested implicating an underlying female endrocrine dysfunction, most likely affecting subcortical hypothalamic central nervous system functions.

In 1975, we proposed two neuropsychological models for consideration (Rau & Green, 1975). Both remain viable today. The first suggests that the lesions responsible for neurogenic bulimia are located specifically in the appetitive centers of the hypothalamus, either resulting in excitation of the eating center or inhibition of the satiation center. Psychological factors were considered as principally secondary, such that they resulted from the primary neurological disturbance. That is, different defensive patterns lead to different coping mechanisms.

Our second model suggests that the primary neurological lesion produces an increase in general drive state in a random dysrhythmic manner, just as epileptic seizures occur in an irregular unpredictable pattern. Whether a person becomes bulimic then depends on unconscious psychogenic factors. More specifically, some persons consciously choose bulimia as a way of attempting to recognize the sudden increase in impulse. Others may choose drinking, drugs, gambling, or fetishes (e.g., Mitchell, 1954).

This model would be supported if subgroups of alcoholics, compulsive gamblers, drub abusers, and so forth were found with EEG dysrhythmias and a positive drug response to anticonvulsant medication. Further research should help lead to a narrowing of the choices among these models and offer a unique opportunity to answer basic brain-behavior issues.

Any such research should be designed carefully. For example, the Wermuth et al. (1977) study, which used a double-blind placebo crossover design, has been interpreted in different ways regarding the effect of Dilantin on bulimic bingeing. Certain shortcomings of the study, however, highlight caution to other researchers in this area. The restriction of the sample to volunteers is unfortunate, as it limits generalizability. The failure to report the 14 + 6 positive spike pattern, even if not regarded as abnormal, makes comparison with other reports impossible. Using their data, 60 percent of their patients (11) improved with Dilantin as measured by a minimum 50 percent reduction in bingeing. Of the 11 patients, seven had "normal EEGs." Were these EEGs entirely free of dysrhythmias? If not, how did such improvement take place? No information was provided as to the effect of Dilantin on neurological soft signs, nor were such data collected. It would have been helpful to have such data. Even without it, Wermuth and colleagues conclude that some patients were helped by Dilantin and did have some form of neurogenic bingeing. It is for future research to clarify these matters and resolve the body-over-mind issues inherent in bulimia.

References

Alajouanine, T., Villey, R., Nehlil, J., *Troubles de L'appetit et Rhinenacephale. Presse Mediche, 61,* 1957, 1385–1400.

American Psychiatric Association. *Diagnostic and Statistical Manual of Mental Disorders,* 3rd ed. Washington, D.C.: American Psychiatric Association, 1980.

Balagura, S. Neuropsychological aspects: Hypothalamic factors in the control of eating behavior. In F. Reichsman, (ed.), *Advances in Psychosomatic Medicine: Hunger and Satiety in Health and Disease,* vol. 7. New York: S. Karger, 1972.

Bruch, H. *Eating Disorders: Obesity, Anorexia Nervosa and the Person Within.* New York: Basic Books, 1973.

Chapman, L. J., & Chapman, J. P. Illusory correlations as an obstacle in the use of valid psychodiagnostic signs. *Journal of Abnormal Psychiatry,* 1969, *74*(3), 271–280.

Crisp, A. H. The possible significance of some behavioral correlates of weight and carbohydrate intake. *Journal of Psychological Research,* 1967, *11,* 117–131.

Crisp, A. H., Fenton, G. W., & Strotton L. A controlled study of the EEG in anorexia nervosa. *British Journal of Psychiatry,* 1968, *114,* 1149–1169.

Dally, P. *Anorexia Nervosa.* New York: Grune & Stratton, 1969.

Davis, K. L., Quallis, B., Hollister, L. E., and Stunkard, A. J. EEGs of "binge" eaters. (Letter to editor.) *American Journal of Psychiatry,* 1974, *131,* 1409.

Gibbs, F. A. & Gibbs, E. L. *Atlas of Electroencephalography,* vol. 3. *Neurological and Psychiatric Disorders.* Reading, Mass.: Addison-Wesley, 1965.

Goor, E. EEG in anorexia nervosa. *British Journal of Psychiatry,* 1954, *6,* 349–351.

Green, R. S., & Rau, J. H. Treatment of compulsive eating disturbances with anticonvulsant medication. *American Journal of Psychiatry,* 1974, *131,* 428–432.

Green, R. S., & Rau, J. H. The use of diphenylhydantoin in compulsive eating disorders: Further studies. In R. A. Vigersky (ed.), *Anorexia Nervosa.* New York: Raven Press, 1977.

Greenway, F. L., Dahms, W. T., & Brag, G. A. Phenytoin as a treatment of obesity associated with compulsive eating. *Current Therapeutic Research,* 1977, *21,* 338–342.

Grosman, S. P. Neurophysiologic aspects: Extrahypothalamic factors in the regulation of food intake. In F. Reichsmann, (ed.), *Advances in Psychosomatic Medicine: Hunger and Satiety in Health and Disease,* vol. 7. New York: S. Karger, 1972.

Hercaen, H. Mental symptoms associated with tumors of the frontal lobe. In J. M. Warren & K. Akert (eds.), *The Frontal Granular Cortex and Behavior.* New York: McGraw-Hill, 1964.

Heron, G. B., & Johnston, D. A. Hypothalamic tumor presenting as anorexia nervosa. *American Journal of Psychiatry,* 1976, *133*(5), 580–582.

Hofstatter, L., Smolik, E. A., & Busch, A. K. Prefrontal lobotomy in the treatment of chronic psychosis. *Arch. Neurol. Chicago,* 1945, *53,* 125–130.

King, A. Primary and secondary anorexia nervosa syndromes. *British Journal of Psychiatry,* 1963, *109,* 470–479.

Kirschbaum, W. R. Excessive hunger as a symptom of cerebral origin. *Journal of Nervous and Mental Disorders,* 1951, *113,* 95.

Klein, D. F., & Davis, J. M. *Diagnosis and Drug Treatment of Psychiatric Disorders.* Baltimore, Md.: Williams & Wilkins, 1969.

Liebowitz, M. R., & Klein, D. F. Hysteroid dysphoria. *Psychiatric Clinics of North America,* 1979, *2*(3), 555–575.

Lindner, R. *The Fifty-Minute Hour.* New York: Rinehart, 1954.

Lundberg, O., & Wolinder, J. Anorexia nervosa and signs of brain damage. *International Journal of Neuropsychiatry,* 1967, *3,* 165–173.

May, R., Angel, E., & Ellenberger, H. F. *Existence.* New York: Simon & Schuster, 1958.

Mitchell, W. Epilepsy with fetishism relived by temporal lobectomy. *Lancet,* 1954, *2,* 626–630.

Moskovitz, R. A., & Lingao, A. Binge eating associated with oral contraceptives. *American Journal of Psychiatry,* 1979, *136*(5), 721–722.

Pyle, R. L., Mitchell, J. E., & Eckert, E. D. Bulimia: A report of 34 cases. *Journal of Clinical Psychiatry,* 1981, *42*(2), 60–64.

Rau, J. H., & Green, R. S. Compulsive eating: A neuropsychologic approach to certain eating disorders. *Comparative Psychiatry,* 1975, *16,* 223–231.

Rau, J. H., & Green, R. S. Soft neurological correlates of compulsive eating. *Journal of Nervous Mental Disorders,* 1978, *166,* 435–437.

Reeves, A. G., & Plum, F. Hyperphagia, rage and dementia accompanying a ventromedial hypothalamic neoplasm. *Arch. Neurol,* 1969, *20,* 616–624.

Remick, R. A., Jones, M. W., & Campos, P. E. Postictal bulimia. (Letter to the editor.) *Journal of Clinical Psychiatry,* 1980, *41,* 7, 256.

Rosenberg, P., Herishanu, Y., & Bellin, B. Increased appetite (bulimia) in Parkinson's Disease. *American Geriatrics Society,* 1977, *25*(6), 277–278.

Sawa, M., Ueki, Y., Arita, M., & Hurada, T. Preliminary report on the amygdaloidectomy on the psychotic patients with interpretations of oral-emotional manifestation in schizophrenics. *Folia Psychiatrica Neurologica Japonica,* 1954, *7,* 309–329.

Schachter, S. *Emotion, Obesity and Crime.* New York: Academic Press, 1971. (a)

Schachter, S. Some extraordinary facts about obese humans and rats. *American Psychologist* 1971, *26,* 129–144. (b)

Schachter, S., & Rodin, J. *Obese Humans and Rats.* Washington, D.C.: Erlbaum, 1974.

Struve, F. A., Saraf, K. R., Arko, R. S., Klein, D. F., & Becka, D. R. Electroencephalographic correlates of oral contraceptive use in psychiatric patients. *Psychiatry,* 1976, *33,* 741–745.

Stunkard, A. J. Eating patterns and obesity. *Psychiatry Quarterly,* 1959, *33,* 284–295.

Stunkard, A. J. Hunger and satiety. *Journal of American Psychiatry,* 1961, *118,* 212–217.

Stunkard, A. J., Grace, W. J., & Wolff, H. G. The night-eating syndrome: A pattern of food intake among certain obese patients. *American Journal of Medicine,* 1955, *19,* 78.

Teitelbaum, P., & Campbell, B. A. Ingestion patterns in hyperphagic and normal rats. *Journal of Comparative Physiological Psychology,* 1958, *51,* 135–141.

Templar, D. Anorexic humans and rats. *American Psychologist,* 1971, *26,* 935.

Terzian, H., & Ore, G. D. Syndrome of Klüver-Bucy reproduced in man by bilateral removal of temporal lobes. *Neurology,* 1955, *5,* 373–380.

Wegner, J. R., & Struve, F. A. Incidence of the 14 and 6 per second positive spike pattern in an adult clinical population: An empirical note. *Journal of Nervous and Mental Disorders,* 1977, *164,* 340–345.

Weiss, T., & Levitz, L. Diphenylhydantoin treatment of bulimia. (Letter to the editor.) *American Journal of Psychiatry,* 1976, *133,* 1093.

Wermuth, B. M., Davis, K. L., Hollister, L. E., & Stunkard, A. J. Phenytoin treatment of the binge-eating syndrome. *American Journal of Psychiatry,* 1977, *134,* 1249–1253.
Whittier, J. R. Asphyxiation, bulimia and insuline levels in Huntington's disease (chorea). (Letter to the editor.) *Journal of American Medical Association,* 1976, *235*(14), 1423.

7

Bulimarexia: Guidelines for Behavioral Assessment and Treatment

C. Tracy Orleans
Linda R. Barnett

This chapter presents guidelines for the comprehensive assessment and treatment of bulimarexic behavior based on a behavioral analysis of binge–purge practices. We use the conceptual framework of a functional analysis of behavior to integrate findings from past studies and clinical reports and to suggest systematic behavioral assessment and treatment approaches. Practical guidelines for the assessment of bulimarexic behavior and related problems are presented. Recommendations for treatment are discussed in the context of a review of past behavioral treatment studies.

Several terms have been used to describe binge–purge practices, including bulimarexia (Boskind-Lodahl & White, 1978), the gorging/ purging syndrome (Rosen & Leitenberg, 1982), bulimia (APA, 1980; Casper, Eckert, Halmi, Goldberg, & Davis, 1980), and bulimia nervosa (Russell, 1979). In this chapter, we use the term bulimarexia to describe the binge–purge practices without wishing to designate a uniform syndrome with a single etiology. We think that debate over whether the binge–purge disorder shall be considered a symptom, a subtype, or a chronic version of anorexia nervosa (e.g., Russell, 1979), or a full-fledged independent psychiatric syndrome (e.g., APA, 1980) is premature. We believe instead that binge–purge practices and their affective and behavioral correlates require more careful study in their own right, as problems that can constitute a serious eating disorder for excessively weight-conscious individuals in obese, normal-weight, and anorexic populations.

Prevalence of Binge–Purge Practices

We know relatively little about the prevalence or demographic correlates of bulimarexic behavior (Lucas, 1981). Binge–purge behavior has been studied most among hospitalized anorexics, occurring in nearly 50 percent of the cases in two samples (Beumont, George, & Smart, 1976; Garfinkel, Moldofsky, & Garner, 1980). However, the prevalence in the general population is hard to estimate. It is commonly assumed that bulimarexic practices are increasingly common among college students, especially women, who acquire them through modeling (Boskind-Lodahl, 1976; Russell, 1979). But data to substantiate this belief are scant and inconclusive, suggesting a range of 3 to 14 percent prevalence rates among college women (Beuf, Dglugash, & Eininger, Note 2; Boskind-Lodahl, Note 3; Chernyk, Note 5). Clement and Hawkins (Note 7) found 4 to 9 percent of normal-weight college students (male and females) reporting vomiting after a binge. In a recent study of psychiatric diagnosis at a large university psychiatric clinic, Stangler and Printz (1980) found that 4.4 percent of 500 students presented with a *primary* complaint of bulimia. The authors note, however, that additional cases of bulimia revealed during the course of treatment for other problems were not included in these figures, and they warn against treating this university prevalence estimate as anything but conservative.

Characteristics of Bulimarexics

Findings to date are insufficient to justify any definitive statement about the relationship of gender and weight status to bulimarexic practices, or about the role of psychosocial and psychopathological factors in the development and maintenance of bulimarexic behavior. Existing findings are limited because they are based on circumscribed investigations, including (1) retrospective comparisons of hospitalized anorexic patients who do and do not exhibit binge–purge practices (Beumont, 1977; Beumont et al., 1976; Casper et al., 1980; Garfinkel et al., 1980; Russell, 1979; Strober, 1982), (2) clinical studies of bulimarexics employing restrictive selection criteria, that is, using only women who exhibit binge–purge problems (Boskind-Lodahl, Note 3; Boskind-Lodahl & White, 1978), and (3) surveys of normal-weight or obese populations to obtain information about binge–purge practices (Barnett, Note 1; Beuf et al., Note 2; Carroll & Leon, Note 4; Clement & Hawkins, Note 7).

We review the general conclusions emerging from this research, however, to note that past findings are entirely compatible with the behavioral or learning theory approach suggested in this chapter and to shed light on important correlates of bulimarexia deserving attention in a comprehensive behavioral assessment and treatment.

Sex and Sex-Role Identity

Bulimarexia appears far more common among women than men and, in fact, only a few instances have been noted among men (Boskind-Lodahl, Note 3; Clement & Hawkins, Note 7; Garfinkel et al., 1980; Russell, 1979). No physiological factors have been suggested to explain this sex difference; rather, the great incidence of bulimarexia among women has been related to stronger cultural norms equating beauty and health to a slender appearance designed to please men (Boskind-Lodahl, 1976; Boskind-Lodahl & White, 1978; Lucas, 1981).

Consistent with this view, Boskind-Lodahl (Note 3; 1976) has observed that bulimarexia is most common among women overly invested in the traditional feminine sex-role stereotype characterized by passive dependency and overly concerned with acceptance and approval of others. This overinvestment in a "feminine" identity often may conflict with overt strivings and achievements in traditionally nonfeminine arenas. Barnett (Note 1), for instance, found an unexpectedly high incidence of binge eating (13.5%), bulimarexic practices (2%), and past anorexia (3.9%) among MD and PhD medical and allied health professionals, and anecdotal evidence suggests that the "traditional" feminine values of many bulimarexics are anomalous and conflictual given their outstanding academic or occupational achievements (Boskind-Lodahl, Note 3; Lucas, 1981; Rovner, 1981; Russell, 1979). It may be that succeeding in nonfeminine domains places a greater premium on appearing feminine in other ways. The relationship between bulimarexic practices, professional ambition or achievement, and role strain among women is an important area for further study and could be examined using measures of conformity to traditional sex-role stereotypes (Bem, 1974).

Weight Status

The hallmark of the bulimarexic is concern with weight and weight control, rather .than any single weight problem. Bulimarexic behavior has been identified among diet-conscious overweight, normal-weight, and underweight groups (Boskind-Lodahl, Note 3; Clement & Hawkins, Note 7; Lucas, 1981). Its frequent association with past or present anorexia in the literature may be an artifact of selection criteria that have maximized similarities between anorexic and bulimarexic populations (Beumont, 1977; Casper et al., 1980; Garfinkel et al., 1980; Russell, 1979).

All existing findings suggest bulimarexic behavior is acquired as a weight control tactic. Retrospective reports trace the origins of bulimarexic behavior to adolescence, where it is related to difficulties dieting to overcome a mild degree of obesity (Beumont, 1977; Boskind-Lodahl & White, 1978; Garfinkel et al., 1980; Russell, 1979). Most studies comparing bulimarexic and nonbulimarexic subgroups of anorexia nervosa patients have documented a greater incidence of premorbid obesity for bulimarexics (Beumont, 1977; Beumont et al., 1976; Garfinkel et al., 1980; Strober, 1982). Several studies have related peer modeling in adolescence to the choice of binge–purge methods, and others have suggested that bulimarexic behavior develops in an atmosphere of excessive family concern about thinness and weight control and/or with familial modeling of weight control difficulties and other substance abuse problems (Carroll & Leon, Note 4; Casper et al., 1980; Garfinkel et al., 1980; Strober, 1982).

Predisposing Personality Factors and Psychosocial Influences

Most data suggest that the origins of bulimarexic practices are related more consistently to difficulties with weight control than to any particular constellation of psychosocial or emotional problems. Unfortunately, there are no prospective data bearing on the question of whether certain personality or psychosocial influences predispose an individual to binge–purge problems. Retrospective reports, however, mostly based on anorexic populations, can be interpreted as supporting this conclusion.

Beumont (1977), comparing anorexics who did and who did not exhibit bulimarexic behavior, found that conventional anorexics more often reported onset at the time of psychological difficulties related to puberty or family problems, while bulimarexics more often cited ·being teased about their weight or joining in competitive sports or dance classes as antecedents. Beumont (1977) found adolescent overweight to be a more important predisposing factor for bulimarexic anorexics than for nonbulimarexic anorexics, and found the reverse to be true for reported life stress and family disturbance. Russell (1979) found such great variability in the premorbid personalities of the 30 bulimarexic anorexic patients he studied that he concluded that there was no one particular type of personality or psychosocial problem consistently tied to the origin of bulimarexic behavior. Only one study (Strober, 1982) has suggested a predisposing psychosocial personality profile involving greater life stress, family discord, and parental psychopathology, including problems of addiction. Unfortunately, these differences were predicted, and interviewers conducting assessments were not blind to these predictions.

We can draw a few cautious conclusions from this limited knowledge of the etiology of bulimarexia. It seems reasonable, at this time, to hypothesize that bulimarexia develops as a faulty weight control practice in an environment where problematic self-control patterns are modeled. Adolescent weight control problems (mild obesity, difficulty dieting) have been reported consistently for bulimarexics and may be tied to a biological predisposition to obesity and/or to acquired eating disorders. Likewise, there are repeated findings of parental problems with weight control or substance abuse, and/or peer modeling of bulimarexic practices. More speculatively, it may be that the bulimarexic has limited opportunities to learn effective weight control practices and many opportunities to observe or acquire unhealthy self-control or stress management techniques involving addictive behaviors.

Only with a comprehensive etiological model, stressing interaction between the individual and the environment, can we clarify and extend these preliminary findings. Clement and Hawkins (Note 7) advance such a model, consistent with the behavioral analysis presented in this chapter. They note the importance of several interactive factors: strong cultural norms equating thinness with attractiveness, a biological predisposition to obesity, and a personality pattern characterized by low self-esteem, limited coping resources, and perceived social incompetence. To these we would add the psychosocial and modeling influences just noted.

Psychological Correlates of Bulimarexia

Several studies suggest a characteristic constellation of emotional and psychological problems accompanying bulimarexic practices. Norm-referenced or standardized personality inventories have been used in a few instances (Beumont, 1977; Casper et al., 1980; Garfinkel et al., 1980), but most reports offer an integrated summary of interview observation and test data. Congruencies in these varied reports suggest a remarkably consistent psychological profile.

Surveys and clinical studies investigating correlates of binge–purge practices among heterogeneous samples (anorexic, normal-weight, obese) have found that the bulimarexic typically manifests

1. A morbid fear of weight gain
2. A fear of losing control of eating and weight and preoccupation with food and eating
3. Body-image dissatisfaction
4. Low self-esteem despite objectively high levels of intelligence, social competence, and achievements
5. Overdependence on approval from others
6. Intense feelings of helplessness about overcoming this eating disorder, accompanied by a passive–dependent social and problem-solving style
7. Underassertiveness
8. A constellation of depressive features, including subjective depression, suicidal ideation, loneliness, social anxiety, and withdrawal (Boskind-Lodahl, Note 3; Carroll & Leon, Note 4; Clement & Hawkins, Note 7; Beumont et al., 1976; Casper et al., 1980; Garfinkel et al., 1980; Rovner, 1981; Russell, 1979). Depressive symptoms appear to vary in intensity with the severity of the eating disorder (Russell, 1979).

Recent studies of bulimarexia in both anorexic and normal populations have suggested generalized impulse control or substance abuse problems, including compulsive stealing and alcohol, tobacco, and drug abuse (Carroll & Leon, Note 4; Casper et al., 1980; Garfinkel et al., 1980; Strober, 1982). Compulsive stealing may serve chiefly to supply adequate amounts of binge foods: More than half of the bulimarexics in one study reported having stolen food specifically for a binge—not surprising, given their estimates that binges cost $10 to $20 each (Carroll & Leon, Note 4). Comparisons of bulimarexic and nonbulimarexic anorexic populations, for the most part, have shown higher levels of psychosexual maturity and extraversion, but greater impulse control problems and more acute distress among the bulimarexic group (Beumont, 1977; Casper et al., 1980; Garfinkel et al., 1980; Strober, 1982).

We need more information about the personality, affective, and behavioral correlates of bulimarexia and their relationship to the etiology and maintenance of bulimarexic behavior. Collecting such information on an individual basis is crucial for defining treatment goals and priorities and for training both the focal behavioral disorder and the associated feelings, cognitions, psychological factors, and behavioral problems that can contribute to, and result from, bulimarexic practices. In other words, the bulimarexic response is usually embedded in a lifestyle that serves to maintain the disorder, and the factors that make up this lifestyle must be assessed—in addition to the problematic binge–purge response.

The value of a comprehensive approach becomes clearer when we consider the complexity of the problem. On the one hand, a passive–dependent orientation and overdependency on approval from others could predispose an individual to bulimarexic practices. On the other hand, repeated failures to overcome this self-perpetuating disorder can reinforce a passive–dependent orientation and contribute to feelings of powerlessness, helplessness, and low self-esteem, which, in turn, would render an individual more dependent upon the approval of others and more dependent upon appearance and weight for self-approval. Similarly, if the bulimarexic maladaptively binges in response to stressful life events, then obsessing about, or engaging in, the binge–purge problem may constitute a reinforcing escape from the "real" problem, or avoidance responses. It is likely that the self-derogation, shame, and guilt that bulimarexics experience as a result of this bizarre eating disorder contribute to depression and social withdrawal. In addition, the bulimarexic pattern, by requiring privacy for bingeing and purging, may contribute to a generalized social avoidance through a process of classical avoidance conditioning. Forcing oneself to adhere to ever-stricter diets is chosen frequently as the path to salvation for these worshippers of slenderness (Chernin, 1981), a solution that only intensifies the problem and guarantees that the bulimarexic will continue to feel out of control.

As these examples illustrate, the binge–purge pattern can overwhelm the bulimarexic's life, intensifying predisposing psychosocial deficits or vulnerabilities, or adding new ones. Therefore, we advise that clinicians and researchers routinely administer objective, standardized measures to assess the psychological correlates of bulimarexic behavior. We suggest either a general personality or psychopathology inventory (e.g., Minnesota Multiphasic Personality Inventory, or California Personality Inventory) or measures of more specific problems of clinical or theoretical interest to the investigator. Such measures might include depression or anxiety rating instruments, measures of social competence and assertiveness (e.g., Levenson & Gottman, 1978; Rathus & Nevid, 1977), sex-role identification (e.g., Bem, 1974), body-image dissatisfaction (e.g., Hawkins & Clement, 1980), preoccupation with food, and fear of loss of control of eating (e.g., Clement, Note 6). In a later section of this chapter we will discuss instruments to assess eating and dieting practices and attitudes associated with bulimarexia. Collecting objective and systematic data stands to greatly advance our understanding of the mechanisms involved in bulimarexic behavior. We routinely administer the MMPI as part of a comprehensive behavioral assessment; our findings illustrate the potential value of incorporating such assessments.

We administered the MMPI to bulimarexic anorexic inpatients and to bulimarexic outpatients and found evidence for a uniform tendency to conform to the traditional feminine sex-role stereotype; this evidence supports the theoretical formulations of Boskind-Lodahl (1976). Figure 7–1 presents the separate and composite profiles of six consecutively seen hospitalized women, aged 17 to 22. All were given a primary diagnosis of anorexia nervosa and were underweight at the time of admission. The relatively low Mf scores (indicating a passive–dependent orientation, an overinvestment in the feminine sex-role stereotype), along with the "V" formed by scales 4 (Pd), 5 (Mf), and 6 (Pa), suggesting a masochistic orientation, were strikingly similar across profiles, despite variable covarying levels of subjective depression (D), manifest anxiety (Pt), social withdrawal (Si), and acute distress (K).

Figure 7-1. Individual and Composite MMPI Profiles of Six Hospitalized Bulimarexic Anorexic Women.

152

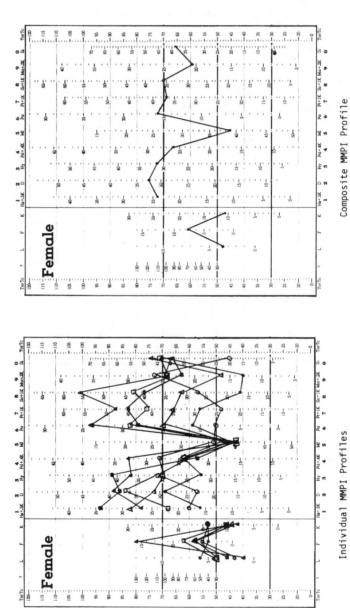

Individual MMPI Profiles

Composite MMPI Profile

———————— Mean

We also tested six nonhospitalized normal-weight bulimarexic women, all aged 21, who were referred consecutively to Dr. Barnett for outpatient psychotherapy. Their profiles are presented in Figure 7–2. Again, we discovered uniformly low Mf scores and similar Vs formed by scales 4, 5, and 6, against a background of variable, covarying levels of anxiety, depression, social withdrawal, and acute distress. Besides providing support for the view that bulimarexic behavior is related to a passive–dependent feminine sex-role orientation, these individual profiles indicated related psychopathology (e.g., depression, social withdrawal) and influenced our choice of treatment goals and priorities.

The Anatomy of Bulimarexic Behavior

The following section of this chapter focuses on the assessment of binge–purge behavior per se. Guided by the conceptual framework of a functional analysis of behavior, we present guidelines for operationalizing bingeing and purging practices and functionally related eating and dieting practices. We provide a referenced summary of these guidelines in Table 7–1 which can be used as an assessment checklist.

We have developed a self-report instrument, the Personal Data Questionnaire (PDQ) to structure a preliminary functional analysis of binge–purge practices on a case-by-case basis (Orleans, Note 8). This questionnaire requests the bulimarexic's descriptions of the circumstances surrounding the onset of bulimarexia; the topography, antecedents, and consequences of bingeing and purging practices; along with ratings of motivation to overcome the problem and descriptions of past control attempts. We use these self-reports to develop an individualized baseline self-monitoring protocol. The questionnaire helps the bulimarexic objectify the binge–purge problem and disclose often embarrassing information prior to a face-to-face interaction. We include this PDQ as a reference in the appendix to this chapter.

Operationalizing Bingeing/Purging Practices

Reliable, objective measures of the frequency and topography of bingeing and purging practices must be obtained. Actually, few researchers or clinicians have assessed these practices carefully,

Figure 7-2. Individual and Composite MMPI Profiles of Six Normal-Weight Outpatient Bulimarexic Women.

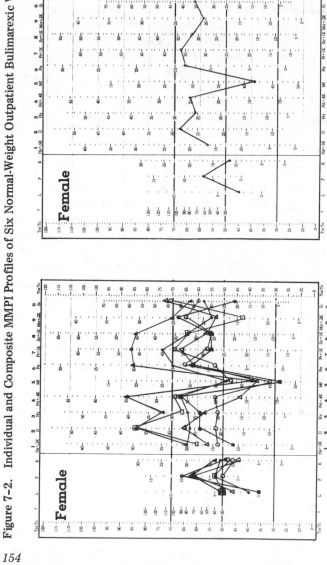

Individual MMPI Profiles

Composite MMPI Profile

——————— Mean

154

Table 7-1. Behavioral Assessment Guidelines

I. Define the problem(s)
  A. Operationalize the bulimarexic response (2, 6, 8, 10, 15, 39, 47, 51–53)
    1. Frequency, duration, interval of binge-purge cycle
    2. Bingeing foods and practices
    3. Purging practices: vomiting, purgatives, fasting, or strict dieting; others
  B. Define related problems and assets (2–4, 6–8, 10, 15–18, 21, 26, 27, 29–32, 35–37, 39–41, 49–53, 56, 64)
    1. Problems related to weight and nutrition: problematic weight status, irregular eating habits, inadequate nutrition, overly strict dieting
    2. Emotional and psychological problems: low self-esteem, depressive features, underassertiveness, morbid fear of weight gain and loss of control
    3. Assets: any normal eating behavior, psychosocial competence and self-control skills, motivation, and environmental resources
    4. Medical complications of bulimarexia
    5. Psychosocial barriers/assets
II. Anatomy of the bulimarexic response
  A. Antecedents of the binge (2, 4, 6–10, 15–18, 29–32, 47, 50–53, 55–56, 62, 64)
    1. Fasting, excessively strict diet
    2. Food-related cues: access to preferred bingeing foods, eating small amounts of "forbidden" foods
    3. Facilitative setting (private, isolated)
    4. Physiological variables: intense hunger, low blood sugar, fatigue medical causes (e.g., neurological defects, hypoglycemia)
    5. Cognitions/emotions: preoccupation with food or eating; feeling deprived; anxiety related to external stress; frustration, disappointment or depression related to self-critical thinking; underassertiveness; interpersonal difficulties or dieting failures
  B. Consequences of the binge (2, 8, 10, 15–18, 35, 36, 39, 48, 51–53)
    1. Positive immediate consequences: (a) negative reinforcement through relief or distraction from antecedent aversive physical and emotional states; (b) positive reinforcement through enjoyment of eating and dissociation mechanisms
    2. Negative delayed consequences: intensely negative self-evaluations and shame, guilt, anguish about the binge; fear or panic about weight gain; "sugar blues" and other uncomfortable physical side-effects
  C. Antecedents of the purge (2, 8, 10, 15–18, 39, 47, 51–53)
    1. Negative delayed consequences of the binge (above)
    2. Facilitative conditions affecting purging method: critical time period; isolated setting; purgatives available
  D. Consequences of the purge (2, 17, 18, 30, 35, 36, 39, 48)
    1. Positive immediate consequences: negative reinforcement through relief from intensely negative physical and emotional consequences, positive reinforcement involving self-talk about the reinstatement of self-control; irrational thinking
    2. Negative delayed consequences: self-critical thinking, depression, shame, helplessness, serious medical complications

using either self-reports *or* objective measures. We review past findings about variations in bulimarexic behavior to suggest assessment targets and methods.

Defining Binge Eating. Past reports, and our own findings using the Personal Data Questionnaire, have indicated considerable variability in the frequency of problematic bingeing or overeating, ranging from once or twice a week to five to 10 times per day (Boskind-Lodahl, Note 3; Carroll & Leon, Note 4; Beumont et al., 1976; Monti, McCrady, & Barlow, 1977; Russell, 1979). As with binge eating in obesity, frequency probably represents the best single index of problem severity (Loro & Orleans, 1981).

The interval of the binge–purge cycle varies. Some bulimarexics binge and purge several times a day, while others binge for several days and then fast or purge for several days. Daily binge episodes often occur late in the day and represent the first "meal" or snack of the day for persons whose eating habits are frequently irregular (Russell, 1979). Many other bulimarexics report overeating a variety of foods over a more extended period of time, for example, over a day, several days, or even a week.

The type and amount of food consumed in a binge, the duration of the binge, and the individual's subjective definition of a binge also vary. Most of our knowledge about these factors comes from the self-reports of bulimarexics (Boskind-Lodahl, Note 3; Carroll & Leon, Note 4; Rovner, 1981). Available findings show considerable variability in the duration of bingeing, both across individuals and over time, for a given individual. For some, a binge extends over several hours (Carroll & Leon, Note 4) and involves eating "as much as the stomach will hold" (Boskind-Lodahl, Note 3). For others, even eating small amounts of "bingeing food" will precipitate vomiting (Chernyk, Note 5). Rosen and Leitenberg (1982) described one bulimarexic who purged both after hour-long binges and after eating only modest amounts of food typically consumed during a binge. The subjective decision that one has eaten "too much" appears more definitive than any objective measure of quantity. Like obese binge eaters, bulimarexics prefer high-calorie junk foods, snack foods, and fast foods (all being foods that are quickly prepared and eaten) and, in some cases, foods like ice-cream, that are easily vomited (Boskind-Lodahl, Note 3; Carroll & Leon, Note 4; Rosen & Leitenberg, 1982; Russell, 1979).

Objective baseline measures of the eating or bingeing should be obtained. Since bulimarexics usually binge in private, self-monitoring represents the most useful measurement strategy. To standardize observations across studies and to obtain a representative sample of bingeing behaviors, we advise using an appropriate validated self-report instrument along with daily self-monitoring. Hawkins and Clement (1980) have developed a Binge Scale that quantifies several important parameters of bingeing behavior (e.g., frequency, duration, rate of eating, and so on), and asks about vomiting following a binge. Gormally, Black, Daston, and Rardin (1982) have constructed a Binge Eating Scale to assess binge frequency and topography and the feelings and cognitions surrounding a binge. These scales go beyond our own Personal Data Questionnaire (see chapter appendix) to identify problematic bingeing practices and associated antecedents and contingencies. Comprehensive daily diet records requiring information about the time, duration, and antecedents of a binge (e.g., location, cognitions, hunger, emotional state, presence of others); the types and amounts of foods consumed; and the physical, cognitive, and emotional consequences of a binge can be adapted easily from those developed to assess behaviors resulting in obesity (Kattell, Callahan, Fremouw, & Zitter, 1979).

Defining Related Eating and Dieting Patterns. Bulimarexia rarely occurs in isolation of more pervasive eating disorders. Irregular eating habits, involving skipping meals or frequent snacking, are the norm (Boskind-Lodahl, Note 3). Bulimarexia can accompany the overeating and underexercising resulting in obesity, or the food restriction and overexercise associated with anorexia nervosa. These related problems should be assessed. For obesity or overweight, physical measures of obesity (weight, adiposity) and diet and exercise records would be appropriate (Loro & Orleans, 1981). For underweight and normal-weight "dieting" bulimarexics, periodic weigh-ins are important. For underweight buimarexics, Garner and Garfinkel's (1979) Eating Attitudes Test is useful to identify eating practices and attitudes associated with anorexia nervosa. For all groups, a review of daily diet records to gauge nutritional adequacy of foods consumed should be considered. Any phobic responses to particular food groups or avoidance of these foods (especially protein and complex carbohydrates) should be noted as factors possibly contributing to dieting or binge–purge patterns and as targets for independent treatment.

Dieting practices must be assessed among bulimarexics because extreme dieting and self-denial are integral to the binge–purge pattern (Boskind-Lodahl, Note 3). Many bulimarexics are chronically on excessively strict diets involving prolonged periods of fasting or self-denial and frequently fast all day (often in reaction to the preceding day's binge). As a result, they inevitably experience intense hunger, feelings of self-deprivation, and fatigue, frequently with concentration difficulties associated with low blood sugar levels. This physical and emotional state of deprivation sets the stage for a binge and heightens its reinforcing consequences. In fact, the relationship between excessively strict dieting and binge eating has been documented repeatedly in normal-weight and obese groups (Gormally et al., 1982; Hawkins & Clement, 1980). Herman and Polivy's (1975) measure of dietary "restraint," or the 14-item Cognitive Factors Scale developed by Gormally et al. (1982) to assess unrealistically strict dieting standards and low-efficacy expectations for staying on a diet, can be used to assess these dieting problems.

Cognitive factors play a crucial role in leading bulimarexics from a slip (just one bite, cookie, etc.) to an all-out binge. Marlatt and Gordon (1979) have advanced a cognitive–behavioral model to describe how abstinent alcoholics, drug addicts, and smokers progress from an isolated slip to a full-blown relapse, and Clement and Hawkins (Note 7) have aptly applied this model to binge eating. Likewise, Herman and Mack (1975) and Spencer and Fremouw (1979) have documented that college students scoring high on Herman and Polivy's (1975) restraint scale ate more when told they had just consumed a high-calorie drink than when told they had just consumed a low-calorie drink.

Variability in eating practices or habits and, in particular, any instances of relatively normal eating should be noted carefully and assessed. The circumstances in which normal eating (without purging) occurs should be studied to identify discriminative stimuli and reinforcers.

Defining Purging Practices. Bulimarexics adopt a wide variety of methods to counteract the fattening effects of a binge (Boskind-Lodahl, Note 3; Carroll & Leon, Note 4; Beumont, 1977; Beumont et al., 1976; Monti et al., 1977; Russell, 1979). Most frequently, binge eaters self-induce vomiting to reverse a binge. In rare cases they use a cathartic, like syrup of Ipecac, to induce vomiting. Many bulimarexics who vomit also occasionally use, or abuse, laxatives or diuretics, and some take amphetamines to counteract the effects of a binge. Each of these purging behaviors generally is peformed in seclusion. As we have noted, fasting or strict dieting after bingeing represents another common "purging" method, used exclusively in some cases (Boskind-Lodahl, Note 3).

Excessive exercise also may be employed. As for bingeing, we recommend daily self-monitoring and recording of target purging behaviors (vomiting, drug use, exercise) and their emotional, cognitive, and locational antecedents and consequences.

Medical Complications. Knowing exactly how purging is accomplished is important from behavioral and medical standpoints. Aside from the health problems of obesity or underweight associated with bulimarexia, purging practices carry their own serious medical risks. Persistent vomiting, laxative abuse, and overuse of diuretics can all cause reduction in serum potassium levels—hypokalemia—which can, in turn, precipitate fatal arrhythmias and dysrrhythmias (Katz, Eckert, & Gebott, 1972; Kolata, 1980; Oster, Materson, & Rogers, 1980; Russell, 1979). Renal problems, a loss of gastric contractility, urinary infections, dental problems resulting from exposure to the highly acidic gastric contents, and swollen salivary glands have been linked to persistent vomiting (Carroll & Leon, Note 4; Russell, 1979). Laxative abuse can be associated with serious gastrointestinal disorders including cathartic colon and a range of renal-electrolyte disturbances (Oster et al., 1980). Diuretic abuse has its own medical complications (Katz et al., 1972; Russell, 1979).

For these reasons, we recommend collaborative medical treatment and regular supervision for any bulimarexia treatment program, and we advise inpatient treatment with close medical supervision for any bulimarexic patient whose potassium levels drift into hazardously low ranges (e.g., 3 to 3.5 meq/L). Also, a careful medical work-up can help to rule out hypoglycemia and certain neuroanatomical defects (Green & Rau, 1973; Rau & Green, 1975) believed to play a role in compulsive eating among a small percentage of binge eaters (Loro & Orleans, 1981) and can indicate appropriate treatment for bulimarexia-related medical problems.

Identifying Personal and Psychosocial Obstacles and Assets

Many bulimarexics possess a self-control motivation and self-observation skills that can be assets in any behavior change effort. Involving the client in planning and implementing all aspects of the treatment allows her to substitute a positive form of self-control for the elusive struggles to achieve control inherent in the binge–purge pattern. Objective data collection methods help the bulimarexic to avoid overly critical self-evaluations.

Social environmental influences should be assessed to determine whether there is ongoing exposure to modeling of problematic self-control and weight management practices (e.g., Carroll & Leon, Note 4; Casper et al., 1980; Garfinkel et al., 1980; Strober, 1982) and possibly inadvertent reinforcement for bulimarexic behaviors (e.g., Minuchin, Baker, Rosman, Liebman, Milman, & Todd, 1975; Stuart & Davis, 1972). Likewise, favorable role models should be identified, and helpful family responses to bulimarexic practices and desirable eating behavior should be modeled, shaped, and reinforced.

Identifying Controlling Antecedents and Consequences in the Binge–Purge Cycle

Controlling stimuli can be identifed only through individualized observation and functional analyses. We have summarized past clinical and research reports to identify the types of antecedents and consequences that commonly maintain the bulimarexic response cycle. Table 7–1 (p. 155) and Figure 7–3 synthesize our discussion and can be used in combination to structure an individual assessment and suggest a treatment program.

The bulimarexic response pattern involves the repetitive creation and relief of highly aversive physical and emotional states, relieved (negatively reinforced) in the first instance by a binge and in the second instance by a purge. Moreover, purging represents an escape from the naturally aversive consequences of bingeing. The bulimarexic's faulty self-control attempts contribute to the self-perpetuating binge–purge cycle. Engaging in self-denial and self-derogation to overcome bulimarexic behavior sets the stage for the next binge–purge cycle.

Antecedents of the Binge.   The stimuli preceding bingeing for bulimarexics appear very similar to those documented among obese binge eaters (Loro & Orleans, 1981). As just discussed, overly strict dieting usually precedes overeating (Boskind-Lodahl, 1976; Russell, 1979) and, for many bulimarexics, dieting involves repeated prolonged periods of fasting or restricting oneself to fluids. Often bingeing occurs after all-day fasting, which produces an extremely dysphoric state of physiological and psychological deprivation: extreme hunger, fatigue, low blood sugar levels and related lethargy, and feelings of depression.

Food-related cues represent another important class of binge

Figure 7-3. Diagram of the Vicious Binge–Purge Cycle.

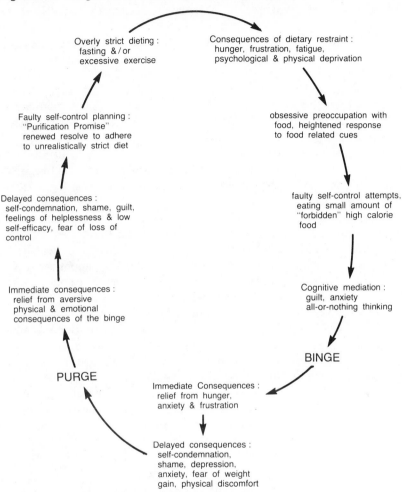

antecedents. Prolonged self-denial probably heightens the bulimarexic's attentional response to food-related stimuli. Access to preferred binge foods, preoccupation with food and eating, and ingestion of even small amounts of "forbidden" or high-calorie foods all
ease the transition from fast to binge (Russell, 1979). Privacy represents a facilitative binge setting, as bulimarexics are most likely
to binge when they are alone (Boskind-Lodahl, 1977; Russell,

1979). Isolation serves the dual purpose of facilitating a binge logistically and of creating an interpersonal vacuum that the bulimarexic tries to fill with food.

External stress and associated feelings of frustration, depression, or helplessness frequently set the stage for a binge. A state of heightened anxiety, for which the bulimarexic lacks effective coping mechanisms, is quite common. Anger and interpersonal conflict for which the individual lacks assertiveness and interpersonal problem-solving skills also frequently set the stage for a binge (Boskind-Lodahl, Note 3; Loro & Orleans, 1981).

Characteristic cognitions mediate between the self-induced dysphoric state described previously and binge eating. The binger–purger often reports an intense preoccupation with food leading to the binge (Boskind-Lodahl, Note 3; Russell, 1979). These thoughts function to displace realistic thinking about the undesired consequences of binge eating; moreover, as Rosen and Leitenberg (1982) note, once the bulimarexic has learned that vomiting will prevent feared binge consequences, thoughts of such consequences lose their power to inhibit a binge. Finally, all-or-none irrational thinking about eating ("Well, as long as I've had one cookie, I may as well go whole hog . . .") also frequently precedes a binge.

Consequences of the Binge. Bingeing has both reinforcing and aversive consequences. Unfortunately, the immediate consequences are reinforcing and thereby exert more control over the bingeing behavior than delayed aversive events.

These immediate reinforcing consequences chiefly involve negative reinforcement. Like obese binge eaters (Loro & Orleans, 1981), bulimarexics experience immediate relief from hunger, feelings of self-deprivation, and high levels of tension. Blood sugar levels increase, precipitously elevating energy level and improving concentration. Likewise, binge eating temporarily takes the person's focus away from uncomfortable emotional states, such as anger, tension, frustration, disappointment, or boredom. In addition, the taste and smell of the food exerts positive reinforcement control. The concern and attention that bingeing receives from significant others actually may have an inadvertent reinforcing effect (Stuart & Davis, 1972). And, since binge eating occurs in private, the individual avoids any immediate negative social consequences.

Strong aversive consequences come into the foreground later, following a pattern similar to that documented for obese binge eaters (Loro & Orleans, 1981). After a binge, the bulimarexic usually experiences anguish, shame, guilt, and self-disgust (Boskind-

Lodahl, Note 3; Russell, 1979). Tension, anxiety, and panic rise, related to intense and irrational fears of weight gain and loss of control (Rosen & Leitenberg, 1982). There is some evidence (Russell, 1979) that bulimarexics employ dissociative mechanisms to minimize their awareness of these delayed aversive consequences while they are bingeing. But, extremely self-critical thinking and a self-derogating preoccupation with weight and fatness reliably follow the immediate positive experiences surrounding the binge itself. In addition, blood sugar levels begin to drop, leading to the so-called "sugar blues," and the uncomfortable physical side-effects of the binge intensify (e.g., bloated stomach, abdominal cramping, headache, fatigue). Any evidence or anticipation of unavoidable weight gain is extremely aversive. Depression and despair related to these physical and emotional states are almost universal (Boskind-Lodahl, 1976; Russell, 1979).

Antecedents of the Purge. Many of the delayed consequences of binge eating constitute critical antecedents for purging. As Rosen and Leitenberg (1982) suggest, vomiting represents an escape response that is strongly negatively reinforced. In the vast majority of cases, purging does not occur in the absence of binge eating or overeating and its usual delayed consequences. Other antecedents are chiefly facilitative, like access to purgatives or being alone in a purging setting during the critical period after a binge during which self-induced vomiting occurs (usually extends 15 to 90 minutes after a binge).

Consequences of the Purge. Negative reinforcement prevails after the purse. Panic about weight gain dissipates immediately following purging, and the physical discomfort associated with bingeing also is relieved. Following negative reinforcements for purging, aversive consequences take over and lead to excessively strict dieting, which in turn sets the stage for the next binge.

Cognitions that follow the purge generally include self-statements resolving to continue to deny oneself and to fast with renewed discipline. Clement and Hawkins (Note 7) have identified a related form of irrational thinking commonly accompanying these postbinge resolutions. They describe it as the "purification promise." The bulimarexic promises herself never again to engage in such uncontrolled eating and also makes the error of redefining *all* her problems as involving uncontrolled eating or overweight. Improved self-control in this area is believed to be the global solution (e.g., "If this is the last time I binge or purge, I will be thin, attractive, and *all* my problems will be solved"). Unfortunately, as we have noted, setting such unrealistic goals and adopting rigid standards for eating and dieting are associated strongly with low self-efficacy (Gormally et al., 1982). Moreover, defining binge–purge behavior as the only problem precludes the recognition and resolution of related problems (e.g., social isolation, external stresses). If the real problems evoke more anxiety, the relief accompanying this faulty assessment may negatively reinforce it.

Consequences of the Binge–Purge Cycle. Each binge–purge cycle reduces the bulimarexic's evaulation of other self-control capabilities. Assuming she possesses limited ability to control her eating, she begins a renewed self-deprivation cycle. Unfavorable self-evaluation, convictions of helplessness, and renewed self-denial, in turn, raise vulnerabilities to outside stresses and dysphoric moods, compromise adaptive problem-solving and coping resources, and increase the likelihood of a binge. Shame, guilt, depression, a paralyzing sense of helplessness, and, in some cases, suicidal thinking are among the debilitating cognitive and emotional consequences of the binge–purge pattern. Not only can they lead to depression, they also can motivate isolation and social withdrawal, which in turn intensify the loneliness, dependence on others for approval, and low self-esteem that fueled the dysfunctional pattern in the first place. This unending cycle of self-derogation helps make the bulimarexic pattern self-perpetuating.

In addition to the self-loathing that follows a purge, the serious medical complications of bulimarexic practices represent aversive bingeing consequences. Striking to us is how frequently the terror experienced by the bulimarexic patient at the thought of weight gain is more motivating than the threat of death itself.

Summary. The self-perpetuating cycle we have just reviewed and outlined in Figure 7–3 presents many opportunities for behavioral intervention using stimulus-control and reinforcement strategies to modify focal bingeing and purging behaviors. Likewise, a comprehensive assessment following the guidelines in Table 7–1 will suggest treatments to alter the feelings, cognitions, psychosocial factors, and behavioral problems that contribute to or result from bulimarexic practices.

Behavioral Treatments

Behavioral treatments for bulimarexia are designed to alter the antecedents and consequences controlling critical responses in the binge–purge cycle. This vicious cycle, depicted in Figure 7–3, may be entered at any point to produce changes in the complex of related responses (Rosen & Leitenberg, 1982). The complexity and variability of bulimarexic behaviors require individualized, multicomponent treatments. We now will discuss and outline several generic behavioral treatment strategies. We do not intend to be definitive or exhaustive. Basically, examples presented in the text and summarized in Table 7–2 involve

1. Binge prevention through
   a. Helping the bulimarexic anticipate, eliminate, and avoid the stimuli triggering binge eating
   b. Altering reinforcements for binge eating to reduce its frequency and help the bulimarexic anticipate, eliminate, and avoid stimuli triggering the purge
2. Altering reinforcements for purging to weaken this behavior and reduce the probability of repeated bingeing

General Principles

In any intervention, we advise teaching self-management skills and involving the client in setting treatment goals, selecting techniques, and monitoring outcomes. Even if treatment entails direct environmental control of controlling stimuli, as in an inpatient contingency management program (Orleans & Barnett, Note 9; Monti et al., 1977), the bulimarexic should be involved maximally in designing contingencies and setting goals. Imparting basic skills in functional analysis and behavioral control and emphasizing positive reinforcement strategies gives the bulimarexic vital self-management and problem-solving skills that may enhance the low self-efficacy and self-esteem so often associated with this intractable eating disorder (Mahoney & Mahoney, 1976).

Assessment Phase

Involving the bulimarexic, of course, begins with the assessment phase. During the first two weeks of assessment we suggest no changes in eating behavior (unless, of course, being underweight presents an immediate health risk). We utilize this time to collect data, administer the Personal Data Questionnaire (see chapter appendix), and obtain a daily eating diary, described earlier, in which the client records what, where, when, and with whom she eats and describes the thoughts and feelings associated with each antece-

Table 7-2. Suggested Behavioral Treatments*

Binge Antecedents	*Antecedent Control*
Fasting, excessively strict dieting and related hunger, frustration, and deprivation	Shape and reinforce sensible regular eating and exercise habits and realistic goal setting (e.g., 33, 42, 57)
Problematic weight status; weight control problems	Shape and reinforce nutritional diet and eating habits appropriate for weight gain, loss, or stabilization (e.g., 10, 11, 33, 42, 47, 57)
Facilitative setting	Stimulus control to restrict access to preferred bingeing foods and settings; social monitoring (e.g., 10, 57)
Obsessive preoccupation with food and eating	Delay therapy; thought stopping (e.g., 22, 45, 61)
Eating small amounts of high-calorie foods	Cognitive restructuring; cognitive ecology; relapse prevention; response prevention (e.g., 10, 42, 44, 56, 61)
Anxiety related to external stress and deficient coping skills	Anxiety management or relaxation training (e.g., 10, 28, 59)
Depression related to self-deprivation, social isolation, harsh self-evaluation	Shape and reinforce increased pleasurable activities; social skill training; cognitive therapy (e.g., 13, 18, 19, 24, 28, 38, 64)
Recurrent interpersonal difficulties including underassertiveness	Assertion and interpersonal problem-solving training (e.g., 18, 19, 28, 64)

Binge Consequences/ Purge Antecedents	*Consequence Control*
Immediate enjoyment of the binge	Aversive conditioning; shame aversion therapy (e.g., 53, 61)
Inadvertent social reinforcement	Family and/or marital treatment (e.g., 46, 57)
Morbid fear of weight gain and loss of control; irrational thinking	Systematic desensitization; rational-emotive therapy; cognitive ecology; exposure plus response prevention (e.g., 13, 24, 28, 42, 51)
Relief from anxiety, hunger, frustration; escape from aversive binge consequences	See Antecedent Control; response prevention (e.g., 51)
Self-condemnation, shame, depression, guilt over bingeing	Shape incompatible problem-solving statements; reframe binge as a learning experience (e.g., 33, 42, 44, 64)
Access to purgatives and preferred purging settings	Stimulus control to restrict access; response prevention (e.g., 43, 57)
Critical time interval	Delay therapy (e.g., 45, 61)

Table 7-2. (Continued)

Purge Consequences	Consequence Control
Immediate relief from aversive physical and emotional consequences of the binge	See Antecedent Control
Self-condemnation, shame, depression, guilt over bingeing, helplessness, low self-efficacy; irrational thinking	Shape incompatible problem-solving skills; reattribution therapy; increase client responsibility for treatment goals and methods; relapse prevention training (e.g., 2, 4, 10, 30, 33, 42, 44, 60, 64)

*Based on A.D. Loro, Jr., and C.T. Orleans, Binge eating in obesity: Preliminary findings and guidelines for behavioral assessment and treatment. *Addictive Behaviors*, 1981, *6*, 155–166.

dent and consequent eating and/or purging event. Feeling "out of control" and experiencing the binge–purge cycle as "uncontrollable," the bulimarexic often is quite relieved upon learning that there are identifiable antecedent and reinforcing stimuli that exert control over bingeing and purging, and that these stimuli can be manipulated to bring about a change in the binge–purge cycle.

Aside from raising expectations that the binge–purge cycle may be controlled, this nonintervention stage frequently has therapeutic impact, even though, or perhaps because, we have forbidden any change of eating behavior. Almost invariably, patients begin to binge less frequently. Information about when the patient is successful in changing a target behavior on her own becomes a useful starting point for planning interventions and pointing to critical controlling variables. Thus, the assessment phase serves as a kind of paradoxical intention (Frankl, 1975) or programmed binge (Loro & Orleans, 1981) during which potentially obstructive rebellious behaviors can be harnessed in the service of treatment goals.

Binge Prevention

The first part of Table 7–2 outlines various binge antecedents and possible control options. These involve teaching normal eating patterns to prevent the excessively strict dieting that precedes the binge, as well as teaching skills to use in dealing with related stress, dysphoria, critical self-evaluation, and obsessive phobic or irrational thinking about eating.

Two reports describe broad-spectrum behavioral interventions employing contingency management and stimulus-control techniques to change and reinforce eating patterns incompatible with bingeing in order to prevent purging and promote weight gain in the bulimic anorexic patient. Monti et al. (1977) examined the effect of positive reinforcement, informational (e.g., caloric intake) feedback, and contingency contracting on weight gain in a 28-year-old bulimic anorexic patient. Results were somewhat ambiguous due to the medical complication of edema, but the patient appeared to benefit from the combined reinforcement of weight gain and caloric intake feedback. Desensitization to thoughts that she was a "bad person," which precipitated bulimic episodes, resulted in a decreased tension rating. Contingency contracting on an outpatient basis resulted in maintenance of weight gain at a six-month follow-up.

In the second report, Orleans and Barnett (Note 9) reported the case of a 19-year-old female bulimarexic hospitalized for excessive weight loss and obsessional fears of weight gain. Reinforcement of weight gain and caloric feedback alone were not effective in eliminating binge–purge practices and producing and maintaining consistent weight gain. However, the addition of punishment (i.e., loss of hospital privileges) for weight loss resulted in stable weight gain and maintenance during hospitalization. Desensitization to feared foods, cognitive ecology to change irrational fears about excessive weight gain, and relapse prevention training also were introduced. However, generalization of new eating and self-control patterns to the disturbed home environment could not be programmed, and at a six-month follow-up the patient had resumed binge–purge practices and lost much of the weight she had gained during inpatient treatment.

These reports suggest that similar behavioral binge prevention strategies may be of considerable benefit. We present some practical guidelines for broad-spectrum treatments of this type.

To prompt and shape appropriate eating and to counteract excessively strict dieting standards and unrealistic goal setting, the bulimarexic should be instructed in a sensible, nutritionally balanced diet and an exercise regimen suitable for her weight status and treatment goals. Nutritional education may present needed information about food values and help to alter misconceptions about avoided foods, such as proteins and complex carbohydrates, which are high in nutritional value but frequently are left out of the strict or faddish diets bulimarexics adopt. Some cognitive restructuring (Beck, 1976; Goldfried & Davison, 1976; Monti et al., 1977; Welch, 1979) of nutritional and diet misconceptions almost always is indicated, since they are likely to play a role in overly strict dieting (Mahoney & Mahoney, 1976). Desensitization to fears of avoided foods may be indicated if such fears help to maintain an inappropriate diet (Goldfried & Davison, 1976).

Contingency management programs developed to alter undereating in anorexia nervosa and overeating in obesity can be incorporated or adapted (Agras, Barlow, Chapin, Able, & Leitenberg, 1974; Jeffrey & Katz, 1977; Mahoney & Mahoney, 1976; Stuart & Davis, 1972). A realistic exercise or conditioning program can replace excessive (or increase insufficient) daily activity levels, reducing body image dissatisfaction and helping to alleviate the anxiety and depression fueling the binge–purge cycle.

Stimulus-control interventions should help the bulimarexic to restrict access to preferred bingeing foods and settings or to arrange for social monitoring to prevent privacy, since most bingeing occurs in isolation. Bulimarexics should be encouraged to avoid fast-food establishments where they obtain bingeing foods, to avoid buying or eating any unusual bingeing food (at least early in treatment, before the ability to eat a limited amount of such foods can be shaped), and to grocery shop with a list of "safe" foods and in the company of a supportive friend. Planning to eat meals with friends or work associates inhibits bingeing. In short, privacy prevention is a major component of binge prevention.

Cognitive stimulus-control strategies also should be considered. Thought stopping (Cautela, 1969) and delay therapy (Meyer, 1973) may be indicated to break the patient's obsessive preoccupation with food, eating, or body weight. Increasing the frequency of nonfood-related activities also may be useful (Jeffrey & Katz, 1977). For instance, Welch (1979) reports the successful treatment of a 28-year-old woman plagued by obsessive thoughts that she was getting fat and by compulsive vomiting. Intervention included cognitive modification and response-delay techniques. Specifically, the woman was asked to confront her irrational thoughts with rational argument by recalling her recorded body weight for the day and subvocally disputing the intrusive obsessive thought. In addition, she was to delay herself at each point in the response chain that led to self-induced vomiting. As a result, vomiting was extinguished by the eighth week of treatment, and intrusive thoughts decreased dramatically with self-reported changes maintained at an 11-month follow-up.

Bulimarexics also may need help to avoid irrational or all-or-none thinking (Ellis, 1962) about the consequences of eating small amounts of high-calorie or "forbidden" foods. For this, Marlatt and Gordon's (1980) relapse-prevention training for addictive problems furnishes a useful model.

Whenever anxiety, depression, and recurrent interpersonal difficulties play a role in triggering binges, binge prevention will involve helping the bulimarexic identify and deal appropriately with these problems. Teaching relaxation skills (Goldfried & Davison, 1976) or general stress-management skills (Suinn, 1977) can improve the bulimarexic's abilities to manage external and self-produced stresses without turning to food. Increasing the frequency of reinforcing or pleasurable activities (Lewinsohn, 1975), social skill training (Bower & Bower, 1976; Goldfried & Davison, 1976), and cognitive therapy (Beck, 1976) can reduce the depression, social isolation, and harsh self-evaluation conducive to bingeing.

Training in assertiveness and communication skills (Bower & Bower, 1976; Goldfried & Davison, 1976) is appropriate whenever passive–dependent nonassertive behavior is implicated in the bulimarexic pattern. New skills enable the patient to deal with interpersonal difficulties in a more efficacious and rewarding manner, reducing avoidance of such difficulties through overconcern with the bulimarexic pattern. The promising reports of Boskind-White and her colleagues (Boskind-Lodahl & White, 1978; White & Boskind-White, in press) illustrate the value of a focus on psychosocial deficits that contribute to the origin or maintenance of bulimarexic practices. They developed and evaluated a short-term experiential–behavioral group program for overly dependent women to alter the cognitions, feelings, and behavioral deficits associated with binge–purge behaviors. Group interactions clarified the purposes bingeing serves in the life of the patient, switching attention from the preoccupation with food itself to the feelings and life situations eliciting the binges or purgation. They repeatedly challenged the assumption that a slim body would solve these problems. Patients were taught assertiveness skills and encouraged to become more aware of their own interests and abilities. Daily monitoring of feelings and antecedents of binges, short-term contracting, and behavioral rehearsal of assertive responding also were utilized in this treatment. Beneficial short-term changes in self-perception were reported.

Altering the Consequences of the Binge/Preventing the Purge

Since binge consequences are purge antecedents, efforts to weaken or extinguish binge eating and to prevent the purge will be related.

Reinforcement control strategies noted in Table 7–2 involve reducing or eliminating the immediate positive consequences of bingeing. Aversive techniques, including shock aversion (Wijesinghe, 1973), covert sensitization (Cautela, 1969), and shame aversion (Serber, 1970) can be used to decrease enjoyment of binges. Since being observed bingeing or purging would be highly aversive or embarrassing for most bulimarexics, shame aversion has unexplored potential in suppressing bingeing.

To prevent inadvertent social reinforcement, parents, friends, roommates, or spouses can be advised to refrain from commenting on the binge–purge behavior they observe or suspect. When clear gains are derived from the bulimarexic's "disorder," more extensive family/marital treatment and therapeutic "reprogramming" are in order (Minuchin et al., 1975).

Once the binge has taken place, the bulimarexic must be equipped to overcome fears of weight gain or loss of control that typically precede the purge. Cognitive ecology (Mahoney & Mahoney, 1976), rational emotive therapy (Ellis, 1962), cognitive restructuring (Beck, 1976), and systematic desensitization (Goldfried & Davison, 1976) represent possible interventions. Likewise, the self-condemnation, shame, depression, and guilt following bingeing must be attenuated. We find it helpful to reframe the binge as a learning experience (Loro & Orleans, 1981) and to teach the bulimarexic to analyze the particular high-risk situation that led to the binge, planning a coping strategy to avoid future bingeing (Marlatt & Gordon, 1980).

Stimulus-control techniques also can be applied to preventing a purge. Purging can be avoided or delayed by teaching the patient to increase the interval between the binge and purgation (Marks, 1978; Stuart & Davis, 1972). This also weakens reinforcement for both the binge (because it requires the bulimarexic to experience the physical discomfort that results from excessive consumption for a longer time) and the purge (because delayed purging is less effective in undoing the fattening effects of the binge). To aid in this delay, the bulimarexic needs a relaxation or cognitive counterattack strategy incompatible with purging and with intrusive obsessions over the consequences of the binge (Welch, 1979). If the patient is hospitalized, access to purging settings can be restricted, preventing the immediate reinforcement of purgation. Self-restriction is advised for outpatient treatments.

Along these lines, Rosen and Leitenberg's (1982) exposure-plus-response-prevention procedure has proven effective in decreasing subjective discomfort after a binge and extinguishing purging and bingeing. Reasoning that vomiting provides a vital escape from the natural aversive consequences of bingeing, Rosen and Leitenberg evaluated a procedure incorporating exposure to bingeing foods plus vomiting-response prevention for a 21-year-old normal-weight chronic bulimarexic. In this highly successful treatment, the subject was instructed to eat amounts of three types of preferred bingeing foods sufficient to produce a strong vomiting urge in supervised treatment sessions. Prevented from vomiting, she focused on the discomfort she felt until the vomiting urge dissipated. Treatment sessions followed a repeated baseline design, with three classes of high-calorie bingeing foods introduced sequentially, and concluded with a home generalization schedule. Over 18 response-prevention sessions, the subject showed decreased post-eating anxiety, decreased time to overcome the urge to vomit, and increased intake of previously "forbidden" foods. These changes were generalized and maintained. Frequency of bingeing decreased dramatically, despite the fact that bingeing was never a target of intervention. Rosen and Leitenberg conclude bingeing might be viewed better as a consequence of vomiting, than vomiting as a consequence of bingeing, since bingeing only occurred when vomiting could provide an escape from its naturally aversive consequences.

Altering the Consequences of the Purge

Reducing the immediate negative reinforcement for the purge can be difficult and may heighten the despair, self-condemnation, and guilt that lead to overly strict dieting, depression, low self-efficacy, and, ultimately, bingeing.

We find it helpful to teach bulimarexics more adaptive, more self-accepting responses to the purge; thus, teaching them how to perform functional analyses and to plan to avoid future bingeing can enhance perceived self-efficacy and self-control and foster attributions for a binge–purge cycle to external precipitants, rather than to dispositional weaknesses (Valins & Nisbett, 1972). This approach is very similar to the personal problem-solving training recommended by Mahoney and Mahoney (1976) and to the relapse-prevention training outlined by Marlatt and Gordon (1980).

Finally, the helplessness that typically follows a purge can be treated by increasing the patient's responsibility for treatment goals and methods (White & Boskind-White, 1981), thereby promoting an increased sense of self-efficacy. Likewise, restructuring the unrealistic cognitions, resolutions, and promises that usually follow the cycle promotes realistic goal setting (Hawkins & Clement, 1980).

Reference Notes

1. Barnett, L. Sex role strain and women in medicine. Unpublished doctoral dissertation, Department of Psychology, University of Kentucky, 1981.
2. Beuf, A., Dglugash, R., & Eininger, E. Anorexia nervosa—A sociocultural approach. Unpublished manuscript, University of Pennsylvania, 1976.
3. Boskind-Lodahl, M. The definition and treatment of bulimarexia: The gorging/purging syndrome of young women. Unpublished doctoral dissertation, Department of Psychology, Cornell University, 1978 (University Microfilms No. 7807776).
4. Carroll, K., & Leon, G. R. The bulimia-vomiting disorder within a generalized substance abuse pattern. In G. R. Leon (Chair), Eating disorders in the context of other habit and social patterns. Symposium presented at the meeting of the Association for Advancement of Behavior Therapy, Toronto, 1981.
5. Chernyk, B. Sex differences in binge-eating and related habit patterns in a college student population. In G. R. Leon (Chair), Eating disorders in the context of other habit and social patterns. Symposium presented at the meeting of the Association for Advancement of Behavior Therapy, Toronto, 1981.
6. Clement, P. F. Correlates of binge eating among college women. Unpublished doctoral dissertation, Department of Psychology, University of Texas at Austin, 1980.
7. Clement, P., & Hawkins, R. C. Pathways to bulimia: Personality correlates, prevalence and a conceptual model. Paper presented at the meeting of the Association for Advancement of Behavior Therapy, New York, 1980.
8. Orleans, C. S. Protocol and procedures for a functional analysis of bulimarexic behavior using the Personal Data Questionnaire.

Unpublished manuscript, Duke University Medical Center, 1980.
9. Orleans, C. T., & Barnett, L. R. Bulimarexia: Guidelines for behavioral assessment and treatment. Paper presented at the meeting of the Association for Advancement of Behavior Therapy, New York, 1980.

References

Agras, W. S., Barlow, D. H., Chapin, H. N., Able, G. G., & Leitenberg, H. Behavior modification of anorexia nervosa. *Archives of General Psychiatry*, 1974, *30*, 279–286.

American Psychiatric Association. *Diagnostic and Statistical Manual of Mental Disorders*, 3rd. ed., Washington, D.C.: American Psychiatric Association, 1980.

Beck, A. T. *Cognitive Therapy and the Emotional Disorders*. New York: International Universities Press, 1976.

Bem, S. L. The measurement of psychological androgyny. *Journal of Consulting and Clinincal Psychology*, 1974, *42*, 155–162.

Beumont, P. J. V. Further categorization of patients with anorexia nervosa. *Australian and New Zealand Journal of Psychiatry*, 1977, *11*, 223–226.

Beumont, P. J. V., George, G. C. W., & Smart, D. E. "Dieters" and "vomiters and purgers" in anorexia nervosa. *Psychological Medicine*, 1976, *6*, 617–622.

Boskind-Lodahl, M. Cinderella's step-sisters: A feminist perspective on anorexia nervosa and bulimia. *Signs: Journal of Women in Culture and Society*, 1976, *2*(2), 342–356.

Boskind-Lodahl, M., & White, W. C. The definition and treatment of bulimarexia in college women—A pilot study. *Journal of the American College Health Association*, 1978, *27*, 84–87.

Bower, S. A., & Bower, G. H. *Asserting Yourself*. Reading, Mass.: Addison-Wesley, 1976.

Casper, R. C., Eckert, E. D., Halmi, K. A., Goldberg, S. C., & Davis, J. M. Bulimia. *Archives of General Psychiatry*, 1980, *37*, 1030–1035.

Cautela, J. R. Behavior therapy and self-control: Techniques and implications. In C. M. Franks (ed.), *Behavior Therapy: Appraisal and Status*. New York: McGraw-Hill, 1969.

Chernin, K. *The Obsession: Reflections on the Tyranny of Slenderness*. New York: Harper & Row, 1981.

Ellis, A. *Reason and Emotion in Psychotherapy*. New York: Lyle Stuart, 1962.

Frankl, V. E. Paradoxical intention and dereflection. *Psychotherapy Theory, Research and Practice*, 1975, *12*, 226–236.

Garfinkel, P. E., Moldofsky, H., & Garner, D. M. The heterogenity of anorexia nervosa. *Archives of General Psychiatry,* 1980, *37,* 1036– 1040.

Garner, D. M., & Garfinkel, P. E. The Eating Attitude Test: An index of the symptoms of anorexia nervosa. *Psychological Medicine,* 1979, *9,* 273–279.

Goldfried, M. R., & Davison, G. C. *Clinical Behavior Therapy.* New York: Holt, Rinehart & Winston, 1976.

Gormally, J., Black, S., Daston, S., & Rardin, D. The assessment of binge eating severity among obese persons. *Addictive Behaviors,* 1982, *7,* 47–55.

Green, R. S., & Rau, J. H. Treatment of compulsive eating disturbances with anticonvulsant medication. *American Journal of Psychiatry,* 1973, *131,* 428–432.

Hawkins, R. C., & Clement, P. F. Development and construct validation of a self-report measure of binge eating tendencies. *Addictive Behaviors,* 1980, *5,* 219–226.

Herman, C. P., & Mack, D. Restrained and unrestrained eating. *Journal of Abnormal Psychology,* 1975, *84,* 666–672.

Herman, C. P., & Polivny, J. Anxiety, restraint, and eating behavior. *Journal of Personality,* 1975, *84:* 666–672.

Jeffrey, D. B., & Katz, R. C. *Take It Off and Keep It Off.* Englewood Cliffs, N.J.: Prentice-Hall, 1977.

Kattell, A., Callahan, E. J., Fremouw, W. J., & Zitter, R. E. The effects of behavioral treatment and fasting on eating behaviors and weight loss: A case study. *Behavior Therapy,* 1979, *10,* 579–587.

Katz, F. H., Eckert, R. C., & Gebott, M. D. Hypokalemia caused by surreptitious self-administration of diuretics. *Annals of Internal Medicine,* 1972, *76,* 85–90.

Kolata, C. B. NIH shaken by death of research volunteer. *Science,* 1980, *209,* 475–479.

Levenson, R. W., & Gottman, J. M. Toward the assessment of social competence. *Journal of Consulting and Clinical Psychology,* 1978, *46,* 453–462.

Lewinsohn, P. M. The behavioral study and treatment of depression. In M. Hersen, R. M. Eisler, & P. M. Miller (eds.), *Progress in Behavior Modification,* vol. 1. New York: Academic Press, 1975.

Loro, A. D., Jr., & Orleans, C. T. Binge eating in obesity: Preliminary findings and guidelines for behavioral assessment and treatment. *Addictive Behaviors,* 1981, *6,* 155–166.

Loro, A. D., Jr., & Orleans, C. T. The behavioral assessment of obesity. In F. J. Keefe & J. A. Blumenthal (eds.), *Assessment Strategies in Behavioral Medicine.* New York: Grune and Stratton, 1982.

Lucas, A. R. Bulimia and vomiting syndrome. *Contemporary Nutrition,* 1981, *6,* 1–2.

Mahoney, M. J., & Mahoney, K. *Permanent Weight Control: A Total Solution to the Dieter's Dilemma.* New York: Norton, 1976.

Marks, I. M. Exposure treatments. In S. Agras (ed.), *Behavior Modification,* 2nd ed. Boston: Little, Brown, 1978.

Marlatt, A., & Gordon, J. Determinants of relapse: Implications for the maintenance of behavior change. In P. O. Davidson & S. M. Davidson (eds.), *Behavioral Medicine: Changing Health Life-Styles.* New York: Brunner/Mazel, 1980.

Meyer, R. G. Delay therapy: Two case reports. *Behavior Therapy,* 1973, *4,* 709–711.

Minuchin, S., Baker, L., Rosman, B. L., Liebman, R., Milman, L., & Todd, T. C. A conceptual model of psychosomatic illness in children. *Archives of General Psychiatry,* 1975, *32,* 1031–1038.

Monti, P. M., McCrady, B. S., & Barlow, D. H. Effect of positive reinforcement, informational feedback and contingency contracting on a bulimic anorexic female. *Behavior Therapy,* 1977, *8,* 258–263.

Oster, J. R., Materson, B. J., & Rogers, A. I. Laxative abuse syndrome. *American Journal of Gastroenterology,* 1980, *74,* 451–458.

Rathus, S. A., & Nevid, J. S. Concurrent validity of the 30-item assertiveness schedule with a psychiatric population. *Behavior Therapy,* 1977, *8,* 393–397.

Rau, J. H., & Green, R. S. Compulsive eating: A neuropsychologic approach to certain eating disorders. *Comprehensive Psychiatry,* 1975, *16,* 223–231.

Rosen, J. C., & Leitenberg, H. Bulimia nervosa: Treatment with exposure and response prevention. *Behavior Therapy,* 1982, *13,* 117–124.

Rovner, S. A fear of fat. *Washington Post,* Sunday, December 13, 1981, K1–K7.

Russell, G. F. M. Bulimia nervosa: An ominous variant of anorexia nervosa. *Psychological Medicine,* 1979, *9,* 429–448.

Serber, M. Shame aversion therapy. *Journal of Behavior Therapy and Experimental Psychiatry,* 1970, *2,* 213–215.

Spencer, J. A., & Fremouw, W. J. Binge eating as a function of restraint and weight classification. *Journal of Abnormal Psychology,* 1979, *88,* 262–267.

Stangler, R. S., & Printz, A. M. DSM-III: Psychiatric diagnosis in a university population. *American Journal of Psychiatry,* 1980, *137,* 937–940.

Strober, M. The significance of bulimia in juvenile anorexia nervosa: An exploration of possible etiologic factors. *International Journal of Eating Disorders,* 1982, *1,* 28–43.

Stuart, R. G., & Davis, B. *Slim Chance in a Fat World: Behavioral Control in Obesity.* Champaign, Ill: Research Press, 1972.

Suinn, R. M. Type A behavior pattern. In R. Williams & W. D. Gentry (eds.), *Behavioral Approach to Medical Treatment.* Cambridge, Mass.: Ballinger, 1977.

Valins, S., & Nisbett, R. E. Attribution processes in the development and treatment of emotional disorder. In G. E. Jones, D. E. Kanouse, H. H. Kelley, R. E. Nisbett, S. Valins, & B. Weiner (eds.), *Attribution: Perceiving the Causes of Behavior*. Morristown, N.J.: General Learning Press, 1972.

Welch, G. J. The treatment of compulsive vomiting and obsessive thoughts through gradual response delay, response prevention and cognitive correction. *Journal of Behavior Therapy and Experimental Psychiatry*, 1979, *10*, 77–82.

Wermuth, B. M., Davis, K. L., Hollister, L. E., & Stunkard, A. J. Phenytoin treatment of the binge-eating syndrome. *American Journal of Psychiatry*, 1977, *134*, 1249–1253.

White, W. C., & Boskind-White, M. An experiential–behavioral approach to the treatment of bulimarexia. *Psychotherapy: Theory, Research and Practice*, 1981, *18*, 501–507.

Wijesinghe, B. Massed electrical aversion treatment of compulsive eating. *Journal of Behavior Therapy and Experimental Psychiatry*, 1973, *4*, 133–135.

Appendix to Chapter 7

Personal Data Questionnaire*

We have designed this questionnaire to help us understand your bingeing/purging habit. Your responses will help us plan and evaluate a treatment program.

First, a few questions about you.

Name: _____ Date: _____
Age: _____Marital status: _____ Children: _____
Education: _____ Occupation: _____
Number of brothers and sisters: _____
Your birth order: _____
Height: _____ Weight: _____ Goal weight: ____

Next, we'd like to ask you a few questions about how your bingeing/purging habit got started.
1. When did your bingeing/purging behavior begin? Please give the month, year, and circumstance. _____
   _____

2. How did you "discover" the purging habit? (Illness? seeing or learning of others with this habit?) _____
   _____

3. What were the circumstances surrounding the onset of this habit? (Check as many as apply and give a brief description for items you check.)
   a. Were you:
      Concerned about your weight or appearance? _____
      _____

      Having problems in a personal relationship? _____
      _____

      Involved in a serious dating relationship? _____
      _____

Changing your living environment (moving to school, away from home, etc.)? _____

Dealing with outside pressures related to family, friends, school, or work? _____

Dieting? _____

b. How much did you weigh at that time? _____
For you, was this overweight? _____
underweight? _____
normal weight? _____

Now a few questions about your typical patterns of bingeing and purging.

4. Briefly describe your eating/purging behavior. (Please describe your typical behavior in the month before starting this treatment program.)

a. How many times a week do you eat/purge or binge/purge?
_____

b. If you binge eat, how often do you do so? _____

c. What do you eat when you binge that leads you to purge? (Please give examples and estimate the total number of calories in a typical "binge.") _____
_____
_____
_____

d. Are there typical times of the day that you binge? If yes, describe. _____

e. Where do you usually binge? (List several common settings.) _____

f. Are you usually alone? _____ or with people you know? _____ or with "anonymous" others? _____

g. How long after you eat do you usually purge? _____

h. What methods do you use to get rid of the food and/or weight? Circle those that apply: forced vomiting, over-the-counter or prescribed medicines, fasting. Please describe in detail: _____
_____
_____

i. Where do you usually purge? (List common settings.) ___
    _____
    _____
    _____

j. How do you usually feel just before a binge? Imagine
    yourself feeling like you're headed toward a binge. Put
    yourself vividly in that situation until you can clearly
    imagine or experience your thoughts and feelings. What
    are you usually feeling? _____
    _____
    _____
    _____

k. What is your frame of mind during and after a binge?
    During and immediately after? _____
    _____
    Later afterwards? _____
    _____

l. How do you usually feel just before you purge? Imagine
    that you have binged and are now planning a purge. Put
    yourself vividly in that situation.
    Usual feelings? _____
    _____
    Usual thoughts? _____
    _____

m. What is your frame of mind immediately after and then
    later after you purge?
    Immediately afterwards? _____
    _____
    Later afterwards? _____
    _____

n. At what times of the day do you usually eat?
    Breakfast _____
    Lunch _____
    Dinner _____
    Snacks _____

o. What do you eat when your meals and snacks do not lead
    to bingeing? In other words, what is an acceptable meal or
    snack? (Please give examples and calorie estimates.) ___
    _____
    _____

5. Who knows of your bingeing/purging or eating/purging behavior, and how have these persons reacted to the problem? ＿＿

＿＿＿＿＿＿＿＿＿＿＿＿＿＿＿＿＿＿＿＿＿＿＿＿＿＿＿＿＿＿

＿＿＿＿＿＿＿＿＿＿＿＿＿＿＿＿＿＿＿＿＿＿＿＿＿＿＿＿＿＿

＿＿＿＿＿＿＿＿＿＿＿＿＿＿＿＿＿＿＿＿＿＿＿＿＿＿＿＿＿＿

＿＿＿＿＿＿＿＿＿＿＿＿＿＿＿＿＿＿＿＿＿＿＿＿＿＿＿＿＿＿

6. When did you first seek help for bingeing/purging, or a related eating problem? ＿＿＿＿＿＿＿＿＿＿＿＿＿＿＿＿＿＿＿＿

7. Describe previous help you have sought for this problem (therapy, friends, physician, parents, pastor, nutritionist, etc.):

＿＿＿＿＿＿＿＿＿＿＿＿＿＿＿＿＿＿＿＿＿＿＿＿＿＿＿＿＿＿

8. How would you rate your current motivation to kick this habit?

							I definitely
I don't care							want to quit
0	1	2	3	4	5	6	7

9. How confident are you that you will succeed in quitting with this treatment?

No chance							I will definitely
I'll succeed							succeed
0	1	2	3	4	5	6	7

10. What is the longest period of time in the past that you have been able to refrain from bingeing/purging? ＿＿＿＿＿＿＿＿＿

11. When you "relapsed" after stopping for awhile, what were the usual circumstances? (Please check all those that apply and then circle the two most common circumstances.)
    a. negative emotional states (e.g., ＿＿＿＿＿＿＿＿＿＿＿)
    b. positive emotional states (e.g., ＿＿＿＿＿＿＿＿＿＿＿)
    c. negative physical states (e.g., ＿＿＿＿＿＿＿＿＿＿＿)
       (including weight gain)
    d. testing personal control
    e. urges and temptations
    f. interpersonal conflict
    g. upsetting or stressful life events (e.g., ＿＿＿＿＿＿＿＿)
    h. social pressures (e.g., ＿＿＿＿＿＿＿＿＿＿＿＿＿＿)
    i. a new social environment (e.g., ＿＿＿＿＿＿＿＿＿＿＿)
    j. other (please describe) ＿＿＿＿＿＿＿＿＿＿＿＿＿＿＿

Thank you for your thoughtful responses. If you think that there are other things we should know about your bingeing/purging pattern in planning a treatment program, please summarize them in the space below.

_____

_____

_____

_____

_____

_____

_____

_____

_____

_____

8

Binge Eating: A Cognitive–Behavioral Treatment Approach*

Albert D. Loro, Jr.

Binge eating is a complex behavioral and psychological problem that often contributes to obesity and complicates comprehensive treatment approaches to weight reduction and weight control (Loro & Orleans, 1981). In slightly overweight and normal-weight populations of weight-conscious clients, binge eating often is followed by vomiting or purging (with laxatives) (Boskind-Lodahl, 1976; Boskind-Lodahl & White, 1978; Lucas, 1981). In addition, the bingeing and vomiting or purging pattern is found frequently in some types of anorexic patients (Beumont, George, & Smart, 1976; Bruch, 1973; Garfinkel, Moldofsky, & Garner, 1980; Russell, 1979). Furthermore, recent surveys indicate that the prevalence of binge eating among undergraduates is surprisingly high, ranging from 49 percent among males to 79 percent among females (Hawkins & Clement, 1980). In one study, Ondercin (1979) found compulsive eating or binge eating was a popular and common undergraduate practice, especially among females. In another report, Boskind-

*Portions of this chapter were presented at the Fourteenth Annual Association for Advancement of Behavior Therapy Convention, New York, 1980, and previously published in A.D. Loro, Jr., & C.S. Orleans, Binge eating in obesity: Preliminary findings and guidelines for behavioral analysis and treatment. *Addictive Behaviors,* 1981, *6,* 155–166.

Lodahl (1976) noted that binge eating with its pernicious sequelae of purging and vomiting is a frequent complaint of distressed young women students.

In spite of the increase in binge eating and its relatively high prevalence on college campuses, few effective treatments or treatment programs have been developed. Recently, however, preliminary results using combinations of cognitive, behavioral, and experiential interventions have produced clinically significant results (Boskind-Lodahl & White, 1978; Meyer, 1973; Morganstern, 1974; White & Boskind-White, 1981; White & Boskind-White, Chapter 4, this volume; Wijesinghe, 1973). Because of these promising results, treatment approaches combining cognitive, behavioral, and experiential approaches to binge eating merit further attention.

The purpose of this chapter is fourfold. The first is to describe briefly the problem of binge eating. The second is to present a conceptual model for analyzing the typical problems of clients who engage in binge eating. Third, we will explain some of the cognitive–behavioral and psychotherapeutic interventions that we have found to be effective in changing and controlling binge-eating patterns. Fourth, we will point out the clinical issues and possible complications in treating clients who binge eat.

Binge Eating

Binge eating is defined as the consumption of excessive or enormous amounts of food in a relatively short period of time.[1] Functional analyses of binge eating have revealed specific response characteristics, antecedents, and consequences to this behavioral pattern (see Chapter 11 by Fremouw & Heyneman). Systematically

[1]There are conceptual as well as practical problems in adequately defining and operationalizing binge eating. In part, this stems from the wide individual variability in how clients define "excessive"/"enormous" and "short period of time." In my clinical behavioral assessments, I ask clients to identify themselves as people who eat "enormous or excessive amounts of food in short periods of time" on a pretreatment self-report questionnaire. Then, during a clinical interview, I ask clients to describe in detail what they *mean* by "binge eating," "enormous"/"excessive," and "short periods of time." I then use my clinical judgment to determine whether the client's description qualifies as binge eating, overeating, snacking, or something else. Generally, binge eating is a relatively short-duration, solitary activity that occurs in the early or late evening. Typically, binge eating occurs in addition to or instead of the traditional meals of breakfast, lunch, and dinner (Loro, 1980).

identifying important featurs of the binge-eating pattern can reveal specific targets for behavior change (Loro & Orleans, 1981). Before presenting some of the common problems of binge eaters and several possible therapeutic interventions to address these problems, I would like to present a conceptual model for the cognitive–behavioral descriptions of these problems.

A Conceptual Model for Describing the Problems of Binge Eaters

The major problems of binge eaters fall into four categories: (1) cognitive, (2) behavioral, (3) emotional, and (4) interpersonal (Barnett & Loro, 1981). Typically, clients who binge engage in cognitive distortions, irrational beliefs, maladaptive behavioral patterns, and fad diet practices (Gormally, Black, Daston, & Rardin, 1982). In addition, they generally experience difficulty identifying and expressing feelings, particularly negative ones, such as anger and frustration (Loro, 1980). Since these and other problems tend to occur in an interpersonal context, complications arise as the client must try to relate to and deal with people in spite of these deficits and difficulties (Barnett & Loro, 1981).

Cognitions, behaviors, and emotions are interdependent and interactive (Hollon & Kendall, 1979); that is, one type of problem usually overlaps with and affects other problem areas. For example, a binge eater may overeat to relieve accumulated emotional stress, then think he/she is disgusting and repulsive for doing this, and then experience intense feelings of self-hatred and worthlessness (Loro & Orleans, 1981). This sequence can occur just prior to a scheduled evening out with friends and may result in the binge eater canceling her/his social engagement. This final act has implications for future social engagements, because a friend who cancels at the last minute with a poor excuse may not be invited out again as readily. It also may set the stage for more binge eating as the client, by his/her own choice, is now faced with an entire evening alone with no scheduled activities. Many clients binge repeatedly under these circumstances (Loro & Orleans, 1981).

This section describes the cognitive, behavioral, emotional, and interpersonal problems of binge eaters. Within each general problem category, I will present a few specific examples of problems that are common in binge eaters.

Cognitive Distortions and Irrational Beliefs

Binge eaters lack correct and adequate knowledge about food and the overall value of eating a well-balanced, varied, and nutritional diet (Barnett & Loro, 1981). They tend to eliminate categorically certain foods (e.g., breads and potatoes) from their diets, because these foods are perceived as "fattening." Generally, their thinking about food and the caloric value of foods is distorted and fallacious. Specifically, they do not accept or understand that a calorie is a calorie whether it is contained in a protein, carbohydrate, or fat food group.

By way of example, most binge eaters I treat hold magical expectations about the miraculous benefits of consuming large amounts of protein-rich foods as opposed to "fattening" carbohydrate foods. Unfortunately, this kind of fallacious thinking is propagated by the multimillion-dollar fad-diet industry.[2] The truth is, a gram of carbohydrate is essentially equivalent to four calories, while a gram of protein is essentially equivalent to four calories. Further, both types of foods are necessary in any nutritionally sound diet, and neither should be eliminated categorically from any diet plan.

At the same time, some binge eaters are aware of foods that "set them off" on binges. For example, one middle-aged woman I treated would binge uncontrollably after consuming *one* Twinkie. Technically, it is not clear whether this loss of eating behavior control is due to a cognitive–behavioral process, a physical reaction such as glucose intolerance, or some other problem. On the one hand, some clinical evidence suggests that avoiding most sweets and refined carbohydrates may be a sign of healthy living and a sensible diet (see Chapter 10, by Hawkins & Clement). In addition, this preplanned avoidance strategy may facilitate eating behavior control. In such cases the binge eater may decide to refrain from eating foods that trigger binge episodes. On the other hand, I find that some binge eaters who stoically deny themselves access to certain desired foods—such as breads, pastries, and ice cream—tend to experience extreme feelings of deprivation related to these foods (Loro & Orleans, 1981). Some clinicians have labeled this dieting tactic the "restrictive approach" to weight control (Stern, Hoch, & Carper, 1976) and note that it often results in generating

[2]See "Step Right Up Suckers," Chapter 12 in T. Berland, *Diets '81*. Chicago: Consumer's Union, 1981.

a list of "forbidden fruits" that become increasingly attractive over time (Mahoney & Mahoney, 1976). In my own clinical work, I often find the specific foods binge eaters have chosen to eliminate completely from their diets are the very foods they ultimately choose for episodic binges.

Most of the binge eaters I treat hold unreasonable expectations about the daily effects of dieting on body weight and fat deposition. They rigidly believe there is a one-to-one ratio between what they eat and how their weight is affected. Many believe that certain foods magically turn to fat in their bodies shortly after consumption, and to prove this belief they often weigh themselves after meals or snacks and note the weight gain. Incorrectly, they assume that the undigested or partially digested food in their stomachs or gastrointestinal tracts has been converted to adipose tissue. They discount and disregard the relatively complex and somewhat lengthy process of digestion, metabolism, and fat deposition. Often they react to the subjective sense of being "full" and the observation that they now are "fatter" than before they ate. One female medical student I treated would examine her stomach closely after a meal and if it "bulged out" too far she immediately would induce vomiting. When carefully questioned about this belief, she revealed two concerns. First, she thought her stomach would remain protruded, which was totally unacceptable to her. Second, she did not like the stuffed, full feeling that coincided with a slightly protruding stomach.

Binge eaters also frequently engage in perfectionistic and all-or-none thinking. They strive to adhere rigidly to whatever diet regimen they are following and experience intense disappointment if they fail to follow their diet perfectly. Since it is impossible to complete any task perfectly, they experience failure when they "break" their diet. Typically, the experience of going slightly off the diet is followed by disappointment in not measuring up to their perfectionistic standards and results in a full-blown binge. In this way, binge eaters continually set themselves up for the disappointment and anguish of unfulfilled personal and diet-related expectations. This cycle is both self-perpetuating and self-defeating. Generally, distorted cognitions and irrational beliefs lead to intense negative feelings which result in binge eating (Loro & Orleans, 1981). For the most part, moderation in food consumption and flexibility in food choices is *not* considered an option.

The final two areas of cognitive distortions and irrational beliefs for binge eaters involve their body and sexuality. Most binge eaters possess a severely distorted body image. This is manifested by an inaccurate and unrealistic view of how their body looks. The majority see themselves as much heavier than they are, and almost all express extreme dissatisfaction with the size, shape, and appearance of their bodies.[3] This type of cognitive distortion and unrealistic thinking is fueled by cultural influences, social pressures, and the media—all of which glorify the excessively thin, svelte, and sylphlike body (Leon, 1980). Many bright, young, and intelligent women fall prey to these influences and pressures and attempt to maintain a body weight *below* what is considered healthy and appropriate for their age, body frame, and lifestyle (Boskind-Lodahl, 1976; Orleans & Barnett, 1980).

Most binge eaters have cognitive distortions and irrational beliefs about sexuality and sexual behavior. Generally, they think sex is "bad" or "scary" and one more way to lose control (Barnett & Loro, 1981). Though sexually active, they have difficulty accepting their sexuality and enjoying sex. This probably is related to other emotional and interpersonal problems as well as their negative feelings about their body. But unlike other individuals who think sex is bad and scary and therefore shun sexual encounters, I find most binge eaters are sexually active in a relatively controlled way. Many of them explain their sexual activity as a way to be close to another or make contact with another person but on their own terms.

One attractive professional woman who frequently binged and vomited typifies these sexual concerns. Early in therapy she revealed a fear of intimacy and preferred to not become emotionally involved with anyone. She did have one ongoing sexual relationship and described her partner as follows: "He is someone I really don't like as a person nor is he very handsome or attractive. But he likes my body, even if I don't, and I do enjoy the feeling of being close to him when we have sex. You see, he agrees to have sex when I want it and he doesn't bug me about the binge eating. . . ." Of course, there are other self-concept and control issues present with this client, but her brief description illustrates some of the

---

[3]I would like to thank my candid women clients, my women colleagues, and especially Dr. Linda Barnett for patiently raising my consciousness about this important women's issue. In my experience, I have found that most male therapists have little understanding of how women feel about their bodies. For example, most women I treat, including relatively normal-weight women (1) hate or intensely dislike their bodies, (2) are severely critical of their physical appearance, and (3) are often phobic about slight gains in their body weight.

dilemmas and conflicts she faces. Specifically, she makes a conscious, deliberate choice to avoid intimacy and pursue involvement with a less-valued partner. At the same time, she realizes her need to enjoy sex but possesses little awareness of the way satisfying intimate sexual encounters can develop with time, trust, and mutual caring (Kaplan, 1979).

Maladaptive Behavioral Patterns and Faddish Diet Practices

Binge eaters frequently engage in eating behaviors that are irregular, bizarre, and extreme. They tend to skip meals, fast for short periods, adhere to one or two food regimens (e.g., eat only grapefruits or water and yogurt), and follow fad diets. Typically, their unusual and extreme behaviors are short-lived because they result in uncomfortable physical or psychological side-effects such as dizziness, headaches, and diarrhea or a sense of boredom or deprivation. Often they follow ritualistic practices that in the past have occurred coincidentally prior to a weight loss. This type of ritualistic practice is sometimes superstitious and unrelated to food intake. One pre-med student I treated reported religiously waking up one hour earlier in the morning after consuming ice cream the evening before because on one occasion she did not gain weight following this practice.

Often, extreme eating and dieting behaviors are paired with rigid and severe exercise regimens. While regular strenuous exercise will facilitate weight loss and weight control (Jeffrey & Katz, 1977), sporadic bursts of physical exertion are ill advised and sometimes harmful. For instance, a binge eater who runs to exhaustion after consuming two dozen chocolate chip cookies may burn up some calories but also puts a severe strain on her/his digestive system. In a similar vein, a client who sporadically performs calisthenics until sore is certainly toning some muscles but also is risking physical injury and unpleasant side-effects.

Emotional Problems

Binge eaters have a variety of emotional deficits and problems that center around a poorly developed capacity to identify feelings accurately and express feelings effectively. These deficits are particularly evident when binge eaters attempt to express anger, frustration, disappointment, sadness, boredom, and other uncomfortable feeling states. For instance, some binge eaters do not make distinctions between negative feelings and hunger or appetite and frequently eat in response to any emotional stress. Other binge eaters have fears of losing control emotionally and so, in order to avoid unleashing anger, frustration, or sadness, stuff down their feelings with food. In many situations, binge eating provides a temporary diversion from experiencing negative feelings; often my clients remark, "Instead of crying, I binged," or "Instead of screaming, I pigged out." In these cases, binge eating serves a useful purpose as an emotional release mechanism.

Frequently, the binge eaters I treat are unaware of their personal needs and limitations. They tend to take poor care of themselves physically and emotionally while overextending themselves to help others. My clients often give up rest and relaxation and push themselves mercilessly to accomplish unreasonable expectations or unrealistic goals. They tend to take on more responsibilities and tasks than they realistically can complete, and this usually results in a disappointing and unsatisfying experience. Generally, binge eaters can be described as individuals who try to do everything perfectly and manage to accomplish little adequately. Throughout these experiences, they report a recurrent feeling of being depleted or burned out. Often, binge eating is a futile attempt to restock depleted emotional stores.

Interpersonal Problems

Binge eaters experience several problems in their relationships with other people (see also Chapter 10, by Hawkins & Clement). Typically, they tend to be nonassertive, socially isolated, counterdependent, and rebellious. Their nonassertiveness presents itself as a poor capacity to say no to others, set limits, and stand up for personal rights. Generally, because of their difficulty expressing negative feelings, they tend to avoid conflicts with others, even at the expense of not exercising their rights and expressing their wishes. Clients often report binge eating after being in a situation where they are unable to be assertive.

Their difficulties in setting limits, in part, stem from holding unreasonable expectations for themselves and from being unaware of personal limitations. Usually, setting limits with others is difficult. It requires diplomacy, firmness, and the ability to express one's rights and point of view verbally. This type of encounter often creates interpersonal tension and uncomfortable feelings in all parties. Again, since binge eaters strive to avoid conflict and negative feelings, they tend to give up and give in quickly, choosing to suffer in silence and swallow their anger, frustration, and dissatisfaction. One client, in describing her interactions with her boss, remarked, "I usually go along with his/her stupid suggestions because if I said what I thought I'd really open up and probably get fired." Their fear of losing emotional control often is tied to skill deficits in setting firm, clear limits and in being assertive.

Previously I noted that most binge eaters overeat alone. Because of their embarrassment and shame about eating, they tend to spend much of their time alone hoping they will not be discovered. Some of this time is spent preparing for a binge, and the remainder is spent actually binge eating and recovering. This preference for solitary binge eating results in social isolation and social withdrawal as binge eaters plan their lives so as to allow time for these episodes. Their social isolation results in fewer and fewer opportunities to relax wtih others and comfortably engage in social interactions, so their already poorly developed social skills grow rusty with disuse and they usually experience intense feelings of social inadequacy and incompetence. These feelings frequently lead to further decisions to socially withdraw. This becomes a self-perpetuating cycle.

Binge eaters also have difficulties asking for help and being dependent on other people. Their counterdependency leads to personal attempts to do everything on their own without seeking help or assistance. They tend to see asking for help as weakness and often equate being dependent on another as being vulnerable to rejection. Their motto is often, "I can do it all my myself." With this interpersonal stance, they avoid the uncomfortable feelings of taking an interpersonal risk. They fear rejection, yet at the same time they deny themselves the opportunity to be accepted and eventually helped in the process. Many also experience strong feelings of personal inadequacy and deficiency, noting, "If other people knew what and how I ate, they would be repulsed and reject me."

One final interpersonal problem is that of rebelliousness (see also Chapter 9, by Coffman). Binge eaters tend to resist taking orders and advice, especially from people they see as powerful and controlling, such as their parents, spouse, or doctor. Often they verbally comply with diet prescriptions and actively rebel by engaging in secret binge episodes. A relatively large number begin this practice early in adolescence or late in childhood when parents try to deny them food. In most cases, the rebelliousness is an indirect (if covert) or direct (if overt) attempt to cope with unexpressed negative feelings such as anger and hostility. Often they seem to be rebelling against cultural and social pressures to be thin that conflict with our ideas of how to be happy and enjoy ourselves. As one binger–vomiter remarked, "Bingeing and throwing up is my way of having my cake and eating it too."

Therapeutic Interventions for Binge Eaters: A Cognitive–Behavioral Approach

Therapeutic interventions for binge eating are targeted for cognitive, behavioral, emotional, and interpersonal problems. Often, successful interventions in one area will have a positive effect on other areas. The interdependent and interactive aspects of cognitions, behaviors, and emotions allow many points of intervention (Kendall & Hollon, 1979). For example, succesfully restructuring a client's thinking about the questionable value of fad dieting and weight loss during a fast may help the client accept a more sensible, nutritional food exchange program and a gradual rate of weight loss (Jeffrey & Katz, 1977; Stuart, 1978).

To treat binge eating, I use a combination of cognitive, behavioral, emotional, and psychotherapeutic interventions. These include training clients in (1) cognitive restructuring, (2) behavioral self-control, (3) emotional expressiveness, (4) anger control, (5) assertiveness, (6) social skills, and (7) time management. I find the needs of clients vary but most binge eaters need information about and instruction and practice in all these areas. Table 8–1 lists the common problems of binge eaters along with some specific examples of each problem. Adjacent to each problem is a suggested therapeutic intervention or strategy. Several of the listed behavior therapy interventions are described sufficently in the clinical and research literature on each, for example, assertiveness training (Bower & Bower, 1976; Linehan, 1979), social skills training (Bellack & Hersen, 1979), and behavioral self-control (Loro, 1982; Mahoney & Thoresen, 1974). In view of this, I will focus here on those interventions that are relatively novel and possibly unfamiliar to most behavior therapists and clinicians.

Table 8-1. Examples of Common Problems and Suggested Interventions for Binge Eaters.

Problems	Suggested Interventions
1. Cognitive distortions and irrational beliefs	1. Cognitive restructuring
a. Incorrect, inadequate nutritional knowledge	a. Providing nutrition education and information
b. Magical dieting and weight-loss goals	b. Challenge unreasonable expectations and assist client in setting realistic weight-loss goals
c. Perfectionistic and all-or-none thinking	c. Systematically investigate client's ideas about perfectionism and playfully challenge the probability of being perfect in an imperfect world; using exaggeration and well-timed humor, question the value of extremist, all-or-none thinking; point out the value of relativistic thinking and of being flexible in regard to dieting and weight loss
d. Exaggerated importance of having an excessively thin body	d. Challenge adherence to cultural stereotypes and media emphasis on the unquestioned desirability of "never being too thin"
2. Maladaptive behaviors and fad-dieting practices	2. Behavioral self-control training, including self-monitoring of intake, weight and eating circumstances; stimulus/situational control; contingency contracting
a. Irregular and unusual eating patterns	a. Identify typical eating and binge-eating patterns with detailed self-monitoring and complete functional analyses of self-report records to determine strategic behavioral interventions
b. Extreme dieting and exercise practices	b. Provide information about fallacies and hazards of fad-dieting and extreme exercise practices; gradually shape moderate, sensible, and consistent food-intake and exercise practices
3. Deficiencies in emotional expressiveness	3. Training in ways to identify and express feelings, especially negative/uncomfortable feelings
a. Expressing sadness, disappointment, anger, and frustration	a. Training in effective interpersonal communication
b. Controlling anger and frustration	b. Training in anger control; instruction in use of humor and exaggeration

(continued) *193*

Table 8.1.   (Continued)

Problems	Suggested Interventions
c. Recognizing individual needs and limitations	c. Instructions in how to take care of oneself via personal needs assessment, value clarification, and setting priorities; instruction in how to manage time
4. Interpersonal issues	4. Training in interpersonal skills development
a. Saying no and setting limits	a. Assertiveness training
b. Social isolation and social withdrawal; fears of social incompetency	b. Social skills training
c. Counterdependency	c. Instructions in how to identify reliable, dependable people; modeling and behavioral rehearsal in asking for help
d. Rebelliousness	d. Paradoxical strategies and interventions to facilitate recognition of self-destructive vs. self-constructive rebellion; programmed binge eating to co-opt resistance

Behavioral Interventions

I would prefer to begin treating a binge eater by carefully examining her/his thinking patterns and belief system and initiating therapy with a series of cognitive interventions (Leon, 1979). However, most binge eaters that present for therapy desperately want to control their eating behavior, so I usually begin with behavioral interventions (Loro, 1982). The first step in a behavioral intervention is completing a behavioral assessment and analysis of a client's eating activity and lifestyle patterns (Loro & Orleans, 1982). I gather these data with an eating pattern questionnaire and self-monitoring records of daily caloric intake (see Figure 8–1). With these data, I can identify what and how a client eats, what the past dieting history is, and most of the client's expectations and beliefs about weight reduction. I then use these data to complete a functional behavioral analysis of the antecedents, consequences, and response topography of a client's caloric intake. In addition, I assess her/his current psychological status with the Minnesota Multiphasic Personality Inventory (MMPI) and a clinical interview. When I compile these results, I usually have a well-rounded de-

Figure 8-1. Caloric Intake Record.

Name _____

DATE	TIME	PLACE	ALONE OR WITH WHOM	ASSOCIATED ACTIVITY	FEELING STATE(S)	FOOD: AMOUNTS, TYPES AND HOW PREPARED LIQUIDS: AMOUNTS AND TYPES (COMPUTE CALORIES)	ASSOCIATED THOUGHTS

195

scription of a client's eating and food-related behavior, as well as some clinical sense of her/his psychological resources.

Following this initial assessment, I recommend that the client keep detailed records of all binge eating episodes and, if present, any purging or vomiting behavior (Orleans & Barnett, 1980). I ask the client to include in these records any thoughts, feelings, fantasies, events, and the like that occur before, during, or after a binge. If a client purges or vomits, I request that she/he keep records on this behavior (see Figure 8–2). After the client records binge-eating data for two to three weeks, I complete another functional analysis focused on the binge-eating pattern (Loro & Orleans, 1981). During this analysis, I pay close attention to the specific antecedents, consequences, and response characteristics of the binge. Often it is useful to compare this analysis to the initial functional analysis of daily eating behaviors. I find these two functional analyses generally provide a wealth of intervention possibilities and point to ways to help the client gain some initial behavioral control over the binge eating. Often the client will recognize personal stragegies to control or reduce the binge eating just by keeping detailed food/binge records. In this way, the reactivity of self-monitoring is clinically useful. I also find that most binge eaters have not attempted in other therapy experiences to learn about the problem before they attempt to solve it. Typically, my "let's keep detailed records so we can learn as much as possible about the problem" approach seems so paradoxical to clients that they will cooperate with me while I build rapport. This paradoxical strategy also serves to disarm the rebellious binge eaters because I do not ask them to stop binge eating—just to keep detailed records of binges. I then focus on the cognitive and emotional aspects of the client's binge eating.

Cognitive Interventions

Frequently, I use the self-monitoring records or clinical interviews just discussed to identify a client's major cognitive distortions, such as perfectionistic thinking, as well as emotional problems. Armed with these data, I begin gradually to reeducate the client about sound nutritional practices, sensible weight-control techniques, and realistic goal setting. When appropriate and possible, and depending on the amount of rapport I have with the client, I begin to confront and challenge a client's cognitive distortions and magical/

inaccurate beliefs about dieting and weight control. I start cognitive restructuring by verbally challenging a blatant cognitive distortion in a systematic yet playful fashion. Frequently, I begin with the client's strong need to be perfect or engage in perfectionistic thinking (a common problem of binge eaters). I might begin this challenge by asking, "How important is it to be perfect . . . and how do you know when you're perfect—I mean how do you really evaluate being absolutely perfect. . . . Do you know anyone now who is perfect. . . ." I then might spend a few minutes asking about how one can tell perfection from excellent imitations. By this time, the client usually is smiling and ready to acknowledge that perfection is more of an abstract ideal and not applicable to reality. Also, we usually are able to agree that perfectionistic thinking, while not productive, is difficult to change. At this point, I emphasize the importance of being imperfect and making mistakes in dieting and behavior control so that one can learn from them. This tends to produce moderate risk taking and facilitates the initiation of self-control. I end this cognitive restructuring sequence by focusing on the subjective meaning of perfection and perfectionism in eating and weight control and point out how difficult and burdensome it is to attempt to be perfect in an imperfect, mistake-prone world. Again, depending on the client and the types of cognitive distortions involved, I might playfully challenge other distortions, irrational beliefs, or fallacious assumptions. Usually I give special attention to any distortions left over from previous dieting and weight-reduction experiences.

A client's concerns and perceptions about her/his body are areas to explore slowly and carefully. For example, the complex, complicated, and multifaceted problem of body image disturbance needs to be examined with care and clinical sensitivity. In my experience, this is a difficult and slow-to-change issue, especially for women. In light of this, I proceed cautiously and gather information systematically about how a client feels about her/his body before attempting to make cognitive interventions concerning body image distortions and issues. To prepare clients for work in this area, I often will recommend specific homework geared toward developing a better body sense and body awareness. I find that asking clients to examine themselves nude in a mirror, take a dance aerobics class, try on new clothes, or go for a body massage can facilitate accurate body image development. In my clinical experience, a lengthy period of time must pass before a client is ready, willing, and able to confront body image issues directly. Some psy-

Figure 8–2. Record of Binge-Eating and Vomiting/Purging Episodes.

Initials _____   Date _____

Estimated Body Weight (1bs)_____

TIME	PLACE	ASSOCIATED ACTIVITIES	FOOD: Amounts & Types LIQUIDS: Amounts & Types	FEELINGS
				Before
				During
				After

THOUGHTS				
Before				
During				
After				

Please note on the reverse side any recollections, i.e., thoughts or feelings you have 1 to 2 hours after the binge.

chotherapists have handled this sensitive area in groups, using structured group exercises with a same-sex therapist (see Chapter 4, by White & Boskind-White), which often is a useful and appropriate approach.

Sexuality

Interventions in matters of sexuality and sexual relationships are difficult, delicate, and dependent on how receptive the client is to dealing with these issues. Often a group therapy setting with access to a same-sex therapist provides more opportunities for therapeutic intervention in sexual areas. White and Boskind-White (see Chapter 4) have reported that bingers and purgers will discuss sexual problems and fears openly in structured group sessions with same-sex participants and a same-sex therapist. If this option is not available and the client is receptive, I will intervene in the area of accepting one's sexuality. I will begin with some basic self-concept-building tasks, such as asking clients what they like to do, excel in, like to read, and so on. I will proceed by discovering what they like about themselves, their families, and the like, and end up by focusing on what they consider attractive about themselves. Since this is a relatively threatening question, I start by asking what others have said they liked about them. I also cover what the clients do not like, enjoy, or prefer in each area and in this process help them develop more balanced self-images.

The clients' sexuality and sexual relationships eventually surface in my questioning, and I then focus on the details of these concerns. Often I will ask clients to complete supplemental reading on sexuality, intimacy, mutual caring, and the like and bring questions about these matters to future sessions. When appropriate, I emphasize the idea that taking good care of oneself (see later discussions of emotional and interpersonal problems) pertains to sexual involvement as well as other areas. Generally, if clients are experiencing sexual conflicts and problems I seek consultation of experienced professionals. Often, to circumvent this conflicted area, I will recommend the binge eaters begin expanding and developing contacts and relationships with like-sexed individuals. I particularly emphasize the need for binge eaters to have supportive social networks (Barnett & Loro, 1981).

As therapy proceeds, I identify other related problem areas, issues, or treatment needs, such as the need for assertiveness training or social skills development (Hersen & Bellack, 1977). Typically, I refer clients to other experienced professionals for short-term structured training programs in these areas. My goal is to connect a client's work in these interpersonal areas to their progress in controlling their eating, weight, and lives.

Emotional Interventions

Much of my therapy time is spent training clients to identify, express, and, if necessary, control anger, frustration, and sadness. In my opinion, a major portion of unexpressed feelings and interpersonal conflicts in affluent, food-abundant countries are played out in eating situations. In general, I teach clients to cope more effectively with feelings in nonfood-related ways. Because this therapeutic process is difficult to describe and because it differs with the client and the situation, I will not attempt to describe my therapeutic approach to emotional interventions in detail. Basically, however, it involves the following: (1) gradually shaping binge eaters to identify and focus on their feelings, (2) teaching clients to distinguish between the need for food and other affectional and emotional needs, (3) training clients to be comfortable with negative feelings, and (4) modeling socially acceptable ways to express feelings. While working in these areas, I use concepts and techniques from available literature on communication effectiveness, problem solving, and assertiveness and social skills training.

In my clinical work, I find that nearly all binge eaters need training in how to control anger. I address this need with anger-control training, a coping-skills therapy developed from the concept of stress inoculation. The concept of stress inoculation, though originally developed to treat anxiety (Meichenbaum, 1977), was extended recently to anger (Novaco, 1977a, 1977b, 1978). Generally, anger control focuses on developing a client's competence to respond appropriately to stressful events. The goal is to reduce the intensity of disturbing emotions so that anger is experienced and often expressed, while behavioral control is maintained. The client learns to prepare cognitively for anger-provoking events and acquires a variety of anger-control techniques. The final step in the training involves applying these acquired skills in role-played or real-life situations. (See Novaco, 1979, for an extensive description of this training approach.)

Along with exploring the preceding emotional issues, I train clients to recognize personal needs for affection, attention, rest, relaxation, time alone, time to eat, and so on. Often I find binge eaters do not allow themselves to satisfy individual needs directly. Instead, they choose to sacrifice their personal needs or devalue their needs relative to the needs of others around them. Generally, I spend therapy time instructing clients in how to take better care of themselves physically, psychologically, and emotionally. I usually point out that they can take better care of others if they take good care of themselves. This training and instruction process involves encouraging binge eaters to identify their important needs; recognize their personal, financial, and familial responsibilities; recognize their limitations and situational constraints; clarify their values; set priorities; make informed choices; and structure/manage their time to accomplish their choices.

Interpersonal Interventions

Finally, I work on interpersonal issues and conflicts. As noted before, I encourage clients to seek further training in assertiveness and social skills if this is appropriate, and I emphasize how important it is from a behavioral self-control perspective to have the skills necessary to solve interpersonal problems. I illustrate the connection between deficiencies in interpersonal problem-solving skills and binge eating, using clients' own records showing binges precipitated by interpersonal conflicts.

Most of the remaining time, I deal with the interpersonal problems of counterdependency and rebelliousness. I approach counterdependency with paradoxical strategies and encourage the binge eater to be as independent and self-sufficient as possible. Often I will self-disclose information about how counterdependent I used to be (which is true). I state that being counterdependent is smart when you have to deal with all the undependable people around today. Usually I help clients develop an informal identification system for finding dependable people. I focus the therapy not so much on the clients' needs to be counterdependent as on their fear of becoming dependent. Often it is necessary to explore their past experiences with dependency in relationships, or their fears about being rejected and exposed by others if they choose to become dependent, ask for help, and reveal their vulnerability. Typically, I draw examples from literature or everyday life to illustrate how people are most human when they allow other caring individuals to help them, that is, be dependent on one another. I note, however, the critical importance of carefully choosing people on whom to depend.

To deal with the problem of rebelliousness or resistance to change in binge eating, I use the therapeutic strategy of programmed binge eating. This is a quasi-behavioral intervention that involves subtle reinforcement control and countercontrol procedures. Programmed bingeing is especially appropriate in cases of rebellious binge eating, which present special problems to the behavior therapist. When authority figures (family members, a physician, or counselor) in an individual's social learning history have provided powerful, often inadvertent reinforcers for bingeing, the behavioral therapist must avoid eliciting similar rebelliousness in treatment.

Programmed bingeing involves using countercontrol tactics like paradoxical injunctions (Watzlawick, Beavin, & Jackson, 1967), intentions (Ascher & Efran, 1978), and prescriptions (Haley, 1976) to gain control of bingeing behavior. These procedures commonly are employed by behavior therapists to minimize reactance or resistance to therapeutic programming, even though they are difficult to analyze within a strict stimulus-response framework (Asher & Efran, 1978; Davison, 1973). Programmed bingeing also may be particularly helpful for clients who perceive themselves as having little control over their bingeing. Finally, programmed bingeing, like Marlatt and Gordon's (1980) programmed relapse for newly abstinent alcoholics, smokers, and heroin users, may prove useful for clients with a history of slips and relapses following a binge-free period.

Basically, programmed bingeing means bingeing under close therapeutic direction. Therapeutic direction is combined with cognitive restructuring in which the clients learn to view their bingeing behavior as a habit under control of antecedent and consequent events rather than the expression of personal weaknesses or a personality deficit. In addition, clients learn to look on a binge or slip as a learning experience rather than as proof of the intractability of this behavior.

The procedure begins with a review of the initial intake records (Figures 8–1 and 8–2). The therapist and client identify preferred binge foods, settings, and high-risk circumstances. Together, they make a written or verbal contract for the client to binge eat in a predetermined fashion, that is, eating slowly, concentrating on the food's taste, and eating in a private setting. The therapist reframes this premeditated binge as a structured learning experience, assuring the client that this structured binge is necessary to understand the entire binge-eating pattern fully (i.e., antecedents, topography, and consequences).

The therapeutic strategy of programmed binge eating is paradoxical in several ways. First, the therapist is asking the client to engage in the problem behavior. This forces the client to perform the behavior on demand and causes the client to think about the behavior in a new and different way. Second, by requesting that the client binge, the therapist implies that the behavior is under the client's control, at least temporarily. Third, bingeing helps the client to experience voluntarily some degree of control over the behavior. Fourth, bingeing under the therapist's supervision frees the client from making destructive self-attributions of personal failure and powerlessness to explain or rationalize the binge, because the therapist is asking the client to binge.

During the programmed binge, the client keeps detailed records about calories consumed and thoughts, feelings, or behaviors preceding, accompanying, and following the structured binge. The therapeutic impact of the programmed binge is far more valuable than its assessment function, however, since bingeing under therapeutic direction differs significantly from self-directed bingeing. The programmed binge usually is discussed in a follow-up appointment scheduled 12 to 24 hours after the binge. Many clients report an inability to follow through with the binge, feeling disinterested in eating, while others are unable to eat as much food as anticipated. When this occurs, the therapist helps the client to identify the techniques she/he used, which can be used later to resist further bingeing. Thus, noncompliance with the programmed binge is mobilized to enhance self-control and therapeutic progress.

When programmed bingeing is skillfully applied, it has a powerful impact on the client's perceptions and feelings of self-control (Bandura, 1977). When used early in treatment for rebellious binge eating, programmed bingeing removes or neutralizes rebellion as a critical therapeutic issue and clears the way for a more direct and straightforward approach to antecedent and consequence control (Goldfried & Davison, 1976). For, whether or not the client complies fully with the programmed bingeing instructions, she/he experiences significant control over a problem behavior previously experienced as "uncontrollable." If the client completes the programmed binge and keeps detailed records, these records provide data for a more detailed functional analysis and behavioral assessment. The paradoxical dilemma placed on the client is that she/he complies at some level, even when not complying. If used appropriately and timed properly, programmed bingeing can be therapeutically productive.

When used at the end of treatment, programmed bingeing can follow Marlatt and Gordon's (1980) guidelines for programmed relapses that prepare clients to avoid full-blown relapses should a single binge or slip occur after treatment. The therapist presents a cognitive and behavioral analysis of the relapse process, helping the client to identify high-risk relapse situations, coping responses, and general problem-solving strategies. In addition, the dynamics of the "abstinence violation effect" can be reviewed beginning with the feelings of guilt and failure following a slip, leading to defining oneself as out of control, and leading in turn to further bingeing (Marlatt & Gordon, 1980). By outlining the abstinence violation effect, the therapist may be able to inoculate the client against the destructive personal attributions of failure associated with a slip. Cognitive restructuring is introduced to define a slip as (1) only a single mistake and (2) an opportunity for new learning. Programmed bingeing under therapeutic direction gives the client experiential knowledge that a single binge can occur without a full-blown relapse.

Problems and Complications in the Treatment of Binge Eating

Frequent episodes of binge eating eventually will lead to an overweight or obese condition, unless the binger chooses to fast, vomit, or purge, in which case some degree of weight control may result but unnecessary weight loss and possible protein-calorie malnutrition could occur. Even though a client's body weight may remain within a relatively acceptable range, frequent vomiting, laxative use, and enemas can lead to serious medical/physical complications, such as dehydration and electrolyte disturbances (Hill, 1970; Lucas, 1981).

The most serious medical complication of binge eating followed by vomiting or purging is hypokalemia (a low level of serum potassium). This condition, if untreated, can lead to cardiac arrest and kidney failure. Chronic vomiting can result in extensive dental-enamel erosion and salivary-gland enlargement. By the same token, chronic laxative abuse could lead to laxative dependence or

addiction and sometimes irreversible changes in lower-gastrointes-
tinal-tract functioning, that is, loss of peristalsis. Generally, specific vitamin and mineral deficiencies do not develop, but these
problems are possible, depending on the nature of the client's caloric intake and the frequency of vomiting or purging (Lucas,
1981).

Menstrual disturbances also may occur in women who binge
and purge. This symptom is more common in anorexic binge eaters
(Casper, Eckert, Halmi, Goldberg, & Davis, 1980), but it also can
occur in relatively normal-weight binge eaters, particularly if the
client has made radical changes in her diet. Because of the strong
relationship between food intake and endocrine and metabolic
functions, other medical or physical problems could develop. In
light of this possibility and the serious medical complications of
frequent binge eating followed by vomiting and purging, it is absolutely essential for therapists to require binge eaters be examined
by a qualified physician prior to treatment. This exam should include routine lab work, with special attention to electrolyte levels.
The therapist and physician consultant also must determine the
type(s) and amount(s) of medications the binge eater is taking and
whether these medications, coupled with bingeing and vomiting,
place the client at medical risk.

If these clinical procedures are not followed closely, the results
could be tragic, as in the case of Bernadette Gillchrist. Ms. Gillchrist, a 23-year-old nursing student, died, presumably of a cardiac
arrest, while participating in a National Institute of Health (NIH)
sleep study (Kolata, 1980). As part of the study's protocol, Ms.
Gillchrist, a chronic vomiter, was required to take lithium and
alpha-methyl-paratyrosine (AMPT). AMPT is an experimental
drug that blocks catecholamine synthesis. In prestudy examina-
tions, Ms. Gillchrist lied about her past medical history, current
psychotherapy, and chronic vomiting problem. What the NIH ex-
perimenters did not know was that she had been diagnosed previously as anorexic and that she periodically self-induced vomiting
as a weight-control technique. On two previous occasions she had
experienced cardiac arrest, and on the first occasion she was in a
coma for two days. Her doctors believed that her cardiac arrests
were a direct result of her vomiting, which caused loss of hydro-
chloric acid from the stomach and led to a compensatory loss of
intracellular potassium. This condition can result in a potassium
imbalance—hypokalemia—which can cause cardiac arrest (Kolata, 1980). Gillchrist's history of self-induced vomiting was espe-

cially ominous because she was given lithium as part of the NIH experiments. Generally, lithium depletes cells of potassium, but not to the extent that is dangerous to people who do not vomit and have normal eating patterns. In the case of a chronic vomiter like Ms. Gillchrist, however, lithium should not be prescribed or given (Kolata, 1980). Ms. Gillchrist's untimely and unfortunate death poignantly illustrates the seriousness of some types of binge eating, especially if vomiting is involved.

Summary

The prevalence of binge eating is increasing at an alarming rate, and traditional psychiatric treatment approaches to this complex problem are not effective for most binge eaters. As an alternative to traditional psychiatric treatments, this chapter has presented a cognitive–behavioral model of binge eating. To illustrate this model, important clinical and behavioral parameters of binge eating have been presented and common cognitive, behavioral, emotional, and interpersonal problems of binge eaters have been described. Based on these descriptions and clinical evidence, a cognitive–behavioral treatment approach to binge eating has been outlined and explained. This therapeutic approach combines training in cognitive restructuring, behavioral self-control, emotional expressiveness, and interpersonal-skill development, plus nutritional counseling and medical consultation to address the multiple problems of binge eaters.

References

Ascher, L. M., & Efran, J. S. Use of paradoxical intention in a behavioral program for sleep onset insomnia. *Journal of Consulting and Clinical Psychology,* 1978, *46,* 547–550.

Bandura, A. Self-efficacy: Toward a unifying theory of behavioral change. *Psychological Review,* 1977, *84,* 191–215.

Barnett, L. R., & Loro, A. D., Jr. Common problems of bulimarexics. Unpublished manuscript, Duke University Medical Center, 1981.

Bellack, A. S., & Hersen, M. (eds.). *Research and Practice in Social Skills Training.* New York: Plenum Press, 1979.

Beumont, P. J. V., George, G. C. W., & Smart, D. E. "Dieters" and "vomiters and purgers" in anorexia nervosa. *Psychological Medicine,* 1976, *6,* 617–622.

Boskind-Lodahl, M. Cinderella's step-sisters: A feminist perspective on anorexia nervosa and bulimia. *Signs: Journal of Women in Culture and Society,* 1976, *2*(2), 342–356.

Boskind-Lodahl, M., & White, W. C., Jr. The definition and treatment of bulimarexia in college women—A pilot study. *Journal of the American College Health Association,* 1978, *27,* 84–86.

Bower, S. A., & Bower, G. H. *Asserting Yourself.* Reading, Mass.: Addison-Wesley, 1976.

Bruch, H. *Eating Disorders: Obesity, Anorexia Nervosa, and the Person Within.* New York: Basic Books, 1973.

Casper, R. C., Eckert, E. D., Halmi, K. A., Goldberg, S. C., & Davis, J. M. Bulimia: Its incidence and clinical importance in patients with anorexia nervosa. *Archives of General Psychiatry,* 1980, *37,* 1030–1035.

Davison, G. C. Counter control in behavior modification. In L. A. Hamerlynck, L. C. Handy, & E. J. Mash (eds.), *Behavior Change: Methodology, Concepts, and Practice.* Champaign, Ill.: Research Press, 1973.

Garfinkel, P. E., Moldofsky, H., & Garner, D. M. The heterogeneity of anorexia nervosa: Bulimia as a distinct subgroup. *Archives of General Psychiatry,* 1980, *37,* 1036–1040.

Goldfried, M. R., & Davison, G. C. *Clinical Behavior Therapy.* New York: Holt, Rinehart & Winston, 1976.

Gormally, J., Black, S., Daston, S., & Rardin, D. The assessment of binge eating severity among obese persons. *Addictive Behaviors,* 1982, *7,* 47–55.

Haley, J. *Problem Solving Therapy.* San Francisco: Jossey-Bass, 1976.

Hawkins, R. C., II, & Clement, P. F. Development and construct validation of a self-report measure of binge eating tendencies. *Addictive Behaviors,* 1980, *5,* 219–226.

Hersen, M., & Bellack, A. S. Assessment of social skills. In A. R. Ciminero, K. S. Calhoun, & H. E. Adams (eds.), *Handbook of Behavioral Assessment.* New York: John Wiley, 1977.

Hill, O. W. Functional vomiting, abdominal pain and diarrhea. In O. W. Hill (ed.), *Modern Trends in Psychosomatic Medicine.* London: Butterworths, 1970.

Hollon, S. D., & Kendall, P. C. Cognitive–behavioral interventions: Theory and procedure. In P. Kendall & S. Hollon (eds.), *Cognitive–Behavioral Interventions: Theory, Research, and Procedures.* New York: Academic Press, 1979.

Jeffrey, D. B., & Katz, R. C. *Take It Off and Keep It Off.* Englewood Cliffs, N. J.: Prentice-Hall, 1977.

Kaplan, H. S. *Disorders of Sexual Desire.* New York: Brunner/Mazel, 1979.

Kolata, G. B. NIH shaken by death of research volunteer. *Science,* 1980, *209,* 475–479.

Kendall, P. C. & Hollon, S. D. *Cognitive–Behavioral Interventions: Theory, Research, and Practice.* New York: Academic Press, 1979.

Leon, G. R. Cognitive–behavior therapy for eating disturbances. In P. C. Kendall & S. D. Hollon (eds.), *Cognitive–Behavioral Interventions: Theory, Research, and Procedures.* New York: Academic Press, 1979.

Leon, G. R. Is it bad not to be thin? *The American Journal of Clinical Nutrition,* 1980, *33,* 174–176.

Linehan, M. M. Structured cognitive–behavioral treatment of assertion problems. In P. C. Kendall & S. D. Hollon (eds.), *Cognitive–Behavioral Interventions: Theory, Research, and Procedures.* New York: Academic Press, 1979.

Loro, A. D., Jr. Binge eating: A clinical–behavioral description. Paper presented at the Fourteenth Annual Association for Advancement of Behavior Therapy Convention, New York, New York, 1980.

Loro, A. D., Jr. Treatment for eating disorders. In P. A. Boudewyns & F. J. Keefe (eds.), *Behavioral Medicine in General Medical Practice.* Reading, Mass.: Addison-Wesley, 1982.

Loro, A. D., Jr., & Orleans, C. S. Binge eating in obesity. Preliminary findings and guidelines for behavioral analysis and treatment. *Addictive Behaviors,* 1981, *6,* 155–166.

Loro, A. D., Jr., & Orleans, C. S. The behavioral assessment of obesity. In F. J. Keefe and J. A. Blumenthal (eds.), *Assessment Strategies in Behavioral Medicine.* New York: Grune & Stratton, 1982.

Lucas, A. R. Bulimia and vomiting syndrome. *Contemporary Nutrition,* 1981, *6*(4), 27–35.

Mahoney, M. J., & Mahoney, K. *Permanent Weight Control: A Total Solution to the Dieter's Dilemma.* New York: W. W. Norton, 1976.

Mahoney, M. J., & Thoresen, C. E. *Self-Control: Power to the Person.* Monterey, Calif.: Brooks/Cole, 1974.

Marlatt, G. A., & Gordon, J. R. Determinants of relapse: Implications for the maintenance of behavior change. In P. Davison & S. M. Davison (eds.), *Behavioral Medicine: Changing Health Lifestyles.* New York: Brunner/Mazel, 1980.

Meichenbaum, D. *Cognitive Behavior Modification.* New York: Plenum, 1977.

Meyer, R. G. Delay therapy: Two case reports. *Behavior Therapy,* 1973, *4,* 709–711.

Morganstern, K. P. Cigarette smoke as noxious stimulus in self-managed aversion therapy for compulsive eating: Technique and case illustration. *Behavior Therapy,* 1974, *5,* 255–260.

Novaco, R. W. Stress inoculation: A cognitive therapy for anger and its application to a case of depression. *Journal of Consulting and Clinical Psychology,* 1977, *45,* 600–608. (a)

Novaco, R. W. A stress inoculation approach to anger management in the training of law enforcement officers. *American Journal of Community Psychology,* 1977, *5,* 327–346. (b)

Novaco, R. W. Anger and coping with stress. In J. P. Foreyt & D. Rathjen (eds.), *Cognitive Behavior Therapy: Therapy, Research and Practice.* New York: Plenum Press, 1978.

Novaco, R. W. The cognitive regulation of anger and stress. In P. Kendall & S. Hollon (eds.), *Cognitive–Behavioral Interventions: Theory, Research and Procedures.* New York: Academic Press, 1979.

Ondercin, P. Compulsive eating in college women. *Journal of College Student Personnel,* 1979, *20,* 153–157.

Orleans, C. T., & Barnett, L. R. Bulimarexia: Guidelines for behavioral assessment and treatment. Paper presented at the Fourteenth Annual Convention of the Association for Advancement of Behavior Therapy, New York, NY, November, 1980.

Russell, G. F. M. Bulimia nervosa: An ominous variant of anorexia nervosa. *Psychological Medicine,* 1979, *9,* 429–448.

Stern, F. M., Hock, R. S., & Carper, J. *Mind Trips to Help You Lose Weight.* Chicago, Ill.: Playboy Press, 1976.

Stuart, R. B. *Act Thin, Stay Thin.* New York: W. W. Norton, 1978.

Watzlawick, P., Beavin, J., & Jackson, D. *Pragmatics of Human Communication.* New York: W. W. Norton, 1967.

White, W. C., Jr., & Boskind-White, M. An experiential–behavioral approach to the treatment of bulimarexia. *Psychotherapy: Theory, Research, and Practice,* 1981, *18,* 501–507.

Wijesinghe, B. Massed electrical aversion treatment of compulsive eating. *Journal of Behavior Therapy and Experimental Psychiatry,* 1973, *4,* 133–135.

9

A Clinically Derived Treatment Model for the Binge–Purge Syndrome

David A. Coffman

The model described in this chapter is a "working" one in that it necessarily will be refined and shaped as additional clinical data become available. The impetus for the model grew out of my clinical experience while treating bulimic women between the ages of 20 and 33 at the University of Texas at Austin, over the past five years (Coffman, Note 2).[1]

Recalling Tolman's (1959) suggestion that all behavior is purposive, the following clinically derived treatment model was developed from a functional perspective. By "functional," it is assumed that bingeing and purging have a purpose, which is most often unconscious, the end result of which is to maintain the integrity of the personality.

The early psychosocial development of the binger–purger seems fairly normal; however, there appears to be a heightened sensitivity beginning in puberty and early adolescence to issues surrounding body image, appearance, food, dieting, and the like.

[1] I agree with Wilson (Chapter 12) that the model I propose here is hypothetical. If I appear to be overly enthusiastic, it is because this hypothesis has been found to be useful empirically in the clinical encounter, time after time. It seems to me that, if a treatment strategy results in consistent successful outcome, then that is its "truth."

I further agree with Wilson that this model has to be hypothetical in the absence

Even more important, there seems to be inadequate independence training and often subtle but significant threats to the bulimic's sense of personal authority, effectiveness, and power (Bruch, 1973) via a "significant other," usually one or both parents. The focus of domination and threat to the bulimic's early developing sense of control is often the father. This clinical profile of the bulimic and her/his family development is quite similar to that found in other research (Boskind-Lodahl & Sirlin, 1977; Strober, 1981).

The excessive emphasis on body image and appearance and feelings of domination and loss of control result in an aggregate of symptoms that includes bingeing and purging. Bulimics often describe themselves as nonassertive, lonely, isolated, helpless, unattractive, overweight, and angry (Boskind-Lodahl & Sirlin, 1977; Dunn & Ondercin, 1981; Garner & Garfinkel, 1979; Hawkins & Clement, 1980; Herman & Polivy, 1975; Loro & Orleans, 1981). This treatment model assumes, on the basis of clinical experience, that these feelings will diminish in frequency and intensity as these individuals experience an increase in their own sense of power, authority, and control (Loro & Orleans, 1981; Seligman, 1975).

It is, in fact, important for the therapist *not* to focus on the bingeing and purging symptom exclusively. As a significant authority, the therapist unknowingly may challenge the weak and fragile sense of control of the bulimic who sees the therapist's clini-

---

of hard clinical data. Clinical validity, of course, will be determined ultimately by therapists who test this hypothesis in clinical settings and compare the outcome (reduction of symptoms) with other treatment methods. I further agree with Wilson that it would be a mistake to suggest prematurely to a bulimic client that they can choose not to eat. This would be an inappropriate thing to suggest to a person with relatively low self-esteem, feelings of helplessness, and a perceived lack of effectiveness. This is why discussion of decision making and choice come later in the process of therapy, as described in my model. After a careful reading of the phases of therapy section, it becomes clear that, initially, the therapist is *not* encouraging the client to choose between bingeing or not bingeing. In fact, as stated before, it is most appropriate for the therapist to focus as little as possible on food and the behavior surrounding eating. The emphasis in this model throughout is on helping bulimic clients in defining, developing, and choosing productive and reasonable life goals, both immediate and long-term, when and only when they are ready to do so. The timing on working on life planning, skill acquisition, and so on is idiosyncratic and may vary dramatically from client to client. After the person begins to initiate action toward short-term, personally defined goals and develops the skills to encounter people differently, then the self-attribution changes and food consumption patterns become simply another arena of planning, choice, and assertion.

cal interest as a demand. This perceived demand will need to be rejected and subverted by maintaining or increasing the bingeing and purging.

The Binge–Purge Cycle

The binge–purge syndrome seems to follow a cycle that is stimulated by a critical event involving a threat to the person's sense of control, a feeling of rejection or isolation, or unfavorable comparisons based on appearance, intelligence, or the like. The stimulus event may be a personal feeling, perception, or idea, or it may be an interpersonal transaction of some kind. After the stimulus event, which may precede the binge by hours or minutes, the bulimic plans the time and place of the binge and type and amount of food. Binges often become ritualistic as to time, place, and food, which seems to discount the "critical event" theory; however, with bulimics where bingeing is regular and ritualized, negative self-statements, perceptions, and attributions always precede a binge. The implication is that chronically low self-esteem may provide a daily stimulus for bingeing.

After a binge, the individual will eliminate the food by vomiting, severe fasting, or the use of laxatives. The emotional aftermath includes fatigue, guilt, depression, and usually a commitment not to binge again. With increased frequency of bingeing, the personal sense of commitment to stop and of self-confidence diminishes. This sets the stage for further bingeing.

Over time, perhaps years, the individual develops a secret lifestyle around bingeing and purging and the symptom often goes unnoticed by family and friends. The request for professional help usually is preceded by growing fears concerning the medical consequences of bingeing and purging or follows having the problem discovered by a spouse, friend, or family member.

Strategies for intervention need to take into account the individual's sensitivity to demands or perceived control; feelings of isolation and loneliness; somewhat sporadic, inconsistent, and problematic relationships with men (since almost all bulimics are women, my discussion will focus on the female); lack of social and assertiveness skills; low self-esteem; and negative body image, often in the absence of being overweight.

It should be noted here that the removal or elimination of the symptomatic response alone is not considered effective treatment (Bruch, 1973; Loro & Orleans, 1981). The goal is to help the person experience more autonomy and control and, as Dollard and Miller (1950) suggest, "to be free within his/her own mind to consider every possible alternative course of action" (p. 249).

Phases of Therapy

Exploration Phase

The goal of this opening is to help the client open up and talk about the problem. Many clients feel embarrassed and humiliated by their bingeing and purging behavior and need to be supported carefully in their attempt to seek help. The counselor should discuss the recent development of interest in bulimia in the professional community. By helping the client understand how bulimia is a problem for many women, the counselor reduces the client's sense of isolation and uniqueness. The counselor also might bring into focus societal and cultural expectations as a backdrop for why many women feel so much pressure to be thin and pretty. From the first session, the counselor should begin to confront the client gently about her assumptions regarding appearance.

The counselor should explore the client's specific pattern and history of bingeing and purging. It is important to know when the problem began and the critical events that surrounded the onset. It is also helpful to know the frequency of bingeing–purging and if any situations, events, or feelings cause the symptoms to abate or increase.

During these initial discussions, the counselor should help the client ventilate feelings of embarrassment, anxiety, anger, and so on, which arise from recalling specific incidents or situations in the past.

After obtaining historical data concerning onset and duration, the counselor should suggest that the client provide some current information, via a food diary, about daily food consumed, including incidents of bingeing–purging. The client should track and record feelings and thoughts that precede a binge and follow a purge. She should be encouraged to bring the food diary to the next session for review and discussion.

It is absolutely imperative that the counselor not appear demanding or judgmental during this exploration phase of therapy.

Bulimic clients are very sensitive to authority and others in power positions. They may misperceive therapeutic interest as an attempt to control them, and so may terminate therapy prematurely.

Assessment Phase

The counselor should go over the food diary with the client, focusing on thoughts and feelings related to bingeing–purging behavior. The client may resist completing the diary and bringing it to the session because she feels embarrassed or apprehensive about the counselor's response. The counselor should explore these feelings in the session and be prepared to eliminate the diary if resistance is great. Some clients will find the diary helpful as a means of tracking their eating behavior, while others cannot bring themselves to complete it. The counselor should be sensitive to these individual differences.

During the assessment phase, the counselor should introduce and go over briefly the Bingeing–Purging Questionnaire (BPQ), presented in full in the appendix to this chapter. The form was designed with the assistance of bulimic clients and is used to provide the counselor with specific details surrounding the bingeing–purging behavior. The form should be taken home, completed, and returned by the client. Again, if there is resistance, the counselor should put the BPQ aside and move on. The BPQ is helpful but not imperative in the treatment plan.

If clients find the food diary a helpful tool, they should be encouraged to continue it. The counselor should carefully avoid giving too much attention to increases or decreases in overall caloric intake or bingeing behavior as indicated in the diary. The role of the counselor should be that of a cohort or consultant, rather than that of a monitoring authority who expects to cure the symptoms.

Developing a Cognitive Map

During this phase, the counselor begins to help the clients learn new ways of thinking about their problems. The goal of this phase is to demystify the bulimic behavior and place it more in the realm of a learned, functional response that can be under control. It is helpful for the counselor to go over the critical items on the BPQ, as a start, and explore the origins of anger, poor body image, loneliness, depression, and so on. Bulimic women often find comfort in learning that their feelings and thoughts are shared by other women with the same problem, as reflected by the questions on the BPQ.

An attempt should be made to reconstruct eary significant relationships, particularly with the parents. Here, we must look for the dominating "authority" or "master" in the client's past. Inquiry is sometimes helpful regarding expectations about appearance, physique, dieting, food, and so on. What are the expectations? Has the client internalized those expectations and tried to make them her own?

The counselor should make a point to explore how much personal control and power the clients felt they had in the past, say early adolescence, and how they feel now. How much decision-making power do they have? Are they in the school, the job, or the relationship that *they* want to be in, or do they feel pressured by outside forces? Many clients feel, for the first time, that they are engaged in activities or have established goals to which they are only minimally committed.

Develop the Master/Slave Model[2]

Summarize the cognitive map and the significance of early relationships in previous session(s). Who, in the past, was the person(s) who expected the most from the client? Were these expectations perceived as demands?

Explore feelings related to being pressured to conform to this controlling "master's" expectations regarding the client's appearance, performance, diet, and so on. Help the client uncover subtle feelings of resentment.

The client may feel the need to defend the "master" at this point. The counselor should explain that the objective is not to find out who was or is at fault, but to verbalize and thereby understand negative feelings which, up to this time, the client has not allowed herself—or others have not allowed her—to express. This feeling or condition of not being allowed to express negative feelings or make independent choices is similar to being subjugated or enslaved.

The counselor should make the connection between the onset of bingeing–purging and the analogy of a "slave revolt." It's a way of saying no to the master or the authority. *As such, it is a statement of determination and integrity.* The revolt is enacted with the

---

[2]For help in fully understanding the master/slave concept, see M. E. P. Seligman's *Helplessness—On Depression, Development, and Death.* San Francisco: Freeman, 1975.

very object that the master often forbids, namely, food. The revolt is never complete, however, because after the defiant gesture (the binge) the individual feels anxious and afraid of disapproval and acquiesces to the master's demands to be thin (by purging). (If the revolution were completed, the problem probably would be obesity rather than bingeing–purging.)

The counselor needs to go over this model carefully and make sure the client understands the functional nature of the bulimia and how it has been and continues to be a mechanism of adaptation and coping, although not a very effective one. Be sure to emphasize that the binge is an angry statement directed at some particular person or persons (the counselor should be able to name who the "master" is by now) and is an indication of the client's strength and determination and reflects a need for integrity and power, which is quite normal.

The counselor should show how real power and control are related to decisions and choices and emphasize how the client is now the locus of control and can choose to eat or not eat, binge or not binge. It's entirely up to her. *She* is the *master* now. Many clients feel a new sense of enthusiasm and power at this phase in therapy; however, this new awareness of the freedom to choose may generate some anxiety, because, for the first time, a client may begin to question lifelong goals. Although they may be ready to reject prescribed goals from the old master, there may be no obvious personal goals to replace them with. The counselor should assist the client in exploring hidden desires, wants, needs, and values that differentiate and separate her from the old master and make her an individual. Some rational problem solving and planning can be done to establish new, attainable short- and long-range goals.

Support Phase

The counselor is needed to give support and encouragement as the client begins to reduce the frequency of the bingeing–purging. Counselors should avoid efforts on the part of the client to give them credit for the changes she is making, referring her instead back to the model. The reduction of the bingeing is due to *her* choices, *her* will and strength, *her* self-control and power.

The reduction in frequency of bingeing–purging may be rather dramatic after the model is explained. The client may be pleasantly surprised and a little puzzled at the reduction in her desire to binge.

When she does backslide and binge, she may feel particularly vulnerable and guilty. The best policy at this stage is simply not to focus on the bingeing behavior, but to reinforce her increased control and decision-making power and to focus instead on life-planning issues such as decisions about a new job, changing college majors, expanding her social network, and using time creatively.

Skill Acquisition Phase

Because of the history of low self-esteem and negative body image, the bulimic may need to develop new personal and social skills. This may be an appropriate time for the counselor to refer the bulimic client to skill groups such as assertiveness training, relationship management, stress management, and relaxation training. This training will help provide specific skills that will implement the attitude change toward a more self-controlling, powerful person.

The client should remain in individual therapy during this skill-building phase so that the counselor can monitor and help the client integrate the multiple changes taking place.

Termination Phase

As the client brings the bingeing well under her control and is able to monitor and reinforce her own behavior, the support of the counselor will become less and less important. The counselor should discuss with the client reasonable strategies for dealing with bingeing–purging behavior that may occur in the future. The client should be cautioned not to panic or feel guilty, but simply use the skills she has acquired to sort it out and move on. Again, the emphasis is not on bingeing and purging, but on developing an appropriate sense of power and control.

It should be noted that the number of sessions required in each of these phases we have just discussed will vary depending on the individual client and her readiness for change, as well as the amount of resistance at different stages in the therapeutic process. It is important for the counselor always to be aware of individual client differences and be prepared to spend additional time in a given phase or drop a homework assignment if it's not working. It also should be pointed out that not all of these phases flow automatically and consistently in the order presented. For example, it may be expeditious to refer a client to an assertiveness-training group after the first individual session. Also, clarification and implementation of new goals seems to be a continuous process across phases and is usually an area that is discussed to some extent in most sessions.

Assessment and Clinical Utility of the BPQ

Some of the problems in the area of assessment and measurement of binge eating have been noted by the other investigators (e.g., Hawkins & Clement, 1980). The Bingeing–Purging Questionnaire (BPQ), presented in the appendix to this chapter, was developed by me, with the help of two previous bulimic clients, as a means of helping clients to develop a cognitive map and increase their awareness of the historical and current conditions and events that directly affect bingeing–purging behavior. The BPQ may be used in the therapy session as a structured interview, or, as is most often the case, it may be given to clients to take home, complete, and return at their next session. All of the items were selected to access some salient feature of binge–purge behavior or the thoughts, feelings, or experiences that impinge on that behavior. The completed BPQ is reviewed carefully by the therapist as a way of learning a great deal about the bulimic client very quickly; any of the items may reveal a helpful piece of information. In my experience, however, I have found particularly salient the responses to items 13, 19, 20, 21, 24, 25, 27, 28, and 30, which often reveal information that the therapist can use as a stimulus for further inquiry and that the client can use toward a greater understanding of the problem. Let's turn now to some actual clinical responses to these items, made by clients we will know as "Dorothy" and "Tracy."

Item 13. Describe your physiological and emotional states before, during, and after bingeing and purging.
  Dorothy: "Usually I don't know what to do with myself as I go to the refrigerator."
  Tracy: "I'm keyed up before, during I feel relieved and uncontrollable, and after I feel depressed and hopeless."
Item 19. What certain situations seem to provoke you to bingeing?

> *Dorothy:* "When I'm lonely, alone, or bored."
>
> *Tracy:* "Being alone or I guess lonely, also being afraid of being alone, being angry with no outlet for it."

Item 20. Are you a perfectionist? . . . What do you think your parents expect of you?

> *Dorothy:* "I want things perfect and neat. My parents expect good grades and success in life, but it doesn't come."
>
> *Tracy:* "Yes. I never feel I'm doing things as well as I could be doing them."

Item 21. Do you ever feel you are doomed to failure?

> *Dorothy:* "Yes, yes, almost always."
>
> *Tracy:* "Yes, all of the time."

Item 24. Does it seem to you like everyone knows how to cope with life but you? . . .

> *Dorothy:* "Yes, I always seem to fall back into feeling I can't cope with my problems."
>
> *Tracy:* "Yes, I often sit and watch people and know how much happier they are and how much better they are at their jobs and making friends."

Item 25. Do you ever enjoy feeling isolated?

> *Dorothy:* "Yes and no. I rarely go out because I don't want anyone to see me, and no because it's lonely and I eat more."
>
> *Tracy:* "Yes."

Item 27. What do you think men look for in women?

> *Dorothy:* "At first appearance (face and body), then personality, sense of humor."
>
> *Tracy:* "A good shape, pretty face."

Item 28. Do you have feelings that everyone you pass on the street is judging your appearance and actions? Did you have this feeling as a child?

> *Dorothy:* "Yes. Yes. People usually do."
>
> *Tracy:* "Yes! Yes! I was scared to death of my classmates as a kid."

Item 30. How long do you usually go before starting the bingeing–purging cycle again?

> *Dorothy:* "It always varies, depending upon my happiness with my life at the time."
>
> *Tracy:* "It used to be every three days, now since coming to college, it's every day almost."

Background

These two typical cases have been selected to illustrate the use of the BPQ as a strategic tool in therapy. A brief biographical and clinical profile is needed for addition background for our discussion.

Dorothy. She referred herself to therapy at the University of Texas Counseling Center. At the time of therapy, she was 20 years old, attractive, and was of normal weight. She was enrolled as a full-time student but had not decided on a major. Dorothy was the youngest of four siblings. Both parents were normal in weight. Her mother was very critical of Dorothy's eating habits and was described as "very watchful." There was a history of continuous dieting since early adolescence because of a tendency to gain weight. No diets ever were really successful. Dorothy binged on highly sugared foods four or five times per week. She purged by vomiting. She had been bulimic for 3½ years, and it began as a means of weight control. She sought treatment because of her concern for her physical health.

Tracy. She also was self-referred for treatment at the University of Texas Counseling Center. She was 21 years old, attractive, and of normal weight. She was a full-time student but undecided about a major. Tracy was the second-oldest of six siblings. Everyone else in the family was overweight, and her father was very critical of any weight gain by Tracy. There was a continuous history of dieting, which never was really successful. She binged on highly sugared foods six or seven days per week. Tracy purged by using large doses of laxatives after each binge. She began bingeing nine months previous to seeking treatment, as a means of weight control. She came to therapy out of her concern for her health.

As one can see, both Dorothy and Tracy conform to the psychosocial developmental pattern of many bulimic women. Both women also report dating very little in high school and recall adolescence as a period of loneliness and isolation. The family history also revealed the significant other in the past who later became the "master" or the "controller" against whom the bulimic had to rebel.

Discussion

As can be seen from the samples presented earlier, the responses of the two women to some items are quite similar. These responses were used in therapy with Tracy and Dorothy in ways described earlier in the cognitive mapping phase of therapy. Responses to items reflecting fear of failure (Item 21), feeling critically judged by others (Item 28), feeling a demand to be perfect (Item 20), for example, were taken directly from the BPQ and used as a stimulus for deeper inquiry and exploration with Dorothy and Tracy. As one can see, many of the responses are clinically very provocative and can lead to further productive inquiry and discussion. The questionnaire is not essential in treating the bulimic from the conceptual model suggested; however, it does provide a means to focus quickly on the key causal elements for the client by tying together early feelings, thoughts, and reactions with current behaviors that include the binge–purge symptoms. By developing this conceptual framework, the client can begin to understand the functional nature of her bulimia in the light of her own personal developmental history. This makes the problem less mysterious and diabolical and puts it into a realm of behaviors that are amenable to intervention and change.

Conclusions

The model described in this chapter assumes that bingeing–purging behavior has some functional utility, mainly the private expression of control and power with food being used as an object with which control is expressed. It is an angry and rebellious gesture, often directed at others who are perceived as domineering or controlling—such as society, spouse, or parents—who make demands that the bulimic cannot or will not comply with to a satisfactory degree. The focus of therapy is not on the eating symptom but on helping the clients clarify their personal values and desires and then begin to establish immediate, attainable medium- and long-range goals. A renewed sense of mastery and control follows.

This model may be contrasted with that of Loro and Orleans (1981), who review several behavioral techniques that focus on helping the person develop specific strategies for controlling the symptom behavior and how they approach food. Some of the antecedent control methods described by Loro and Orleans, such as stress management, relaxation training, assertiveness training, and rational problem-solving techniques, fall in the realm of skill acquisition and are included as treatment options in the model espoused in this chapter. A multicomponent treatment approach seems essential in bulimia because of the different areas of functioning affected, for example, cognitive, affective, behavioral, and social.

The problems with a behavioral intervention that focuses on symptom reduction are described in the first part of this chapter and by Loro and Orleans (1981). Because food is quite often an object of rebellion, the bulimic may perceive well-intentioned offers of help by a spouse, friend, or therapist as a threat to control, with the result that the bingeing behavior can—and often does—increase. To counter this resistance to therapy, Loro and Orleans suggest a "quasi-behavioral technique" called programmed bingeing where the bulimic individual is guided through a controlled binge to help her to experience direct and personal control of a binge when the contingencies for bingeing are not present. This exercise reduces the fear and anxiety surrounding a binge and is a structured act of self-control.

The model described in this chapter is sensitive to this issue of resistance and deals with it by not focusing on the bulimic symptom to any great extent. Bulimia, in one sense, is not an eating disorder. It is a problem related to an underdeveloped sense of mastery, control, and power; treatment must take place at this level. Most bulimic women are experts concerning nutrition, diets, food planning, and so on. If progress is made in therapy (1) in helping the individual to clarify and implement personal life goals and plans that previously seemed impossible and (2) in acquiring assertiveness skills and the ability to express appropriate anger and resentment, then the need to rebel with food fades quickly and a near-normal diet almost always is resumed. As Tracy, one of the women described in this chapter, said at the termination of successful therapy, "Eating doesn't interest me anymore the way it used to, now that I'm choosing to do other things with my life."

Reference Notes

1. Clement, P. F. & Hawkins, R. C., II. Pathways to Bulimia. Paper presented at the Fourteenth Annual Convention of the Association for the Advancement of Behavior Therapy, New York, 1980.
2. Coffman, D. A. Unpublished data. Counseling-Psychological Services Center, The University of Texas at Austin, 1981.

References

Boskind-Lodahl, M., & Sirlin, J. The gorging–purging syndrome. *Psychology Today,* 1977, *11,* 50.

Bruch, H. *Eating Disorders.* New York: Basic Books, 1973.

Dollard, J., & Miller, N. E. *Personality and psychotherapy: An analysis in terms of learning, thinking, and culture,* New York: McGraw Hill, 1950.

Dunn, P. K., & Ondercin, P. Personality variables related to compulsive eating in college women. *Journal of Clinical Psychology,* 1981, *37,* 43–49.

Garner, D. M., & Garfinkel, P. E. The Eating Attitudes Test: An index of the symptoms of anorexia nervosa. *Psychological Medicine,* 1979, *9,* 273–279.

Hawkins, R. C., II, & Clement, P. F. Development and construct validation of a self-report measure of binge eating tendencies. *Addictive Behaviors,* 1980, *5,* 219–226.

Herman, C. P., & Polivy, J. P. Anxiety, restraint, and eating behavior. *Journal of Abnormal Behavior,* 1975, *84,* 666–672.

Loro, A. D., Jr., & Orleans, C. S. Binge eating in obesity: Preliminary findings and guidelines for behavioral analysis and treatment. *Addictive Behaviors,* 1981, *6,* 155–166.

Seligman, M. E. P. *Helplessness—On Depression, Development, and Death.* San Francisco: Freeman, 1975.

Strober, M. The significance of bulimia in juvenile anorexia nervosa: An exploration of possible etiological factors. *International Journal of Eating Disorders,* 1981, *1,* 28–43.

Tolman, E. C. Principles of purposive behavior. In S. Koch (ed.), *Psychology: A Study of Science,* Vol.2. *General Systematic Formulations, Learning, and Special Processes.* New York: McGraw-Hill, 1959.

Appendix to Chapter 9

Bingeing–Purging Questionnaire (BPQ)

1. Do you plan a binge around a time and place you plan to purge?
2. Do you become obsessed mentally with certain foods just before you binge?
3. Do you binge in the company of others, or is it primarily something you do when you can be alone?
4. If you are alone, how do you react if someone interrupts you?
5. Are there certain foods that especially attract you?
6. What if these are unavailable? What are some of the least desirable foods you have resorted to eating if nothing better was around?
7. About how much of your time is spent on a binge, planning a binge, and purging?
8. How did you get the idea to start purging?
9. What were the circumstances that made you first binge and purge? Had you ever had an eating problem before, or any trouble with your weight?
10. When did you first decide you wanted to be skinny? What motivated this decision?
11. When did you first begin to feel guilt about your eating habits?
12. If you have ever been drunk, does the "high" (if any) you get from food in any way resemble what you feel after drinking?
13. Describe your physiological and emotional states before, during, and after bingeing and purging.
14. Do you ever feel completely lacking in energy and interest necessary to cope with even simple daily tasks?
15. Do you ever end up bingeing longer than you had planned?
16. What if things don't go as planned in order to purge? To what extremes, if any, have you gone to find a time or place to make yourself purge?

17. Do any of your friends or relatives know about this compulsion? What do you think their reaction would be if they knew?

18. What other means do you use to keep weight off in addition to purging (drugs, fasts, etc.)?

19. What certain situations seem to provoke you to bingeing? Do you ever binge for no real reason except that you have a blinding urge to eat certain foods?

20. Are you a perfectionist? Are any of your close relatives perfectionists? What do you think your parents expect of you?

21. Do you ever feel like you are doomed to failure? Does thinking about the prospects of the future (in regard to job, marriage, family, supporting yourself) make you want to eat?

22. Does it ever get hard, even impossible, to make yourself purge?

23. Do you ever binge even when you know you are not going to be able to purge?

24. Does it seem to you like everyone knows how to cope with life but you, and are you frustrated to see people with less capability than you, seeming to get more out of life than you do?

25. Do you ever enjoy feeling isolated?

26. Do you ever have times when you are completely indifferent to your physical appearance (not washing hair, not brushing teeth, etc.)?

27. What do you think men look for in women?

28. Do you have feelings that everyone you pass on the street is judging your appearance and your actions? Did you have this feeling as a child?

29. Can you remember being especially concerned about your physical appearance as a child?

30. How long do you usually go before starting the bingeing–purging cycle again? Do you notice any progression in your compulsion—do the binges seem to get more frequent or more intense? Do you find that your tolerance for binge foods increases?

31. Have you ever wanted desperately to stop the bingeing–purging cycle, only to find yourself doing it again within a couple of weeks?

32. Do you feel that knowledge of the detrimental effects of these compulsions on the body would help you stop?

III.

Research and Theory

10

Binge Eating: Measurement Problems and a Conceptual Model*

Raymond C. Hawkins II
Pamelia F. Clement

The pattern of compulsive overeating called "bulimia" has been recognized by clinicians for many years (Bruch, 1973; Stunkard, 1959). Boskind-Lodahl and Sirlin (1977), however, triggered a "binge" of research studies as a result of their provocative clinical investigation asserting that bingeing was but one component of a larger behavioral syndrome ("bulimarexia") that was purported to be very prevalent among young women, characterized by alternating periods of binge eating and rigid dieting and accompanied by low self-esteem, poor body image acceptance, and a fear of rejection in heterosexual relationships. (For a review of this literature, see Mitchell & Pyle, 1982; Wardle & Beinart, 1981.)

Despite the *DSM-III* (APA, 1980) diagnostic criteria for bulimia, however, there is still little compelling evidence of a coherent behavioral syndrome (Halmi, Falk, & Schwartz, 1981). In an

*An earlier version of this paper, entitled "Pathways to Bulima," was presented at the Fourteenth Annual Convention of the Association for the Advancement of Behavior Therapy, New York, 1980. Part of the data and conceptualization of this paper are drawn from Pamelia Clement's doctoral dissertation.

earlier study, we reported the development and preliminary construct validation of our Binge Scale, intended to provide more descriptive and quantifiable information about the behavioral and attitudinal parameters of bulimia (Hawkins & Clement, 1980). Over two-thirds of normal-weight college-age females and nearly one-half of the males reported binge-eating occurrences. The severity of binge eating was associated with degree of dieting concern ("restraint," Herman & Mack, 1975) and inversely related to self-image acceptance.

In this chapter, we wish to present some new data replicating and extending the construct validation of the Binge Scale to include additional psychosocial correlates of binge eating, namely, depressive mood and self-perceived social competence/assertiveness in dating situations. We examined these relationships in three primarily female samples of normal-weight college students and in one clinical sample of overweight students treated in a behavioral weight control program (Setty & Hawkins, Note 11.)

To provide a conceptual framework for these data, let us consider three paradigmatic strategies for studying bulimic behavior. The first strategy, following methodological behaviorism, is concerned with the functional analysis of binge-eating behaviors in terms of antecedent–consequent relationships. While we have no empirical data to present from this viewpoint, the model to be presented later in this chapter will address this issue conceptually.

The second strategy, the "psychometric" or "quantitative trait" approach, best describes the rationale for the selection of items for the Binge Scale. These items seemed to lend themselves to a quantitative, continuous measure of the severity of binge eating and thus could be summed accordingly to yield a "total score" for the Binge Scale having satisfactory internal consistency and test–retest reliability (Hawkins & Clement, 1980). The chief advantage of the psychometric, or norm-referenced, approach is that it allows investigation of the bulimia syndrome in a sample of normal-weight and overweight female college students, none of whom ostensibly display clinical psychopathology. One drawback of the psychometric approach is that the widespread prevalence of self-reported binge eating (i.e., two-thirds of college females), while emphasizing pervasive psychosocial processes, seems to belie the clinical significance of binge eating. This approach may be well suited for exploratory research and construct validation studies, but less useful for epidemiological investigations concerned with the detection of clients at risk for serious psychopathology.

The third strategy emphasizes the qualitative, "state-like," and discontinuous nature of bulimic episodes and utilizes a criterion-referencing procedure for assessing prevalence. For example, Garner and Garfinkel (1979) developed the Eating Attitudes Test (EAT) to differentiate a clinical sample of females with anorexia nervosa from samples of normal-weight and overweight females, and from normal-weight males. Other investigators recently have estimated the prevalence of appetite disorders in women on college campuses by utilizing Garner and Garfinkel's (1979) decision rule on an EAT total score in excess of 30 points (e.g., Gelwick, Note 5.) This strategy obviously requires the specification of a clear-cut criterion for the phenomenon or condition. Hospitalization for life-threatening anorexia nervosa constitutes an acceptable criterion for validation of the EAT; however, there is no essential, agreed-upon criterial characteristic for bulimia. Hawkins and Clement (1980) speculated that self-induced vomiting after a binge, which occurs with a frequency of about 5 percent in college normative samples of women, may represent such a criterion for the gorge–purge process.

The present study first delineates, from the psychometric ("quantitative trait") perspective, the psychosocial correlates of binge eating tendencies. It then considers, from the criterion-referenced ("qualitative state") perspective, the differences among binge eaters who do—versus those who do not—report self-induced vomiting after a binge, and between women who obtain EAT scores in excess of 30 versus those with scores of less than 30. (The prevalence of bulimia or appetite disorders from this more restrictive definition will be presented.) Finally, this study offers a conceptual model, the Pathways to Bulimia, that suggests a synthesis of the three paradigmatic strategies just mentioned for the study of bulimia.

Method

Subjects

The subjects in the three normal-weight samples included 231 females, 276 females, and 156 females (the third sample also contained 39 males) drawn from several undergraduate classes. The clinical sample of overweight students, averaging over 40 percent overweight, comprised 86 females participating in a broad-spectrum cognitive–behavioral weight control program (Setty & Hawkins, Note 11.)

Measures

The instruments administered included the following:

1. The nine-item Binge Scale (Hawkins & Clement, 1980)
2. The Eating Attitudes Test (Garner & Garfinkel, 1979), which was subdivided into a restrictive dieting subscale (DIET) and a second subscale (LOCO) that reflected preoccupation with food and fear of loss of control of eating (Clement, Note 1; Garner, Olmsted, Bohr, & Garfinkel, 1982
3. The 12-item Negative Self-Image Scale (Nash & Ormiston, 1978)
4. The Beck Depression Inventory (Beck, 1970)
5. The "neuroticism" scale from the Maudsley Personality Inventory (Jensen, 1958)
6. The Dating and Assertion Questionnaire (Levenson & Gottman, 1978), which yielded two subscales (Dating and Assertion)
7. An experimental measure called the Dating Relationships Questionnaire (Clement, Note 1), which was designed to assess a subject's perception of being "one down" in a dating relationship.

The sample of overweight women received only the Binge Scale. All samples also were administered the dieting Restraint scale (Herman & Mack, 1975). Further information on these instruments is available upon request.

Results and Discussion

Descriptive Characteristics of Binge-Eating Tendencies

Table 10–1 presents the frequencies of responses to the individual items of the Binge Scale for the combined samples of normal-weight females, a group of normal-weight males, and a clinical sample of overweight females.

Approximately 85 percent of normal-weight females reported binge eating, but only 66 percent of the males. A slightly higher

Table 10-1. Frequency Table of Binge Scale Item Responses (scoring weights in parentheses).

Item	Norm. Wgt. Females (N = 663); Freq. %		Norm. Wgt. Males (N = 39); Freq. %		Ovwgt Females (N = 86); Freq. %	
1. Do you ever binge eat?						
a. yes (0)	568	85.7	26	66.7	81	94.2
b. no (0)	95	14.3	13	33.3	5	5.8
2. How often do you binge eat?						
a. seldom (0)	229	38.6	17	65.4	8	9.9
b. once or twice a month (1)	193	32.5	4	15.3	25	30.9
c. once a week (2)	137	23.0	3	11.5	34	42.0
d. almost every day (3)	35	5.9	2	7.8	14	17.3
3. What is the average length of a binge-eating episode?						
a. less than 15 minutes (0)	256	43.1	17	65.4	19	23.5
b. 15 minutes to one hour (1)	276	46.5	7	26.9	42	51.9
c. one hour to four hours (2)	54	9.1	2	7.7	16	19.8
d. more than four hours (3)	8	1.3	0	0.0	4	4.9
4. Which of the following statements best applies to your binge eating?						
a. I eat until I have had enough to satisfy.	325	54.7	19	73.1	23	28.4
b. I eat until my stomach feels full. (1)	177	29.8	4	15.4	18	22.2
c. I eat until my stomach is painfully full. (2)	49	8.3	1	3.8	26	32.1
d. I eat until I can't eat anymore. (3)	43	7.1	2	7.7	14	17.3
5. Do you ever vomit after a binge?						
a. never (0)	553	93.6	25	96.2	78	93.0
b. sometimes (1)	34	5.8	1	3.8	3	3.7
c. usually (2)	0	0.0	0	0.0	0	0.0
d. always (3)	4	.6	0	0.0	0	0.0
6. Which of the following statements applies to your eating behavior when bingeing?						
a. I eat more slowly than usual. (0)	0	0.0	0	0.0	0	0.0
b. I eat about the same as I usually do. (0)	349	58.8	16	61.5	29	35.8
c. I eat very rapidly. (1)	245	41.2	10	38.5	52	64.2
7. How much are you concerned about your binge eating?						
a. not bothered at all (0)	147	24.7	17	65.4	2	2.5
b. bothers me a little (1)	197	33.2	7	26.9	13	16.0
c. moderately concerned (2)	154	25.9	2	7.7	32	39.5
d. a major concern (3)	96	16.2	0	0.0	34	42.0

Table 10-1. (Continued)

Item	Norm. Wgt. Females (N = 663); Freq. %		Norm. Wgt. Males (N = 39); Freq. %		Ovwgt. Females (N = 86); Freq. %	
8. Which best describes your feelings during a binge?						
a. I feel I could control eating if I chose. (0)	331	55.7	17	65.4	26	32.1
b. I feel I have at least some control. (1)	210	35.4	8	30.8	24	29.6
c. I feel completely out of of control. (2)	53	8.9	1	3.8	31	38.3
9. Which of the following describes your feelings during a binge?						
a. I feel fairly neutral, not too concerned. (0)	232	39.1	21	80.8	9	11.1
b. I am moderately upset. (1)	259	43.6	4	15.4	26	22.1
c. I hate myself. (2)	103	17.3	1	3.8	46	56.8
10. Which most accurately describe your feelings after a binge?						
a. not depressed at all (0)	218	36.7	21	80.8	4	4.9
b. mildly depressed (1)	212	35.7	4	15.4	23	28.4
c. moderately depressed (2)	120	20.2	1	3.8	30	37.0
d. very depressed (3)	44	7.4	0	0.0	24	29.6

percentage of the overweight females reported binge eating (94%). These figures are comparable, but slightly higher, than data reported by Hawkins and Clement (1980).

For the normal-weight females, the "modal characteristics" of binge eating were as follows: Binge eating was reported to occur "seldom" or at most "once or twice a month," with a duration of "15 minutes to one hour," with binge eating continuing until the point of "satisfaction" or until the "stomach felt full." Only about 6 percent of normal-weight women reported ever inducing vomiting after a binge. The speed of eating was reported to be the same as "usual." Binge eating bothered these women "a little," but there was a feeling the eating could be controlled if they chose to. After a binge, feelings were reported to be "fairly neutral," "not too concerned," or, at most, "moderately upset." "Mild depression" was reported following the binge, however.

Visual inspection of these frequency data shows that males reported very mild binge-eating tendencies, if indeed the label "binge" is appropriate to describe their behavior at all. Binges occurred "seldom," usually lasted for less than 15 minutes, were concluded when the point of "satisfaction" had been reached, and rarely terminated with vomiting, while the speed of eating was approximately the same as usual. Males were "not bothered at all" by binge episodes, felt they could control eating "if they chose to," were "not too concerned" after a binge, and were "not depressed at all." On the other hand, the clinical sample of overweight women reported more pronounced binge-eating tendencies. The "modal binge" for this group occurred once a week and lasted from 15 minutes to one hour, and eating was terminated only when the stomach was "painfully full." Interestingly, however, the frequency of self-induced vomiting among the clinically obese women was lower than that for the normal-weight women (i.e., 3.7%). Sixty-four percent of the overweight women reported eating very rapidly when they binged, that binge eating was a "major concern," and that they felt "completely out of control," "hated" themselves, and were "moderately depressed," with a substantial minority (approximately 30%) feeling "very depressed" after a binge.

Personality Correlates of Binge-Eating Tendencies

Since 85 percent of the normal-weight women reported binge eating, we were concerned whether this self-attribution would meaningfully differentiate subgroups of subjects' scores on the various personality measures. Table 10–2 presents descriptive statistics for the three samples of normal-weight females, divided according to the answer to the question, "Do you ever binge eat?"

We see that women reporting no binge eating obtained significantly more positive, lower scores on the Negative Self-Image Scale, lower "restraint," lower scores on the Eating Attitudes Test, expressed less fear of loss of control of eating, and tended to be less neurotic and to report more assertiveness and dating competence.

The psychosocial correlates of binge eating are shown in Table 10–3. These data come from Clement's (Note 1) doctoral dissertation sample. We see that the total score on the Binge Scale was significantly positively correlated with dieting restraint. Moreover, binge-eating tendencies were associated with compulsive dieting efforts and weight preoccupation (i.e., DIET scale) and with fear of loss of control of eating (i.e., LOCO scale). In addition, we found that

Table 10–2. Descriptive Statistics for Three Samples of Normal-Weight Females.†

Variable	Group	Sample 1 N	Sample 1 M ± SD	Sample 2 N	Sample 2 M ± SD	Sample 3 N	Sample 3 M ± SD
NSI	Binge	193	7.9 ± 5.8	231	9.4 ± 6.6	128	8.3 ± 5.6
	No binge	36	○5.4 ± 3.9	43	○4.8 ± 3.1	12	6.0 ± 6.6
RSTS	Binge	194	16.2 ± 5.5			129	16.3 ± 6.2
	No binge	36	○11.6 ± 5.9			16	○9.9 ± 5.4
EATTS	Binge	195	16.4 ± 11.1	233	16.8 ± 12.3	131	16.0 ± 10.1
	No binge	36	*11.7 ± 6.6	43	○11.8 ± 7.5	16	*10.3 ± 10.7
DIET	Binge	195	3.7 ± 4.1	233	3.4 ± 4.1	132	3.4 ± 4.0
	No binge	36	2.7 ± 3.6	43	2.6 ± 3.6	16	○1.0 ± 3.9
LOCO	Binge	195	2.1 ± 2.8	233	2.4 ± 2.9	131	1.8 ± 1.9
	No binge	36	*1.1 ± 1.4	43	*1.4 ± 1.1	16	1.5 ± 2.6
WGTPERC	Binge	194	101.4 ± 14.5	232	100.4 ± 11.1		
	No binge	36	97.2 ± 11.4	42	○95.1 ± 6.5		
ASSERT	Binge	183	30.6 ± 5.5			139	27.7 ± 4.9
	No binge	36	○28.0 ± 5.0			16	27.7 ± 3.2
DATING	Binge	183	27.5 ± 4.8			139	27.8 ± 5.2
	No binge	35	○29.8 ± 6.0			16	27.5 ± 4.8
NEUROT	Binge			232	29.0 ± 10.1	130	28.0 ± 10.7
	No binge			42	○24.5 ± 9.9	16	23.9 ± 12.6

*p < .05 (t-test)
○p < .01 (t-test)
△p < .001 (t-test)
†Subjects are subdivided according to whether they "binge" or have "no binge."

Table 10-3. Pearson Correlations among the Various Measures of Compulsive Eating, Perceptions of Dating Self-Confidence, Assertiveness, and Body Weight (N = 204).*

Measures	RESTR	DIET	LOCO	NSI	BDI	DRQTS	ASSERT	DATING	WGTPERC
BSTS	.61‡	.26‡	.44‡	.45‡	.15**	.13	-.13	-.20†	.28‡
RESTR		.54‡	.34‡	.63‡	.17**	.23‡	-.07	-.18†	.40‡
DIET			.20†	.32‡	.08	.03	.04	-.06	.12
LOCO				.38‡	.21†	.14**	-.15**	-.14**	.05
NSI					.37‡	.30‡	-.28‡	-.37‡	.40‡
BDI						.24‡	-.33‡	-.22‡	.16**
DRQTS							-.33‡	-.36‡	.17**
ASSERT								.54‡	.04
DATING									-.14**

*See Clement, Note 1.

**Significant at the .05 level, two-tailed test.
†Significant at the .01 level, two-tailed test.
‡Significant at the .001 level, two-tailed test.

binge eating was correlated with dissatisfaction with physical appearance (i.e., NSI scale), and there was a modest but significant relationship to depression (BDI scale). Finally, there were significant intercorrelations among these indicants of compulsive eating tendencies (i.e., BSTS, RESTR, LOCO) and various measures of self-perceived social competence (i.e., ASSERT and DATING). Divergent validity is suggested, however, in that compulsive dieting efforts and weight preoccupation (i.e., the DIET scale) were uncorrelated with assertiveness and self-perceived dating competence.

Table 10–4 presents Pearson correlations among the various measures from a pilot sample of females (N = 161, although only 106 subjects had complete data), providing a cross-validation and replication of these personality correlates of binge eating.

A series of hierarchical stepwise multiple-regression analyses (Nie, Hull, Jenkins, Steinbrenner, and Bent, 1975) were performed on these data, revealing that Negative Self-Image, Depression, Assertiveness, and Dating scales all accounted for significant amounts of variance in Binge Scale scores and fear of loss of control (LOCO) scores, after controlling statistically for excess body weight percentage and dieting tendencies (DIET scale scores).

These relationships are quite interesting, since they expand the nomological network for the bulimia syndrome to include the "social meaning" context of binge eating for women. It is undoubtedly the case that any individual will show counterregulaton or reactance to rigid diets; however, overeating or binge episodes become a problematic, recurring lifestyle when accompanied by a negative body image. This combination may bring about a perseveration or "reverberation" of a positive feedback loop, that is the gorge–purge cycle, as theorized by Boskind-Lodahl & Sirlin (1977). The central contribution of body image dissatisfaction to a related appetite disorder, anorexia nervosa, has long been recognized (Bruch, 1973). These data suggest the importance of negative affect for the body as a critical diagnostic characteristic of bulimia as well. Binge-eating tendencies, rigid dieting tendencies, and body image dissatisfaction emerge as three separate but interrelated theoretical constructs. The next stage of research will need to address the causal mechanisms interrelating these components of the bulimia syndrome.

Figure 10–1 presents one model for binge eating, hypothesizing a weak causal ordering of these psychosocial components suitable for path analysis (McCrary, Note 10). According to this model, being overweight or unassertive causes one to develop a negative

Table 10–4. Pearson Correlations among the Various Measures of Compulsive Eating, Perceptions of Dating Self-Confidence, Assertiveness, and Body Weight (N = 106).

MEASURES	RESTR	EATTS	DIET	LOCO	NSI	DRQTS	ASSERT	DATING	WGTPERC
BSTS	.68†	.49†	.33†	.48†	.66†	.38†	-.38†	-.30**	.28**
RESTR		.68†	.56†	.54†	.71†	.39†	-.24*	-.21*	.29**
EATTS			.79†	.55†	.53†	.21*	-.22*	-.22*	.16
DIET				.19	.29**	.02	-.05	.01	.15
LOCO					.64†	.49†	-.40†	-.44†	.21*
NSI						.57†	-.51†	-.49†	.29**
DRQTS							-.44†	-.53†	.13
ASSERT								.66†	-.10
DATING									-.18

*Significant at the .05 level, two-tailed test.
**Significant at the .01 level, two-tailed test.
†Significant at the .001 level, two-tailed test.

Figure 10-1.   A Restricted Model for Binge Eating, Hypothesizing a Weak Causal Ordering of Psychosocial Correlates.

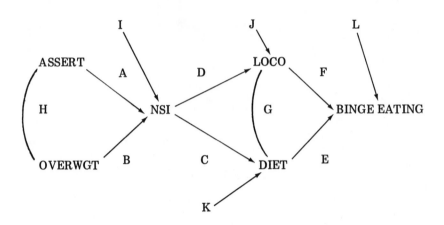

For the large sample (N = 231), this model as a whole was statistically significant (chi-square = 33.9, $p < .01$). For the pilot sample (N = 106), the model was also significant (chi-square = 29.44, $p < .01$), although many of the hypothesized paths were not significant in this sample. (From A.R. McCrary, Pathways to binge eating, unpublished manuscript, The University of Texas at Austin, 1981; See McCrary, Note 10.)

self-image. A negative self-image causes the individual to become either afraid of losing control of her impulses to overeat (LOCO) or to become preoccupied with food and dieting (DIET). Increases in dieting or in fear of loss of control eventually lead to binge eating. Separate path analyses were performed on data from the two correlation matrices (Tables 10–3 and 10–4). For the larger sample (N = 231), each of the hypothesized paths was significant. For the pilot sample (N = 106), however, only the paths connecting ASSERT and NSI (A) and NSI and LOCO (D) were significant. One nonhypothesized path between NSI and binge eating was also significant. Despite the lack of replicability of this initial model as a whole, the paths connecting ASSERT and NSI, and NSI and LOCO appear to be reliable, suggesting the importance of these psychological factors (unassertiveness, negative self-image, fear of loss of control of eating) antecedent to binge eating, rather than to being overweight per se (McCrary, Note 10.)

Criterion-Referenced Distinctions

Although the psychometric approach is undoubtedly well suited for exploratory research, clinical applications of these instruments measuring binge tendencies concern the detection of clients at risk for serious psychopathology. We were skeptical of 85 percent of normal-weight female undergraduates displaying clinical bulimia; therefore, we decided to estimate the prevalence of clinically significant appetite disorders by means of more restrictive criteria. We decided to use the presence of self-induced vomiting and scores on the Eating Attitudes Test in excess of 30, since Garner & Garfinkel (1979) showed that this cut-off score significantly differentiated normal-weight female controls from females with clinical anorexia nervosa. We also predicted that subjects scoring at least 30 on the EAT and reporting self-induced vomiting tendencies would obtain higher scores on the various personality test measures tapping the components of the bulimia syndrome.

The data pertaining to these predictions are presented in Table 10–5 and Table 10–6. Between 11 and 15 percent of the normal-weight females obtained EAT scores of at least 30. This range of frequencies is consistent with the 13-percent figure reported by Garner and Garfinkel (1979) in the validation study of the EAT. Those subjects scoring at least 30 on the EAT obtained significantly higher negative self-image scores and showed stronger binge-eating tendencies, more dieting "restraint," more neuroticism, and more depression relative to those women who had EAT scores less than 30 (Table 10–5).

If one assumes that self-induced vomiting is a pathognomonic sign for bulimia, then about 6 percent of the normal-weight females in these samples were clinically at risk for the gorge–purge syndrome. An examination of Table 10–6 reveals that vomiters obtained significantly higher Negative Self-Image scores in two of the three samples and reported significantly stronger binge-eating tendencies, more dieting "restraint," higher EAT scores (especially on the LOCO subscale), and more neuroticism.

Although these findings are consistent with predictions that EAT scores of at least 30 and reported self-induced vomiting are criterial characteristics of appetite disorders such as bulimia, there are some problems meriting caution: (1) on both the EAT and the Binge Scale, items tapping self-induced vomiting shared very little common variance with other items and (2) the fact that subjects obtaining EAT scores exceeding 30 also report more severe compul-

Table 10-5. Descriptive Statistics for Three Samples of Normal-Weight Females.†

Variable	Group	Sample 1		Sample 2		Sample 3	
		N	M ± SD	N	M ± SD	N	M ± SD
NSI	Lo EAT	206	6.7 ± 4.7	236	7.6 ± 5.6	127	7.3 ± 5.4
	Hi EAT	23	°14.8 ± 7.7	39	°15.4 ± 6.6	17	°12.1 ± 6.8
BSTS	Lo EAT	203	4.9 ± 3.8	236	5.1 ± 4.1	139	5.3 ± 4.1
	Hi EAT	23	°10.3 ± 3.9	39	°9.8 ± 5.0	17	°9.3 ± 5.4
RSTS	Lo EAT	207	14.7 ± 5.5			133	14.8 ± 6.1
	Hi EAT	23	°22.4 ± 3.5			16	°22.3 ± 4.7
DIET	Lo EAT	208	2.8 ± 3.3	238	2.1 ± 2.7	134	2.5 ± 2.5
	Hi EAT	23	°10.7 ± 3.8	39	°10.3 ± 4.4	17	°10.2 ± 5.0
LOCO	Lo EAT	208	1.5 ± 1.9	238	1.5 ± 1.8	133	1.9 ± 2.3
	Hi EAT	23	°6.4 ± 4.0	39	°6.2 ± 3.8	17	°3.6 ± 3.1
WGTPERC	Lo EAT	207	100.4 ± 13.9	236	99.2 ± 10.8		
	Hi EAT	23	104.2 ± 16.0	39	101.5 ± 10.4		
ASSERT	Lo EAT	197	28.6 ± 5.0			143	27.9 ± 4.7
	Hi EAT	21	*26.3 ± 6.1			17	26.8 ± 5.6
DATING	Lo EAT	197	28.1 ± 5.0			143	27.9 ± 5.1
	Hi EAT	21	*21.5 ± 5.3			17	26.8 ± 6.1
NEUROT	Lo EAT			234	27.6 ± 10.0	133	26.8 ± 10.8
	Hi EAT			39	°32.8 ± 10.2	17	*33.1 ± 10.3
BDI	Lo EAT	206	8.1 ± 5.7				
	Hi EAT	23	°12.1 ± 5.6				

†Subjects are subdivided according to whether their score on the Eating Attitude Test was at least 30 ("Hi EAT") vs. less than 30 ("Lo EAT").
*p < .05 (t-test)
°p < .01 (t-test)
△p < .001 (t-test)

242

Table 10–6. Descriptive Statistics for Three Samples of Normal Weight Females.†

Variable	Group	Sample 1 N	Sample 1 M ± SD	Sample 2 N	Sample 2 M ± SD	Sample 3 N	Sample 3 M ± SD
NSI	No Vomit	196	7.8 ± 5.7	227	9.0 ± 6.3	131	7.6 ± 5.8
	Vomit	15	9.0 ± 5.4	12	○13.7 ± 9.3	13	*10.5 ± 4.7
BSTS (no #4)	No Vomit	198	5.7 ± 3.8	228	6.3 ± 4.0	127	6.1 ± 4.1
	Vomit	15	*7.7 ± 4.9	13	○12.5 ± 6.8	13	*8.2 ± 4.0
RSTS	No Vomit	197	15.7 ± 5.5			138	15.3 ± 6.5
	Vomit	15	*18.9 ± 5.9			11	*19.5 ± 3.6
EATTS	No Vomit	198	15.8 ± 10.8	228	15.9 ± 11.5	137	14.8 ± 10.3
	Vomit	15	19.9 ± 10.8	13	○28.4 ± 17.7	13	19.5 ± 9.0
DIET	No Vomit	198	3.6 ± 4.0	228	3.1 ± 4.0	138	3.0 ± 3.9
	Vomit	15	5.3 ± 4.9	13	○7.0 ± 5.0	13	4.1 ± 2.7
LOCO	No Vomit	198	2.0 ± 2.8	228	2.2 ± 2.7	137	1.6 ± 2.0
	Vomit	15	2.7 ± 2.0	13	○4.5 ± 4.4	13	*3.0 ± 1.9
WGTPERC	No Vomit	197	100.7 ± 14.2	227	99.9 ± 10.9		
	Vomit	15	106.1 ± 17.8	13	104.4 ± 14.4		
ASSERT	No Vomit	187	27.9 ± 4.9			147	28.1 ± 4.7
	Vomit	13	*31.4 ± 5.5			13	*25.7 ± 4.3
DATING	No Vomit	187	27.6 ± 5.0			147	28.2 ± 5.0
	Vomit	13	28.6 ± 3.7			13	○23.6 ± 5.6
NEUROT	No Vomit			226	28.5 ± 10.3	140	27.1 ± 11.0
	Vomit			13	*33.4 ± 6.6	10	*33.0 ± 8.4

†Subjects are subdivided according to whether they "vomit" or show "no vomit."
*p < .05 (t-test)
○p < .01 (t-test)
△p < .001 (t-test)

sive overeating tendencies (on the Binge Scale) conceptually calls into question the relationship between anorexia nervosa and bulimia, at least in the subclinical manifestations in a college population. Earlier in this report we argued that the EAT does not distinguish compulsive dieting tendencies and weight preoccupation from fear of loss of control of overeating impulses (i.e., the DIET versus LOCO subscale distinction). Further research clearly is indicated to determine the extent to which anorexia nervosa and bulimia share common behavioral, cognitive, or physiological mechanisms (cf. Casper, Ekert, Halmi, Goldberg, & Davis, 1980; Garfinkel, Moldofsky, & Garner, 1980; Russell, 1979; Strober, 1981).

Pathways to Bulimia: A Conceptual Model

Figure 10–2 presents a conceptual framework that may permit a synthesis of the three paradigmatic strategies for studying bulimia (i.e., the psychometric "trait" approach, the criterion-referenced "state-like" perspective, and the functional analysis of discrete binge-eating behavioral episodes in terms of long- and short-term antecedent conditions.)[1] More important, this figure shows measures (both published and unpublished scales) that may be useful operationalizations of these conceptual processes.

The first figure represents two of the pathways to bulimia:

[1]Figure 10–2 represents two of the pathways to late-adolescence-onset bulimia: "negative psychosocial processes" and "pathogenic predispositions and resultant personality." We start out by postulating certain normative psychosocial processes that are ubiquitous in our Western, postindustrialized culture for both males and females, but especially salient for females. Chief among these processes are social-role stereotypes, namely, that thinness is socially desirable and that obesity is undesirable. It is relatively easy to elicit these negative sterotypical attitudes toward obese individuals, using semantic differential scales (Doell & Hawkins, Note 3). Although the negative obese stereotype is pervasive in our culture, in our research we have found that individual differences in "masculine" (instrumental) and "feminine" (expressive) traits (Spence & Helmreich, 1978) may relate to dieting behavior and thus serve as one mediating link for the "personal compliance" with the cultural expectation for weight-consciousness that is so prevalent among many young women today (Hawkins, Turell, & Jackson, 1983). A related cultural prescription is the use of certain foods as sources of comfort during periods of emotional stress (e.g., for anxiety avoidance). Individual differences in susceptibility to such "mood eating" can be measured and correlated with changes in eating behavior and body weight in short-term longitudinal studies (e.g., Jackson & Hawkins, Note 8). Useful measures of a woman's personal compliance with the slimness ideal include the Restraint Scale (Herman & Mack, 1975), the DIET subscale of the EAT (Clement & Hawkins, Note 1), and behavioral measures of dieting (Hawkins & Wilkenfield, Note 7; Hawkins, 1979).

Figure 10-2. Pathways to Bulimia, Part 1.

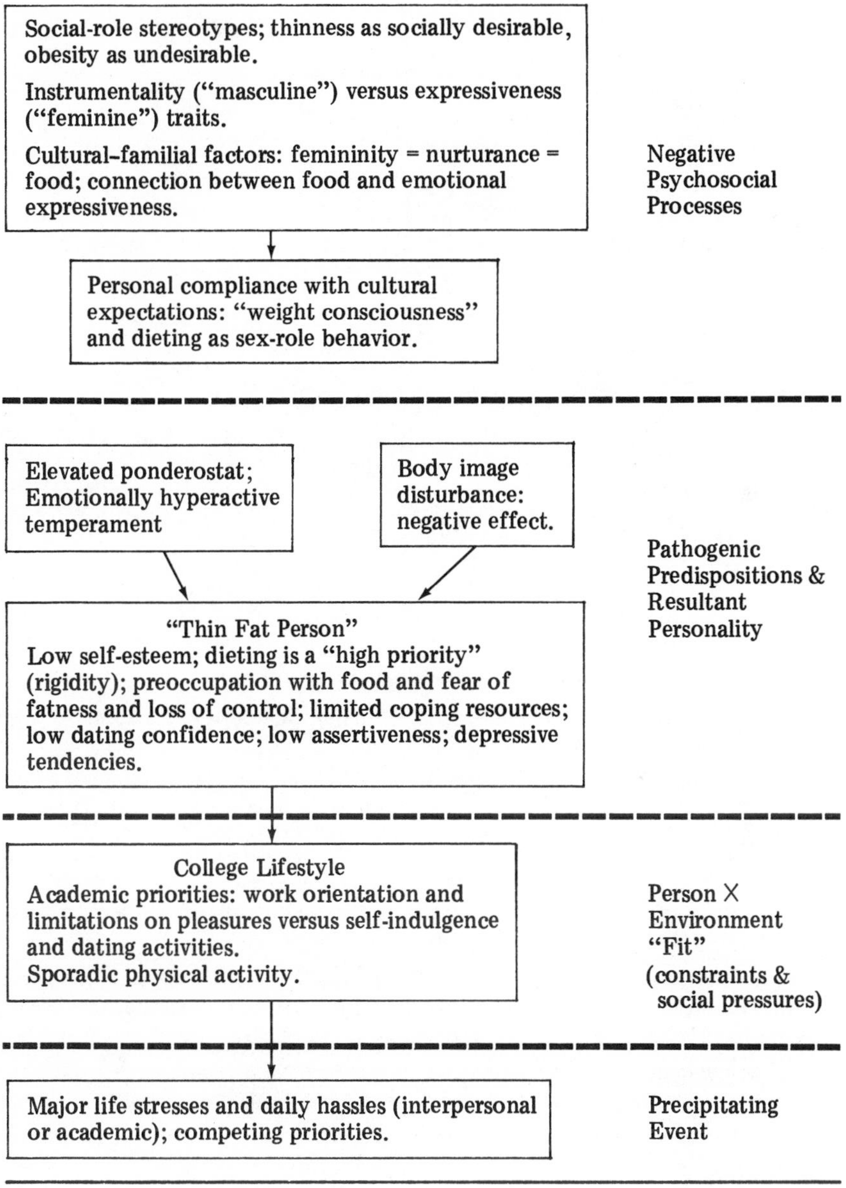

Social-role stereotypes; thinness as socially desirable, obesity as undesirable. Instrumentality ("masculine") versus expressiveness ("feminine") traits. Cultural–familial factors: femininity = nurturance = food; connection between food and emotional expressiveness.	Negative Psychosocial Processes

Personal compliance with cultural expectations: "weight consciousness" and dieting as sex-role behavior.

Elevated ponderostat; Emotionally hyperactive temperament Body image disturbance: negative effect. "Thin Fat Person" Low self-esteem; dieting is a "high priority" (rigidity); preoccupation with food and fear of fatness and loss of control; limited coping resources; low dating confidence; low assertiveness; depressive tendencies.	Pathogenic Predispositions & Resultant Personality

College Lifestyle Academic priorities: work orientation and limitations on pleasures versus self-indulgence and dating activities. Sporadic physical activity.	Person X Environment "Fit" (constraints & social pressures)

Major life stresses and daily hassles (interpersonal or academic); competing priorities.	Precipitating Event

"normative psychosocial processes" and "pathogenic predispositions and resultant personality." We start out by postulating certain normative psychosocial processes that are ubiquitous in our Western, postindustrialized culture for both males and females, but especially salient for females. Chief among these processes are social-role stereotypes, namely that thinness is socially desirable and that obesity is undesirable. It is relatively easy to elicit these negative stereotypical attitudes toward obese individuals (Doell & Hawkins, Note 3). Although the negative obese stereotype is pervasive in our culture, in our research we have found that individual differences in masculinity-femininity traits may relate to dieting behavior and thus serve as one mediating link for the "personal compliance" with the cultural expectation for weight-consciousness, which is so prevalent among many young women today (Hawkins, Turell, & Jackson, 1983).

Note that we are assuming that these normative psychosocial processes contribute to a more problematic path when there exist in addition certain "pathogenic predispositions." These predispositions may be either one or both of two sorts:

1. Biological: an elevated "ponderostat" (Nisbett, 1972) or "set point" for body fat (Hawkins, 1977, 1980), perhaps accompanied by an emotionally labile temperament (Strober, 1981)
2. Cognitive: a body image disturbance with its perceptual distortion and self-loathing, which may develop around the time of pubescence (Stunkard & Mendelson, 1967) and may predispose an individual to difficulties in permanently maintaining a "normal" weight in adulthood.

A particular personality pattern—called the "thin fat person" by Hilde Bruch (1973)—may result from these pathogenic predispositions coacting with the normative psychosocial processes. The personality attributes include low self-esteem dieting "restraint" (Herman & Polivy, 1975) with decreased meal frequency (Hawkins, 1979), preoccupation with food and a fear of loss of control of eating, limited coping resources (Hawkins, Note 6), and perceived incompetence in social situations such as dating or when assertiveness is appropriate. Depressive tendencies, as in Leibowitz & Klein's (1979) concept of "hysteroid dysphoria," may recur sporadically, particularly at times of real or threatened interpersonal rejection. Most of these personality correlates we have described already.

But where is the "trigger" or environmental stress that pre-cipitates the binge-eating episode? Figure 10–3 presents a contin-uation of the pathways-to-bulimia flowchart, in which we see that the "person × environment fit" (the constraints and social pres-sures) may set the occasion for a particular precipitating event and a faulty cognitive appraisal that may flip the switch for the young woman to enter the gorge–purge interactional cycle.

We have begun to assess the nature of the "person × environ-ment fit" and the importance of the college lifestyle. In all likeli-hood the college lifestyle may pose a particular tension between work orientation and dating concerns for the late-adolescent fe-male. The range of pleasurable activities experienced may be lim-ited and/or sporadically indulged in an "all-or-nothing" fashion (Doell & Hawkins, 1982). Unpleasant life events (Sarason, John-son, & Siegel, 1978) and "daily hassles" (Coyne & Lazarus, Note 2) in the form of interpersonal problems—such as rejections in ro-mantic relationships or academic difficulties—then may precipi-tate overeating mediated by a faulty cognitive appraisal of the

Figure 10-3. Pathways to Bulimia, Part 2.

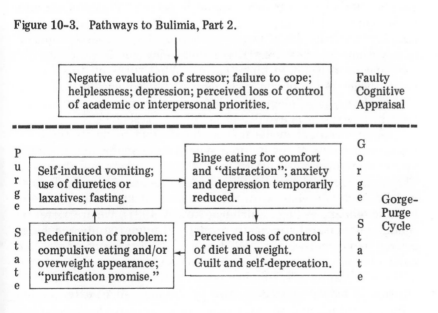

stressor. Thus, the person perceives a loss of control over academic or interpersonal priorities along with thoughts that "Eating will make me feel better," "Who else cares about me, anyway?" and "I might as well eat."

To complete the description of this flowchart, depending largely upon clinical observation (which hopefully would be amendable to cognitive–behavioral functional analysis, despite the secrecy of the activity) (Hawkins & Wilkenfield, Note 7; Johnson & Larson, Note 9), we postulate that binge eating may serve somewhat of a comforting and also "distracting" function, in that anxiety and depression from interpersonal or academic stress may be temporarily reduced during the gorging phase of the cycle. Of course, this reduction of anxiety and distraction from life problems is temporary and is followed by a perception of loss of control over dieting and weight priority, with feelings of guilt and self-deprecation after the binge. The young woman then may make the logical error of redefining her problem as being the uncontrolled overeating itself, or the overweight appearance, rather than the original interpersonal or academic difficulty. She then makes what we call the "purification promise": "If only I could lose 20 pounds, or if only I would never eat any more sweets, then all my problems would be solved." This promise may be accompanied by (or preceded by) purging efforts, such as self-induced vomiting, use of laxatives or diuretics, and fasts. Unfortunately some of these restrictive diets may set the occasion for reactance and renewed binge eating. What turns off this gorge–purge cycle? Some of the cycle may be physiologically self-limiting; however, psychologically, the cycle may persist until the external life stressor is avoided or no longer present.

This conceptual model makes the attempt to clarify the theoretical constructs of the bulimia syndrome to enable more systematic and programmatic efforts by basic researchers and clinicians. The framework also implies different points and strategies for prevention and intervention in the development and maintenance of bulimic tendencies (e.g., Fairburn, Note 4, 1981). We are currently conducting naturalistic, short-term longitudinal studies of binge eating in normal-weight and overweight samples of women. Of particular interest is scrutinizing discrete binge episodes in terms of the topography of eating behaviors, such as the nutritional composition of foods ingested as well as the antecedent external and internal stimuli and consequent events (Hawkins & Wilkenfield, Note 7).

Reference Notes

1. Clement, P. F. Correlates of binge eating among college women. Unpublished Ph.D. dissertation, The University of Texas at Austin, 1980. Separate factor analyses (SPSS, PA1 type) of EAT items in two samples of undergraduate women yielded similar factors entitled DIET (i.e., dieting behavior, avoidance of carbohydrates, etc.) and LOCO (i.e., fear of loss of control of eating, eating binges, etc.). The EAT items comprising these essentially nonoverlapping subscales are listed in the chapter appendix.

2. Coyne, J. C. & Lazarus, R. The ipsative–normative framework for the longitudinal study of stress. Paper presented at the American Psychological Association annual convention, New York, 1980.

3. Doell, S. R., & Hawkins, R. C., II. Obesity, slimness, and self-serving bias: A semantic differential analysis. Paper presented at the American Psychological Association convention, Los Angeles, 1981.

4. Fairburn, C. G. The place of a cognitive behavioral approach in the management of bulimia. Paper presented at the Toronto Conference on Anorexia Nervosa, Clarke Psychiatric Institute, September, 1981.

5. Gelwick, B. Incidence and severity of eating disorders on two campuses. Paper presented at the American Psychological Association convention, Montreal, 1980.

6. Hawkins, R. C., II. Binge eating as coping behavior. Paper presented at the annual convention of the American Psychological Association, Washington, D.C., 1982.

7. Hawkins, R. C., II, & Wilkenfield, J. Ingestive behaviors of individuals reporting binge eating tendencies. Paper presented at the convention of the Association for the Advancement of Behavior Therapy, Toronto, 1981.

8. Jackson, L. J., & Hawkins, R. C., II. Stress related overeating among college students: Development of a Mood Eating Scale. Paper presented at the annual convention of the Southwestern Psychological Association, Oklahoma City, 1980.

9. Johnson, C., & Larson, R. Anorexia nervosa in the context of daily experiences. Paper presented at the annual convention of the American Psychological Association, Los Angeles, 1981.

10. McCrary, A. R. Pathways to binge eating. Unpublished manuscript, The University of Texas at Austin, 1981. This paper presents the findings of path analyses for the correlational data of the present study. As a caveat for these analyses, it should be acknowledged that it is quite difficult to determine causality when dealing with variables that are measured at one point in

time and have no intrinsic causal ordering. Longitudinal data are needed.

11. Setty, R. M., & Hawkins, R. C., II. Factors predicting success in a broad-spectrum behavioral weight control program after treatment and at follow-up. Paper presented at the American Psychological Association convention, Montreal, 1980.

References

American Psychiatric Association. *Diagnostic and Statistical Manual of Mental Disorders,* 3rd. ed. Washington, D.C.: American Psychiatric Association, 1980.

Beck, A. T. Depression: Causes and treatment. Philadelphia: University of Pennsylvania Press, 1970.

Boskind-Lodahl, M., & Sirlin, J. The gorging–purging syndrome. *Psychology Today,* 1977, *11,* 50.

Bruch, H. *Eating Disorders.* New York: Basic Books, 1973.

Casper, R. C., Ekert, E. D., Halmi, K. A., Goldberg, S. C., & Davis, J. M. Bulimia: Its incidence and clinical importance in patients with anorexia nervosa. *Archives of General Psychiatry,* 1980, *37,* 1030–1034.

Doell, S. R., & Hawkins, R. C., II. Pleasures and pounds: An exploratory study. *Addictive Behaviors,* 1982, *1,* 65–69.

Fairburn, C. A cognitive behavioral approach to the treatment of bulimia. *Psychological Medicine,* 1981, *11,* 707–711.

Garfinkel, P. E., Moldofsky, H., & Garner, D. M. The heterogeneity of anorexia nervosa: Bulimia as a distinct subgroup. *Archives of General Psychiatry,* 1980, *37,* 1036–1040.

Garner, D. M., & Garfinkel, P. E. The eating attitude test: An index of the symptoms of anorexia nervosa. *Psychological Medicine,* 1979, *9*(2), 273–279.

Garner, D. M., Olmstead, M. P., Bohr, Y., & Garfinkel, P. E. The Eating Attitudes Test: Psychometric features and clinical correlates. *Psychological Medicine,* 1982, 871–878.

Halmi, K. A., Falk, J. R., & Schwartz, E. Binge-eating and vomiting: A survey of a college population. *Psychological Medicine,* 1981, *11,* 697–706.

Hawkins, R. C., II. Learning to initiate and terminate meals: Theoretical, clinical and developmental aspects. In L. M. Barker, M. Best, & M. Domjan (eds.), *Learning Mechanisms in Food Selection.* Waco, Tex.: Baylor University Press, 1977.

Hawkins, R. C., II. Meal/snack frequencies in college students: A normative study. *Behavioural Psychotherapy,* 1979, *7,* 85–90.

Hawkins, R. C., II. A diathesis-stress model for the study of psychosocial risks: The prediction of infantile obesity. In Sawin, D. B., Hawkins, R. C., II, Walker, L. O., & Penticuff, J. H. (eds.), *Exceptional Infant,* Vol.

4. *Psychosocial Risks in Infant–Environment Transactions.* New York: Brunner/Mazel, 1980.

Hawkins, R. C., II, & Clement, P. F. Development and construct validation of a measure of binge eating tendencies. *Addictive Behaviors,* 1980, *5,* 219–226.

Hawkins, R. C., II, Turell, S., & Jackson, L. J. Desirable and undesirable masculine and feminine traits in relation to students' dieting tendencies and body image dissatisfaction. *Sex Roles,* 1983, *9,* 705–713.

Herman, C. P., & Mack, D. Restrained and unrestrained eating. *Journal of Personality,* 1975, *43,* 647–660.

Jensen, A. R. The Maudsley Personality Inventory. *Acta Psychologica,* 1958, *14,* 314–325.

Leibowitz, M. R., & Klein, D. F. Hysteroid dysphoria. *Psychiatric Clinics of North America,* 1979, *2,* 555–575.

Levenson, R. W., & Gottman, J. M. Toward the assessment of social competence. *Journal of Consulting and Clinical Psychology,* 1978, *46,* 453–462.

Mitchell, J. E., & Pyle, R. L. The bulimic syndrome in normal weight individuals—a review. *International Journal of Eating Disorders,* 1982, *1,* 61–73.

Nash, T. D. & Ormiston, L. H. *Taking charge of your weight and well being,* Palo Alto, Calif.: Bull Publishing Co., 1978.

Nie, N. H., Hull, C. H., Jenkins, J. G., Steinbrenner, K., & Bent, D. H. *Statistical Package for the Social Sciences,* 2nd ed. New York: McGraw-Hill, 1975.

Nisbett, R. E. Hunger, obesity, and the ventro-medial hypothalamus. *Psychological Review,* 1972, *79,* 433–453.

Russell, G. Bulimia nervosa: An ominous variant of anorexia nervosa. *Psychological Medicine,* 1979, *9,* 429–448.

Sarason, I. G., Johnson, J. H., & Siegel, J. M. Assessing the impact of life changes: Development of the Life Experiences Survey. *Journal of Consulting and Clinical Psychology,* 1978, *46,* 932–946.

Spence, J. T., & Helmreich, R. L. *Masculinity and Femininity: Their Psychological Dimensions, Correlates, and Antecedents.* Austin, Tex.: The University of Texas at Austin Press, 1978.

Strober, M. The significance of bulimia in juvenile anorexia nervosa: An exploration of possible etiological factors. *International Journal of Eating Disorders,* 1981, *1,* 28–43.

Stunkard, A. J. Eating patterns of obese persons. *Psychiatric Quarterly,* 1959, *33,* 284–292.

Stunkard, A. J., & Mendelson, M. Obesity and body image: I. Characteristics of disturbances in the body image of some obese persons. *American Journal of Psychiatry,* 1967, *123,* 1296–1300.

Wardle, J., & Beinart, H. Binge eating: A theoretical review. *British Journal of Clinical Psychology,* 1981, *20,* 97–109.

Appendix to Chapter 10

Subscales of the Eating Attitudes Test
Resulting from Item-Factor Analyses*

DIET Subscale of the EAT

1. Am aware of the caloric content of foods that I eat.
2. Particularly avoid foods with a high carbohydrate content (e.g., bread, potatoes, rice, etc.).
3. Exercise strenuously to burn off calories.
4. Avoid foods with sugar in them.
5. Eat diet foods.
6. Feel uncomfortable after eating sweets.
7. Engage in dieting behavior.

LOCO Subscale of the EAT

1. Become anxious prior to eating.
2. Find myself preoccupied with foods.
3. Have gone on eating binges where I feel that I may not be able to stop.
4. Feel that food controls my life.
5. Display self-control around food. [*Reverse scored.*]
6. Give too much time and thought to food.
7. Have the impulse to vomit after meals.

*Eating Attitudes Test from Garner, D. M. and Garfinkel, P. E. The Eating Attitudes Test: An index of the symptoms of anorexia nervosa. *Psychological Medicine,* 1979, *9,* 273-279. For explanation of item factor analyses, see Clement, Note 1.

11

A Functional Analysis of Binge Episodes

William J. Fremouw
Nicholas E. Heyneman

The establishment of bulimia as a *DSM-III* (APA, 1980) diagnostic category acknowledges the slowly emerging recognition that binge eating is a distinct, serious eating disorder that exists across the spectrum of body weights. The three defining characteristics of bulimia are (1) recurrent episodes of ingesting large amounts of food within a short period of time, (2) with accompanying fears of not being able to stop, and (3) depressed mood and self-deprecating thoughts following the eating binges. Preliminary studies estimate that bulimia is present in 47 percent of individuals with anorexia nervosa (Casper, Eckert, Halmi, Goldberg, & Davis, 1980), 23 percent of obese individuals (Gormally, 1980), and 5 percent of normal-weight college students (Spencer & Fremouw, 1980). More recent research on the definition and prevalence of bulimia is presented elsewhere in this book.

Although clear agreement about the prevalence of bulimia has not emerged yet from the research, there is concurrence about the seriousness of bulimia as a complication in the treatment of the obese (Stunkard, 1976; Wilson, 1976) as well as a risk to health among the nonobese (Russell, 1979). The importance of explaining and treating this eating disorder has produced a range of theories of bulimia ranging from neurological and dynamic to cognitive and psychosocial approaches that are discussed in this book.

While much work has begun on factors that predispose a *person* to experience bulimia, little work has appeared on the actual problem *behavior* itself, the binge episode. A behavioral approach to binge eating emphasizes the factors that maintain the problem behavior and deemphasizes the more general etiological factors. Based on the assessment model introduced by Kanfer & Saslow (1969), a functional analysis of a behavior assesses the antecedent conditions of the binge episode, the characteristics of the binge episode, and the consequences of the episode to determine a functional relationship with binge eating. The antecedent conditions include environmental stimuli such as time, place, and other people, plus intrapersonal stimuli such as perceived hunger, stress, emotionality, and cognitions. Consequences include attention from others and changes in stress, emotionality, hunger, or cognitions. Careful analysis of the antecedents and consequences of a binge episode are the first step in controlling the problem through the manipulation of these variables. If a factor such as stress is demonstrated to increase the probability of a binge episode, then interventions can be directed either to reduce the amount of stress experienced, to remove this antecedent, or to learn new means of coping with stress, such as physical exercise, which is a response incompatible to binge eating. The goal of functional analyses of problem behaviors is to identify variables that can be manipulated to change the rate, intensity, or duration of the binge behavior.

Preliminary Research

Because a functional analysis is the first step in behavioral treatment, several researchers have begun to organize data into a functional analytic framework. In Chapter 10, Hawkins and Clement's final two steps in their analysis of pathways to bulimia (Figure 10–2) describe antecedents to a binge episode. Precipitating events such as major life changes and daily stresses are speculated to lead to faulty cognitive appraisal (Figure 10–3). The person negatively evaluates the stressor, feels helpless, and then experiences depression. These feelings of helplessness and depression are presumed to precipitate the binge-eating episode as a distraction from the stressors and as a means to reduce depression. The immediate consequences for binge eating are assumed to be the positive reinforcement from the taste of the food and the negative reinforcement from the reduction of depression through eating. However, negative cognitions then are experienced as the person becomes aware of the amount of excess food consumed, its effects on his/her weight, and the failure to maintain the diet. These perceptions lead to feelings of guilt and self-deprecation, which are the antecedents for a period of fasting or purging to reduce the negative consequences of the previous binge episode.

While consistent with clinical observations of the binge cycle, this formulation is based on general observations by binge eaters. A systematic, finely detailed analysis of the immediate antecedents and consequences of a binge episode is needed for a more definite functional analysis. Some of the suggested variables await empirical demonstration, such as the proposal that increased stress precipitates the binge or that depression is the emotional antecedent for bingeing. The pathways-to-bulimia model offers a rich heuristic framework for further, more in-depth research on each of the potential factors associated with bulimia.

To identify the specific antecedents and consequences of binge episodes, Loro and Orleans (1981) employed a structured self-report questionnaire administered to 280 obese adults admitted to a residential treatment program. Their retrospective descriptions of their typical binge-eating episodes lead to the following conclusions: Bingeing generally occurs in private, with specific, high-calorie, favorite foods, following stressful events, and the bingeing produces negative emotions and cognitions. The binge episode is generally 15 to 60 minutes with 1000 to 10,000 calories consumed.

The consequences of bingeing include positive reinforcement from the enjoyment of the food and negative reinforcement from the reduction of negative emotional states such as anger, depression, or boredom. Sometimes bingeing is reinforced by the attention, albeit often negative, from significant others.

While those forms of reinforcement appear to maintain the binge-eating behavior, Loro and Orleans (1981) report that about one-half of their sample frequently felt upset and angry, and one-third reported hating themselves after a binge. Apparently the immediate reinforcement derived from the taste of the food and the reduction of negative emotions is more controlling than the eventual experience of negative feelings about the binge episode.

This functional analysis is based primarily on responses to a multiple-choice questionnaire completed by their large sample. While this format insures standardized coding, it limits the respondents' descriptions of typical binge patterns by forcing them to select from preestablished response alternatives. This procedure is efficient in describing general patterns among large samples, but it does not permit a careful examination of specific binge episodes nor does it permit individually generated alternatives.

Functional Analysis of Binge Episodes

The following sections describe a functional analysis of binge episodes based on behavioral diaries completed immediately following binge eating. This type of data should be a more valid description of a binge episode than a general retrospective description of typical patterns. Furthermore, data from these diaries can be examined to test the previously reported features of binge episodes, such as location, duration, or antecedent mood. In addition, binge episodes are compared to snack episodes by the same respondent. The identification of variables that distinguish a binge episode from a snack may help focus further assessment and intervention on those unique defining characteristics of a binge and not just the general characteristics of food consumption between formal meals.

Diary Data

Binge-eating and snacking data were collected from nine obese subjects participating in a weight reduction program at West Virginia University. Subjects were a mean of 31.1 pounds overweight (range = 13 to 61) and a mean of 30 years of age (range = 19 to 48). All subjects were considered to be at least moderate binge eaters as assessed by the Eating Habits Checklist (Gormally, 1980). Six of the nine subjects scored above the seventy-fourth percentile for moderate binge eating, while the remaining three subjects scored above the fiftieth percentile.

Subjects were asked to keep daily diaries for 2½ weeks to self-monitor eating episodes and associated cognitive and affective information. Diary information included a description of the food consumed; a judgment of whether the eating episode was a meal, snack, or binge; the time, place, and number of people present during the episode; and a 0 to 7 rating of overall perceived stress just prior to eating. In addition, the diaries contained two separate sections to assess cognitions and affect before and after an eating episode. This information consisted of a rating of perceived hunger (0 to 3 scale), an eight-alternative forced-choice rating of mood[1] listing a predominant self-statement, and the subject's rating of the valence of that self-statement. Valence is a rating of how positive or negative the self-statement is on a scale from −5 to +5, with zero being neutral. Through this procedure, a measure of the emotional impact of the cognition for the subject was obtained.

Prior to the diary data collection period, all subjects had received five weekly sessions of a modified behavioral weight reduction program (e.g., Stuart & Davis, 1972) that included a brief discussion of binge eating. However, subjects were not given standardized definitions of binges and snacks to use in completing the diaries; instead, they labeled eating episodes according to their individual definitions of snacks and binges. Subjects were instructed in self-monitoring of both behaviors and cognitions and were familiarized thoroughly with the diary format and contents.

Quantitative Data

Tables 11–1 and 11–2 present a summary of the quantitative data, obtained from the diaries, comparing binges and snacks. The nine subjects reported 27 binges in 17 days, or a mean of 1.2 binges per person per week. For each binge reported, the next snack reported by the same subject was selected for comparison. This intrasubject comparison allows for each subject to function as her own control. The results on Table 11–1 show that snacking and binges were not discriminated along the dimensions of the time of onset of eating, location of eating, and whether the episode occurred alone or with others. More specifically, both snacks and binges occurred most frequently between the hours of 4 and 8 P.M., in the kitchen, and with only the individual binger present. In addition, subjects' ratings of perceived hunger both prior to and following eating were not significantly different for binges and snacks. Hunger ratings in general were quite low ($\overline{X} = 1.5$), suggesting that hunger may be a relatively unimportant antecedent for between-meal eating episodes.

While the location or time of eating did not discriminate bingeing from snacking, cognitive, affective, and stress data presented

[1]Subjects were asked to record which of the following descriptions best characterized their mood immediately prior to and following eating: happy, depressed, guilty, neutral, frustrated, bored, anxious, or angry.

Table 11-1. Eating Episode Situational Variables.

	Time of Onset (%)				Duration (%)				Location (%)					Eating Alone (%)
	8–12 AM	12–4 PM	4–8 PM	8+ PM	½ hr	½–1 hr	1–2 hr	2+ hr	Kit	BR	Den	LR	Other	
Binge N = 27	0	18	45	37	11	67	17	5	45	0	18	14	23	60
Snack N = 26	4	19	42	35	59	35	6	0	38	5	14	23	10	56
Statistical analysis	$X^2 = 1.0$ ns				$X^2 = 9.31$ $p < .05$				$X^2 = 4.11$ ns					$X^2 = .11$ ns

Table 11-2. Self-Ratings before and after Eating Episodes.

	Stress (0–7 scale)	Hunger (0–3 scale)	Self-statement valence (−5 to +5)	Mood* (%)		Hunger (0–3 scale)	Self-statement valence (−5 to +5)	Mood* (%)		Self-statement valence (−5 to +5)
				Positive/ Neutral	Negative			Positive/ Neutral	Negative	
Binge N = 27	$\bar{x} = 3.1$ sd = 2.4	$\bar{x} = 1.3$ sd = 1.1	$\bar{x} = -3.4$ sd = 2.3	28 Mode = happy (24)	72 Mode = frustrated (24)	$\bar{x} = 0.1$ sd = 0.4	$\bar{x} = -3.4$ sd = 2.8	12 Mode = happy (12)	88 Mode = guilty (42)	$\bar{x} = -3.4$ sd = 2.8
Snack N = 26	$\bar{x} = 1.8$ sd = 2.2	$\bar{x} = 1.6$ sd = 0.8	$\bar{x} = +0.1$ sd = 3.5	66 Mode = happy (52)	34 Mode = bored (10)	$\bar{x} = 0.3$ sd = 0.6		48 Mode = happy (26)	52 Mode = guilty (22)	$\bar{x} = -1.5$ sd = 2.9
Statistical analysis	$t = 2.48$ $p < .05$	$t = .185$ ns	$t = 2.96$ $p < .05$	$X^2 = 6.9$ $p < .01$		$t = .013$ ns		$X^2 = 7.0$ $p < .01$		$t = 2.06$ ns ($p < .07$)

*Positive/neutral includes happy, neutral; negative includes depressed, guilty, frustrated, bored, anxious, and angry.

in Table 11–2 clearly were discriminative. Ratings of the valence of self-statements generated just prior to eating differed significantly ($p < .05$) for snacks and binges. On a scale from -5 to $+5$ with zero being neutral, the mean rating self-statement preceding a binge was -3.4, while the mean for a snack was 0.1 or essentially neutral. Interestingly, the mean valence rating of self-statements generated following a binge was -3.4, identical to the mean value reported preceding a binge. The mean valence rating following a snack was -1.5. This result approaches statistical significance ($p < .07$). It also can be noted that, while the magnitudes of the valence ratings following eating differed for binges and snacks, both produced negative self-talk.

To clarify analysis of the affective data, the eight mood types the subjects recorded were divided into two categories: positive/neutral or negative. The positive/neutral category included simply the "happy" and "neutral" ratings, while the negative group consisted of the combined "guilty," "depressed," "frustrated," "bored," "anxious," and "angry" ratings. Chi-square analyses for moods prior to and moods after eating were both significant ($p < .01$). Overall, ratings of mood both prior to and following eating were significantly more negative for binges and significantly more positive/neutral for snacks.

The modal negative emotion rated just prior to bingeing was "frustration" (24%), and the combined frequency of the negative mood types accounted for 72 percent of all ratings. This can be contrasted with ratings prior to snacking, where "happy" and "neutral" accounted for 66 percent of all ratings.

For ratings of mood reported just following a binge, the combined frequency of the negative mood types was 88 percent, with the modal negative emotion being "guilty" (42%). Following snacks, however, "happy" (28%) and "neutral" (22%) accounted for nearly half of all ratings.

Ratings of perceived stress prior to eating were significantly different for binges and snacks ($p < .05$). The mean rating for stress prior to a binge was a surprisingly low 3.1, or less than the midpoint on the eight-point scale. Stress appeared to be nearly neglible prior to snacking, with a mean rating of only 1.8.

The duration of snacks and binges differed significantly ($p < .05$), with 59 percent of snacks requiring less than 1/2 hour but 67 percent of the binges requiring 1/2 to one hour to complete.

Qualitative Data

Although subjects did quantify their self-statements by providing a rating of valence, it is informative to examine the statement contents. Table 11–3 presents a sample of representative self-statements and their associated valence ratings.

Self-statements recorded just prior to a binge seem to demonstrate a conflict between the urge to eat and an awareness of the negative consequences. Interestingly, the majority of self-statements recorded prior to bingeing present cognitions that reflect that the decision to eat already has been made. This is consistent with the identical mean valence ratings obtained before and after bingeing, in that before the urge has occurred behaviorally, its

Table 11-3. Representative Self-Statements and Their Associated Valence Ratings.

	Self-Statements Prior	*Valence (–5 to +5)*	*Self-Statements Following*	*Valence (–5 to +5)*
Binge	"I want these but shouldn't."	–3	"What a pig."	–5
	"I love nuts, I really shouldn't but will."	–3	"I feel like an ass, don't know why I did that."	–5
	"I'm so hungry, I just can't help myself."	–5	"Good, but wasn't worth it."	–2
	"I'm going to be bad."	–5	"My lessons didn't work, but I just had to have that chocolate—I just hate myself."	–5
Snack	"This should keep me from worse snacking."	+1	"That was good."	+1
	"I should wait till I eat dinner."	–4	"I didn't need that."	–4
	"I'll eat popcorn to keep from eating nutbread."	+1	"I needed something to tide me over—tasted good—didn't stuff myself."	+3
	"I'm very hungry, I need something better than a candy bar."	+1	"Pig, disgusted."	–5

occurrence is acknowledged cognitively. In this sense, the cognitive damage is done before any eating actually takes place.

Self-statements generated following a binge were uniformly negative, with some being strongly self-deprecating, such as, "What a pig," or ". . . I just hate myself." Self-statements prior to and following snacks were more variable than for binges. In some instances it was difficult to distinguish between a snack and a binge. As can be seen from Table 11–3, however, some statements associated with snacking were positive.

For this initial study, no attempt was made to use calorie counts in order to measure the quantities of food consumed during snacks and binges. An informal inspection of the data, however, reveals several interesting features. First, while snacks and binges did appear to differ predictably in terms of food quantity, binges were not excessive in calories. A typical binge might be two sandwiches, or a plate of lasagna, or some crackers and Kool-Aid. In one instance, a binge consisted of only half of a chocolate bar. Snacks were even more moderate: two cookies, pretzels, or an orange. Massive caloric intake reported in classic bulimia was not found here. Food type did not generally discriminate binges from snacks; both often contained similar high-calorie foods. The only exception is that fruits and vegetables did appear more frequently in snacks than in binges.

Despite the relatively modest caloric intake involved in these binges, subjects' reports of negative and self-deprecating cognitions and moods were extreme. Almost any eating, regardless of whether it contained sufficient calories to undermine a diet, appeared cognitively and emotionally disastrous. For example, the subject who ate half a candy bar subsequently reported that she hated herself. It does not appear that the behavioral lapse justified the magnitude of the cognitive punishment. This initial finding, if supported in future research, would suggest some type of cognitively oriented reattribution training. The client who eats half a candy bar and considers this only a minor lapse in an otherwise intact diet might be more likely to succeed than the client who considers this eating a disastrous personal failure.

Summary and Conclusions

This detailed comparison of binge and snack episodes for obese binge eaters reveals results that support earlier research and clarify some previous findings. Self-defined binge episodes are distinguished from snacks primarily by the negative self-statements and moods that precede and follow the binge episode. These negative experiences may be the product of the significantly higher stress levels reported prior to bingeing. The self-statements prior to binge-ing generally reflect an approach–avoidance conflict about the de-sire to eat versus its negative effects. In contrast, self-statements prior to snacking reflect snacking as a deliberate avoidance of more deleterious binge-eating foods. Neither the setting nor time of day discriminate between snacking and bingeing. Based on these initial findings, interventions could be explored to reduce stress and to alter the negative self-evaluations that occur prior to the binge epi-sode. Much more research is needed on binge-eating behaviors to permit effective treatment of this eating problem.

References

American Psychiatric Association. *Diagnostic and Statistical Manual of Mental Disorders,* 3rd ed. Washington, D.C.: American Psychiatric Association, 1980.

Casper, R., Eckert, E., Halmi, K., Goldberg, S., & Davis, J. Bulimia: Its incidence and clinical importance in patients with anorexia nervosa. *Archives of General Psychiatry,* 1980, *37,* 1030–1035.

Gormally, J. The assessment of binge eating severity among obese per-sons. Paper presented at the Association for the Advancement of Be-havior Therapy, New York, November 1980.

Kanfer, F. H., & Saslow, G. Behavioral diagnosis. In C. Franks (ed.), *Behavior Therapy: Appraisal and Status.* New York: McGraw-Hill, 1969.

Loro, A. D., & Orleans, C. S. Binge eating in obesity: Preliminary findings and guidelines for behavioral analysis and treatment. *Addictive Behav-iors,* 1981, *6,* 155–166.

Spencer, J., & Fremouw, W. J. A broad band assessment of binge eating among the nonobese. Paper presented at the Association for the Ad-vancement of Behavior Therapy, New York, November 1980.

Stunkard, A. J. *The Pain of Obesity.* Palo Alto, Calif.: Bull Press, 1976.

Stuart, R. B., & Davis, B. *Slim Chance in a Fat World: Behavioral Control of Overeating.* Champaign, Ill.: Research Press, 1972.

Wilson, G. T. Obesity, binge eating, and behavior therapy: Some clinical observations. *Behavior Therapy,* 1976, *7,* 700–701.

12

Toward the Understanding and Treatment of Binge Eating

G. Terence Wilson

This volume is timely and important. It is timely because of the relatively sudden upsurge of interest, among professionals and the public alike, in the causes and cure of binge eating. For better or for worse, the most recent revision of the American Psychiatric Association's *Diagnostic and Statistical Manual of Mental Disorders* (APA, 1980) included a description of bulimia (binge eating) as an eating disorder that is distinct from anorexia nervosa, obesity, or any other known physical disorder. Classification of bulimia as an independent, specifiable psychiatric disorder will ensure that increasing professional attention will be directed toward its diagnosis and treatment. Even prior to the recognition accorded this disorder in *DSM-III*, a handful of investigators, most of whom are contributors to this anthology, had indentified binge eating as a surprisingly common and serious problem, particularly among women, and had begun the necessary conceptual and therapeutic analyses of phenomenon (Boskind-Lodahl & White, 1978; Rau & Green, 1975). Public interest in binge eating was an immediate response to articles that appeared in the popular press. White and Boskind-White, in their chapter in this volume, indicate the "overwhelming" public response to descriptions of their work in magazines such as *Psychology Today* and *Glamour*. By October 1981, a lengthy and informative article on binge eating and purging by Jane Brody (1981) made front-page news in the Science Times section of the *New York Times*. Brody reported a huge public demand for more information and treatment throughout the United States and in Britain following media coverage of the topic, and cited psychotherapists' judgments that binge eating had reached epidemic proportions on college campuses. Consistent with this sort of report and with what I hear from my colleagues at different universities, the Office of Psychological Services at Douglass College of Rutgers University recently described as "tremendous" the response of female students to group programs for problems of binge eating and purging.

The present volume is important on several counts. By assembling a group of the most active and knowledgeable therapists and researchers in this developing area, the editors have pulled together what we currently know about binge eating and purging and have created a convenient single source that will serve as a useful reference text for some time.[1] Although there is a distinct cognitive–behavioral emphasis in this book, alternative or complementary approaches stressing psychodynamic (Chapter 9, by Coffman), experiential–behavioral (Chapter 4, by White & Boskind-White), and organic perspective (Chapter 6, by Rau & Green) also are included. This would seem to be a wise choice, given the rudimentary understanding we have of the problem and given the rough consensus that seems to be emerging that we require a multifaceted approach to the various phenomena encompassed by bingeing and purging.

There is also a more general sense in which this volume on binge eating is important. It is noteworthy that the different contributors have addressed the problems of binge eating in people who are variously underweight, of normal weight, and overweight. As such, it bears in part on the related eating disorders of anorexia nervosa and obesity. I concur with Wooley and Wooley (1981) when they suggest that "The binge–vomiting syndrome epitomizes the abusive use of food and is an instructive disorder to study as it contains nearly every element seen in other eating disorders: a

---

[1] I am most grateful to the editors and individual authors for allowing me the privilege of reviewing their various chapters before recording my own thoughts about the current status of treatment of binge eating.

fear of overweight as pronounced as that seen in any form of anorexia nervosa, as excessive a food intake as seen in any of the forms of overeating" (p. 46).

Finally, there is the complex and still-unresolved issue of whether or not binge eating is an addition or an example of an obsessive–compulsive disorder. As I suggest in my comments that follow, the analysis and modification of binge eating are likely to be informed by a careful consideration of the treatment of addictive and compulsive disorders. It is not unreasonable to assume that, by using the problems of binge eating as something of a testing ground for concepts and procedures that have been developed in the treatment of other disorders, we also might expand our knowledge of other forms of substance abuse and compulsive rituals.

Definitions and Description

My main purpose in this chapter is to comment on the therapeutic strategies that have been proposed, to summarize some of my own clinical experience with binge eaters, and to speculate on directions for future research and practice. Before pursuing these issues, however, I wish to make a few suggestions about problems of definition. I believe that Hamilton, Gelwick, and Meade (Chapter 1) are correct in predicting that "it is clear that, for some time, research on bulimia will be burdened with the lack of definitional clarity and the use of more terms than are necessary or helpful" (p. 7). Bulimia, bulimarexia, binge eating, compulsive eating, and the gorging–purging syndrome are terms that all are likely to have some play in the literature. Hamilton et al. in Chapter 1 make the sensible suggestion that the *DSM-III* definition be adopted whenever possible and offer several reasons for this choice. In addition, the field will benefit if researchers and therapists routinely provide detailed and comprehensive descriptions of the problems they encounter. Simply relying upon a label such as bulimia, even with strict reference to *DSM-III*, is by itself insufficient. I favor Hamilton et al.'s recommendation about the value of a standardized assessment battery. At a minimum this would include a specific binge-eating scale (e.g., Gormally, Black, Daston, & Rardin, 1982; Hawkins & Clement, 1980), and index of more general levels of functioning (e.g., the MMPI or the shorter SCL-90-R; see Derogatis, 1977), and observations that will allow judgments to be made about possible neurological causes using the criteria spelled out by Rau and Green (Chapter 6). Further descriptive referents of the subjects or clients in question might include a measure of assertiveness (e.g., Rathus, 1973) and the Beck Depression Inventory (Beck, 1976). The chief purpose of such a battery would be to facilitate comparisons among different research and treatment reports. An additional benefit would be that any of these sources of information might be useful in formulating treatment strategies. Nevertheless, for guiding therapeutic intervention, there is no substitute for a detailed behavioral assessment of the specific factors that maintain each individual's problem. A number of the chapters in this volume reveal the unique advantages of a careful behavioral analysis of the client's presenting problem (e.g., Chapter 3, by Gormally; Chapter 7, by Orleans & Barnett; Chapter 8, by Loro; and Chapter 11, by Fremouw & Heyneman).

Two caveats must be issued regarding the definition and conceptualization of binge eating. First, I want to underscore White and Boskind-White's (Chapter 4) concern that this problem not be viewed as a disease process. This does not mean that biological factors need to be overlooked; indeed, given Rau and Green's (Chapter 6) clinical findings, we need to screen effectively for cases of neurologically based eating disorders. The negative consequences of erroneously viewing other behavioral or emotional problems, such as obessive–compulsive disorders (Rachman & Hodgson, 1980), as quasi-disease entities has been documented amply (Bandura, 1969; Ullmann & Krasner, 1975). Similarly, the conceptualization of addictive disorders such as alcohol abuse as a biomedical disease often has proven counterproductive (Marlatt, 1979; Wilson, 1978). It appears that, in the majority of cases, binge eating is a learned response, albeit a complex one that is refractory to modification.

My second caveat, related to the first, is that we must avoid the trap of searching for "the bulimic personality." The futile and wasteful quest for "alcoholic personality," to take another form of substance abuse, should serve as a sobering reminder of the inherent limitations of such a research strategy. Although the foregoing chapters each paint a very similar picture of the binge eater, it would be a mistake to tag such clients with trait labels such as "passive dependency." The data base is still too thin and clinical samples too small to permit broad generalizations. Moreover, trait descriptions explain little and are not particularly useful for directing therapy (Mischel, 1968). Then there is Orleans and Barnett's (Chapter 7) point that it is reasonable to hypothesize that similarities in the "psychosocial profiles" of current bulimarexics are in large part a result, rather than a cause, of this intractable eating disorder." Analysis of the specific psychosocial and biological variables that maintain binge eating or purging in individual clients is the assessment strategy of choice.

An Addiction or a Compulsion?

The extent to which binge eating should be viewed as an addictive or compulsive disorder is an issue that frequently crops up in discussions of the problem. The present volume is no exception. Gormally, in Chapter 3, suggests that binge eating shares characteristics of both addictive and compulsive disorders.

The Secret Addiction

Binge eating takes place in secrecy and isolation. This feature is so characteristic of binge eating that bingeing has been dubbed "the secret addiction." The addictive aspect is virtually taken for granted.

Among others, I too have been impressed by the apparent similarity between binge eating and alcohol abuse. The clients I have treated for binge eating often sound indistinguishable from alcoholics as they describe their "craving," the "loss of control" following "the first bite," the rationalizations and other cognitive distortions that facilitate their self-defeating substance abuse, the postconsumption guilt and depression, the degree to which involvement with the substance (acquiring it, consuming it, agonizing over it) dominates their lives, and the high relapse rate, to name some common characteristics. Having had a good deal of experience in the treatment of alcohol abuse, I find it helpful to use examples and analogies from that disorder in conveying to binge eaters my understanding of their own problems.

All of the characteristics of addictive disorders that I have just noted are not unique to substance abuse, however. As Marlatt (in press) persuasively argues, these issues of acquiring and maintaining regulation of behavior that had been out of control also are pertinent to problems such as gambling and even sexual paraphilias, which do not involve the ingestion of a specific substance. The implications of Marlatt's model for binge eating will be taken up shortly. Our confidence in conceptualizing binge eating as a specific form of physical addiction would be increased by evidence of the development of tolerance and withdrawal symptoms. I know of no descriptions of withdrawal symptoms, but Wooley and Wooley (1981) have referred to the development of tolerance in binge eaters. Specifically, they suggest that binges get worse; that is, progressively more of the substance is required to produce the same subjective effect because the repeated binge–purge cycle disrupts the body's ability to detect satiation. This explanation relies on the theory and findings on conditioned satiety and overeating. According to Booth (1980), conditioned sensory control of food intake has its major effect toward the end of a meal. In binge eaters who also purge, since the food is regurgitated before its metabolic effects are experienced, "one would predict that sensory cues of foods should come to elicit larger meal sizes" (Wooley & Wooley, 1981, p. 61). The explanation for binge eating without purging is less obvious from this perspective, although the Wooleys speculate that repeated shifting between weight loss and weight gain can lead to "erratic conditioning histories" and hence impaired functioning of sensory satiety mechanisms.

Hyperlipogenesis, the accelerated conversion of food into body lipids following a period of severe caloric restriction, is another process that may account for deregulation of eating in a manner that may resemble the development of tolerance in other forms of substance abuse. As Wooley and Wooley (1981) put it,

> If after weight loss, the dieter finds it impossible to feel satisfied by customary amounts of food, he or she may intensify efforts at self-control, diet more stringently, employ vomiting, take laxatives, or resort to hyperactivity to control weight gain. Without such measures, the individual must maintain restraint or tolerate weight gain until lipogenesis is slowed and new equilibrium is achieved. . . . The phenomenon of adaptive hyperlipogenesis creates a situation similar to that occurring in drug tolerance. . . . But whereas tolerance is reduced by substance abstinence, hyperlipogenesis is intensified by food restriction. [p. 63]

If we conceptualize binge eating as a form of addictive substance abuse, it follows that therapeutic strategies that have proved effective in the treatment of other addictive disorders, such as alcoholism, might be applicable. Self-control methods have been used widely to treat addictive disorders, and it is not surprising, therefore, to see extensive discussion in the foregoing chapters of cognitive–behavioral self-control strategies for containing binge eating. One of the most exciting trends in the conceptualization and treatment of addictive disorders is the application of Marlatt's (in press) relapse-prevention model. Given what we currently know, the extension of Marlatt's model to binge eating is as desirable as it is inevitable. Several of the foregoing chapters detail the way in which this model is relevant to understanding and modifying binge eating (Chapters 3, 7, 8, & 11).

Some aversion conditioning techniques have proved successful in the treatment of alcoholism (Cannon, Baker, & Wehl, 1981; Olson, Ganley, Devine, & Dorsey, 1981) and cigarette smoking (Lichtenstein & Rodriques, 1977). Should similar methods be applied to binge eating? Orleans and Barnett (Chapter 7), entertain the possibility of using different aversive methods, including shame aversion. Despite the few case examples to the contrary, I see no use for aversive methods in the treatment of binge eating. Aside from the necessity of treating the whole person, I believe that any resort to aversive methods involving electric shock or even images of nausea or shame will be counterproductive. The binge eater comes to treatment with a low sense of self-efficacy, burdened with shame a sense of helplessness. She/he requires treatment aimed directly at restoring self-esteem and personal respect. Whatever the therapist's rationale, and I am familiar with the argument that gaining control over a problem is an effective means of restoring self-confidence, it is hard to imagine how the use of an aversive method will not be viewed by this particular type of client as a punitive measure that will contribute indirectly to a further erosion of self-esteem (Wooley, Wooley, & Dyrenforth, 1979).

The general implications for treatment of conceptualizing binge eating as a form of addictive disorder seem clear. Cognitive–behavioral treatment strategies and a specific concern for prevention of relapse along the lines that Marlatt (in press) has detailed are the way to proceed. Not as obvious, however, are the therapeutic implications of assumptions about faulty conditioned satiety mechanisms or adaptive hyperlipogenesis. What can be done to regulate the physiology of food intake, as apparently is required, given these assumptions? The sketchy suggestion put forward by Wooley and Wooley (1981) is to help the binge eater "maintain restraint or tolerate weight gain" until the food regulatory system achieves a new equilibrium. But what is meant by restraint, and for how long must it be maintained? What sort of weight gain must be tolerated? This is an area that is high priority for research aimed at providing therapists with some guidelines about what can be expected and how the reconditioning is to be accomplished.

Binge Eating as a Compulsive Disorder

The case for conceptualizing binge eating as a form of compulsive disorder is succinctly stated by Gormally in Chapter 3. He refers to Rachman and Hodgson's (1980) recent analysis of obsessive–compulsive disorders, noting that their definition of a compulsion is "a repetitive, partly stereotyped type of behavior that is preceded or accompanied by a sense of pressure, that usually provokes internal resistance, is at least partly irrational, and often causes distress or embarrassment" (p. 110). The analogy between compulsive disorders such as hand washing and binge eating extends to a range of common characteristics, including the complexity of the disorders and the difficulty therapists traditionally have had in treating them.

The importance of linking binge eating to compulsive disorders lies in the implications for treatment. Behavior therapists have achieved a notable breakthrough in developing very promising treatment methods for compulsions, which hitherto have remained refractory to psychodynamic and biological therapists alike (Rachman & Hodgson, 1980; Rachman & Wilson, 1980). The treatment methods of choice are *in vivo* exposure and response prevention, as Gormally (Chapter 3) notes. In view of their potential value for treating binge eating, and given that relatively little attention is devoted to them in the foregoing chapters, I will elaborate on these methods in the following section.

Treatment Considerations

I concur with the view expressed by most of the contributors to this volume that the treatment of binge eating is necessarily multifaceted in nature. As Gormally, Loro, Orleans, and Barnett, White, and Boskind-White point out in their chapters, treatment is typically focused on the behavioral, cognitive, emotional, and interpersonal dimensions of binge eaters' functioning. The methods that are used to make changes in these diverse aspects of psychological functioning include, at a minimum, training in assertiveness, social skills, and communication competencies; behavioral self-control strategies; cognitive restructuring; methods for coping more constructively with emotions such as anxiety, anger, and depression; and shaping and reinforcement for appropriate, nonabusive eating behavior. Other behavioral procedures that are mentioned include delay therapy, aversion techniques, and programmed binges. Beyond this broad-spectrum behavior-therapy approach, innovative procedures such as White and Boskind-White's (Chapter 4) emphasis on guided group experiences merit attention. In those cases where binge eating appears to be neurologically based, drug treatment is recommended (Rau & Green, (Chapter 6).

My treatment of binge eating essentially has followed the broad cognitive–behavioral framework that I have noted here. There is no need to restate the overall treatment approach, the details of which are presented adequately in some of the preceding chapters (e.g., Gormally; Loro; Orleans & Barnett; White & Boskind-White). Rather, I wish to comment selectively on particular problems I have encountered in using this approach and to share some tentative observations on the use of exposure and response-prevention methods. Before turning to these issues, however, it is necessary to comment on the treatment model presented in Coffman's chapter.

One emphasis that sets aside Coffman's model from a cognitive–behavioral approach is his insistence on the "master/slave" model. It is one matter to prompt the recognition of hidden resentment, to encourage assertion as opposed to submission, and to question personal or societal pressure for conformity to inappropriate sex-role stereotypes (Chapter 4, by White & Boskind-White). It is quite another procedure to insist on the central importance of a "slave revolt." Coffman goes beyond available data in making emphatic declarations, to the client no less, about a binge being "a statement of determination and integrity," and "an angry statement directed at some particular person or persons" whom the therapist is supposed to identify. No evidence of any kind is offered to support these contentions. In the time-honored tradition of psychodynamic, interpretive psychotherapy, an interesting *hypothesis,* that may well need to be examined critically, is elevated to the status of a *de facto* truth on which imposing therapeutic edifices then are constructed. Suffice it to state that from a social learning perspective, if individual assessment indicates that problems with unrecognized or unresolved anger seem to be related to binge eating or any other disorder, then there are well-established procedures for helping the client to identify the anger and express it more constructively. Realizing that I can point to little by way of compelling empirical evidence, I nevertheless might add that I do not believe that binge eating is inevitably a function of repressed resentment toward some "master" or that resolution of such hidden emotions is necessary for therapeutic improvement.[2] For example, it is quite possible for a specific disorder such as binge eating to coexist with broader problems of role conflict. The binge eating might even exacerbate the role conflict, but the two need not be related in a simple causal manner.

Coffman would have the therapist "emphasize how she [the client] is now the locus of control and can choose to eat or not eat, binge or not binge. It's entirely up to her. *She* is the *master* now" (p. 217). In behavior therapy, emphasis on self-control and self-attribution of change is most important in facilitating the maintenance of therapeutically produced change (Wilson, 1979). Coffman, however, presents this interpretation (exhortation?) about the client being the "master" as an early means of producing change. This tactic raises several issues. Coffman reports that the "reduction in the frequency of bingeing–purging may be rather dramatic after the [slave master] model is explained. The client may be pleasantly surprised and a little puzzled at the reduction in her desire to binge" (p. 217). No data are provided to support these encouraging findings. Coffman's unusual success in this regard may well have to do with the nature of the specific sample of clients he has treated. Given the clients I have seen, I remain skeptical about the power of this or any other interpretation or insight to effect changes in so refractory a problem as binge eating. This skepticism seems to be shared by other contributors to this volume. If real change has not occurred, an emphasis on how the binge eater suddenly has the power to choose to binge or not binge, to make a rational, voluntary decision, may result in untoward consequences. Unless the client has achieved genuinely demon-

---

[2]I, too, have noticed that the women I treat for binge eating usually are unassertive. In several clear-cut instances, however, where I have addressed the unassertiveness directly and seen dramatic improvement in this sphere of functioning, concomitant changes in binge eating did not occur. Whether or not submissiveness is associated with the development of binge eating as a disorder, it seems clear that therapeutically induced changes in assertiveness and ability to express anger do not necessarily affect binge eating.

strable control over her binge eating or vomiting, these therapeutic assertions about her being able to choose may backfire and result in what I have called a negative rebound effect. Look at the situation from the client's perspective. She is informed, authoritatively, that she can choose. Yet she continues to binge. Her conclusion is likely to be that she really does not want to stop and so she will blame herself even more. Or she might conclude that her inability to stop indicates the unusual severity of her problem and that she is beyond help. As I have indicated elsewhere in a discussion of attribution and illusory control (Wilson, 1979), "Expectations of control can be assumed to function like other therapeutic expectations. They comprise a double-edged sword. On one hand, positive expectations appear to facilitate outcome; on the other hand, if subsequent experience is not consonant with the expectations the therapist has created and success does not immediately follow, the client may see in this disconfirmation of expectations yet another affirmation of the hopelessness of his or her plight" pp. 79–80).

We must be particularly careful about psychological interpretations of the meaning, conscious or unconscious, of binge eating. What if Wooley and Wooley (1981) are correct in suggesting that the understanding of this disorder "is to be found primarily in study of the physiology of the regulation of food intake and of the conditioning of anxiety reduction?" (p. 50). Or what if the problem is neurologically based as Rau and Green have suggested in Chapter 6? Insisting then on the client's capacity to choose to binge or not to binge not only would be inaccurate but also would be unfair. The point is that, at best, we have relatively crude working hypotheses about the causes of binge eating and purging. As Wooley, Wooley, and Dyrenforth (1979) have argued with respect to the treatment of obesity, it makes sense to explain "the facts" to our clients, including our current uncertainty about etiology and treatment outcome. Different hypotheses, including Coffman's, can be examined in this more constructive climate of mutual problem-solving, with a reduced risk of false interpretations unnecessarily compounding the client's problem.

Self-Control and Cognitive Restructuring

As the authors of Chapters 3, 7, 8, and 11 have made clear, distorted and self-defeating cognitions feature prominently among the antecedents of binge eating and purging. In particular, Gormally et al.'s (1982) emphasis on the combination of unrealistically stringent dietary standards and low self-efficacy for coping with threats to this rigid eating code as a precursor to binge eating incisively captures what I have observed in the binge eaters I have seen. Given this fragile cognitive set, the binge eater then views any transgression from the self-imposed standard as a disaster, as Chapter 11 indicated. The cognitive error is familiar (variously called "all-or-nothing" or "dichotomous thinking"), and the consequence, typically, is further substance abuse. This is known variously as "the abstinence violation effect" (Marlatt, 1979), the "counterregulatory effect" (Polivy, 1976), or the "cognitive claustrophobia" syndrome (Mahoney & Mahoney, 1976).

The similarity between this analysis of antecedents of binge eating and Marlatt's (in press) more general cognitive–behavioral model of addictive disorders such as alcoholism and cigarette smoking is striking. The therapeutic implications of this model are clear and eminently testable. Gormally and Loro, in Chapters 3 and 8, provide specific details of the logical treatment interventions. Loro's account of the therapeutic possibilities of a "programmed binge" is most instructive. Although this method derives directly from Marlatt's suggestions for minimizing the negative psychological sequelae of a dietary slip, Loro's analysis shows that the same procedure would receive an enthusiastic reception from nonbehavioral, strategic therapists like Haley and Watzlawick. Here, undoubtedly, is an illustration of "prescribing the symptom" in an effort to undercut therapeutic resistance. It is my opinion that future investigation and refinement of this line of thinking has considerable promise.

The applicability of cognitive restructuring to the treatment of binge eating is clear, but my clinical experience suggests that it may often be limited in impact. Before addressing the limitations of cognitive restructuring, I need to describe, albeit in abbreviated form, the way in which I use this approach. To ensure active involvement in the treatment process, I have clients write out cognitions that we have identified as probable antecedents of binge eating, indicate the type of cognitive distortion (e.g., "all-or-nothing" thinking), and rewrite the thought in a more rational way that is likely to facilitate self-control.[3] In some instances I ask clients to

---

[3]Among others, a book by Burns (1980) is appropriate for clients and contains useful suggestions for carrying out cognitive restructuring along the lines of Beck's (1976) cognitive–behavioral approach to therapy.

use a tape-recorder in following the same sequence. I emphasize that cognitive restructuring requires a significant commitment of time, effort, and concentration; and I stress the necessity for daily cognitive stock-taking and reevaluation.

A major goal of my treatment is to identify particular high-risk situations or conditions in which the probability of binge eating is greatly increased. With the client's help I develop specific plans for coping with the high-risk situation, including contingencies for what the client might think, feel, and do. Using guided imagery, I have the client conjure up the situation, encounter the anticipated problem, and rehearse appropriate coping strategies. One cognitive strategy is to pair each negative or self-defeating thought with a realistic and credible reinterpretation. I teach clients to anticipate high-risk situations, to plan, and to rehearse their coping strategies before the actual situation is fully upon them. For example, I had a client for whom a consistent high-risk situation was returning home from work in the late afternoon. For a period of roughly an hour she would be alone and had the time to herself. A binge was a high probability under these circumstances. She reported that often the prospect of being alone with time to relax automatically elicited the urge to eat. If this occurred, she claimed, attempts at rational reinterpretation of her thoughts usually proved futile and were abandoned quickly. Once a powerful urge developed, cognitive control appeared to be ineffective. Accordingly, in typical behavioral fashion, I explained how self-control is accomplished most easily by intervening early in the response chain, when the unwanted urge is still relatively weak or even nonexistent. Specifically, she was to spend a few minutes rehearsing cognitive strategies before entering the house on these high-risk occasions.

The approach that I have sketched briefly here demands considerable cooperation from the client. It requires that she be ready and willing to identify the immediate precursors of a possible binge and to institute promptly the necessary coping strategies. Not surprisingly, noncompliance with these therapeutic requirements is a frequent problem. A number of different factors might be responsible for noncompliance, including the complexity or incomprehensibility of the treatment instructions, inappropriate expectations on the part of the client, and problems in the therapist–client relationship (see Franks & Wilson, 1980, for a fuller discussion of compliance). Noncompliance also may have to be analyzed for client resistance to therapeutic change. In general, I find this aspect of treatment to be among the most challenging and important of the therapist's tasks. Resistance may take different forms, and there are various strategies for combating it (Lazarus & Fay, in press; Meichenbaum, in press; Wilson & Evans, 1977). Coffman (Chapter 9) calls attention to an early and critically important form of noncompliance or resistance in noting that some clients balk at self-monitoring of binge–purge behavior and the thoughts and feelings associated with it. I have described my own response to this not unfamiliar obstacle to progress elsewhere (Wilson, 1980). Suffice it to say here that I am likely to confront the client with repeated failure to self-monitor. Insufficient cooperation by the client on this task significantly undermines the ability of the therapist to carry out an adequate functional analysis of the eating disorder. Moreover, noncompliance (resistance) at this initial stage of therapy bodes ill for future success. In a study that examined reasons for failure in the behavioral treatment of obesity, Dubbert and Wilson (in press) found that incomplete self-monitoring during the first few weeks of the treatment program was related significantly to unsuccessful outcomes. As I mentioned earlier, Loro (Chapter 8) describes the uses of a paradoxical treatment strategy (programmed binge eating) as a means of overcoming resistance, an approach that merits serious consideration and evaluation.

In the case of the binge eater I referred to previously, use of the cognitive self-control strategies that we had decided upon mutually usually proved effective in heading off a binge. On some occasions, however, she simply failed even to try to implement demonstrably effective self-regulatory actions. My attempt to uncover the reasons for this noncompliance was unsuccessful. Her comment was, "I guess I really wanted to eat and therefore I did nothing to stop it." She disavowed any conscious intent to undermine or go off the program and expressed considerable frustration over her inability to control her binges reliably and hence maintain weight loss. On these occasions when she failed to implement previously successful cognitive self-regulatory strategies, it seemed that she already had made up her mind to overeat (binge) before she had any real chance to think ahead. Any opportunity for exercising rational self-control strategies had been preempted. In this "dissociative" state (see Chapter 7), the client had no awareness of the negative consequences of eating or the possibility of interrupting the habitual pattern.[4] She attributed her puzzling behavior to a "subconscious desire" to eat.

Bingeing as an Affective Reaction

I had another client for whom cognitive self-control methods usu-ally were effective in controlling binge eating. On occasion, how-ever, she would lapse and fail to implement the procedures, in a manner similar to that of the client just described. She would find herself committed to a binge or, indeed, actually in the process of overeating before any thought of controlling the response occurred to her. Her explanation for this reliable pattern of behavior was that "the hand is quicker than the mind!"

Are the two examples of noncompliance that I have just de-scribed to be viewed as instances of unconscious resistance? I do not believe that there is much to be gained by pursuing this hy-pothesis. What does one do next? I know of no satisfactory evidence showing that interpreting this resistance to the client, or confront-ing it, leads to behavioral improvement. Rather than resistance, I wish to suggest that unchecked binge eating of the sort I have referred to here may be an example of a primary affective reaction that is partly or even wholly independent of conscious cognitive control.

This avowedly speculative analysis leans heavily on Zajonc's (1980) provocative conceptualization of the relationship between feeling and thinking. According to his scheme, affect and cognition are "under the control of separate and partially independent sys-tems." In contrast to cognitive judgments, affective reactions are "primary . . . basic . . . instantaneous . . . automatic . . . precogni-tive . . . holistic . . . dominant . . . and difficult to verbalize" (p. 154). These characteristics seem clearly descriptive of the driving, uncontrollable urges that binge eaters experience. Typically, cli-ents suffering from addictive or compulsive disorders find great difficulty in describing what their urges or cravings feel like.

It is the therapeutic implications of Zajonc's analysis that are

---

[4]At other times, in this client, and others, there is an awareness of a conflict between the desire to eat versus the ultimately negative consequences. Fremouw and Heyneman (Chapter 11) document the latter pattern. I'm suggesting that when there is an anticipatory awareness of the binge, cognitive self-control strategies are most likely to be effective. A lack of awareness, or "automatic" binge eating, may require alternative treatment interventions, such as those in the next section.

of interest here. If I am correct in likening urges to binge to primary affective reactions, it is understandable how treatments based on insight or cognitive restructuring would be ineffective. Cognitive restructuring methods such as self-instructional training (Meichenbaum, 1977) and rational–emotive therapy (Ellis, 1977) are based on the assumption that affect is postcognitive. Yet this assumption is simplistic and often inconsistent with the evidence (see Mahoney, 1980, for details on this issue). In an analysis of the general therapeutic implications of Zajonc's model of the interaction between thinking and feeling, Rachman (1981) has the following to add:

> If it is true that our affective reactions are instantaneous and automatic and that they are determined by stimulus characteristics that are extremely difficult to identify, then our attempts at self-understanding and indeed of therapeutic insight are bound to be unsatisfactory; particularly as they so often rely largely or entirely on cognitive analyses and the verbal mode. . . . Repeated attempts to trace connections between an affective reaction and specific cognitions may in time give way to alternative tactics in which the therapist and patient strive to find more direct and appropriate techniques for modifying the affective reaction within the affective system rather than across the border from the cognitive system. [pp. 286–287]

It is to methods that might influence primary affective reactions directly that I now turn.

Stimulus Exposure and Response Prevention

Zajonc does not address himself to the modification of affective reactions, although he does refer to findings indicating that affective changes occur after repeated stimulus exposure, even in the absence of conscious recognition. The reference to stimulus exposure is of particular interest to behavior therapists. Therapeutic procedures that rely upon prolonged exposure to the stimuli that typically trigger an emotional problem are a significant component of the behavior therapist's armamentarium in treating different disorders, especially phobic and obessive–compulsive disorders (Marks, 1981; Rachman & Hodgson, 1980). Moreover, the data convincingly show that *in vivo* exposure is the treatment of choice in the majority of such cases. Why exposure works has yet to be explained satisfactorily (Wilson & O'Leary, 1980). It is not unreasonable to assume that exposure modifies primary affective reactions directly (Bandura, 1969; Rachman, 1981).

I have noted already that binge eating has been viewed as a type of obsessive–compulsive disorder. On a pragmatic basis alone it can be argued that methods that are effective in eliminating compulsive checking and hand-washing also might be successful in treating a compulsive eating disorder. Actually, it might make little difference whether or not binge eating is conceptualized as compulsive or addictive behavior in this instance. Stimulus-exposure methods have been applied to the treatment of alcoholism with encouraging effects, although the evidence is restricted to uncontrolled case reports (Blakey & Baker, 1980; Hodgson & Rankin, 1976). If urges to binge are primary affective reactions, and if exposure methods are an effective means of modifying affective responses directly, then there is also a theoretical rationale for using these procedures, particularly in those cases where cognitive self-control strategies fail.

The most powerful treatment program for compulsive disorders requires prolonged exposure to the cues that elicit the urges or craving without allowing the client to engage in the compulsive behavior itself (e.g., hand-washing, drinking, or binge eating). The latter actions are viewed as escape or avoidance responses that reduce the discomfort or anxiety of the urges/craving and thereby, through the process of negative reinforcement, increase the probability of similar self-destructive behavior in the future. Preventing the escape/avoidance response eliminates the negative reinforcement and results in gradual extinction of the underlying urge, craving, or anxiety. Gormally (Chapter 3) alludes to the use of exposure and response-prevention methods in his discussion of emotional coping in noting the importance of the binge eater learning to tolerate anxiety and to delay the impulse to eat. Wooley and Wooley (1981) present essentially the same behavioral analysis of binge eating when they suggest that the binge eating reduces anxiety (only in the short run, of course; it increases the anxiety in the long term). Vomiting or temporary stringent dieting (see Hawkins & Clement's "purification promise," Chapter 10) reduces the anxiety, guilt, or discomfort brought on by the binge eating. Wooley and Wooley (1981) emphasize that the entire binge–purge sequence has an anxiety-reducing effect and is used as a form of self-control or dieting.

Scattered clinical reports encourage the view that exposure

and response-prevention methods might be effective with some cases of binge eating and vomiting. Loro (Chapter 8) and Orleans and Barnett (Chapter 7) describe case studies by Meyer (1973) and Welch (1979) in which response delay (a variation of response prevention; see Rachman & Hodgson, 1980) was used to break the association between an obsession with food or weight and compulsive binge eating. A more systematic evaluation of exposure and response-prevention in the treatment of "bulimia anorexia" was conducted by Rosen and Leitenberg (1982). The client was a 21-year-old female college student, just over 5′ tall, who weighed 95 pounds. She reported binge eating at least once a day and vomited several times daily. Drawing an explicit parallel to the behavioral treatment of obsessive–compulsive disorders, Rosen and Leitenberg reasoned that

> . . . binge eating and self-induced vomiting seem linked in a vicious circle by anxiety. As in anorexia nervosa there is a morbid fear of weight gain. Eating elicits this anxiety (binging dramatically so); vomiting reduces it. Once an individual has learned that vomiting following food intake leads to anxiety reduction, rational fears no longer inhibit overeating. Thus the driving force of this disorder may be vomiting, not binging; binging might not occur if the person could not vomit afterwards. [p.118]

Accordingly, in each treatment session, the client was instructed to eat an amount of food that caused her to feel a strong urge to vomit, to the point where she ordinarily would vomit. Not permitted to vomit, she was instructed to focus attention on her discomfort (anxiety) until the urge to vomit disappeared.[5] The effects of these therapy sessions were assessed carefully using a multiple-baseline design across different classes of food stimuli. The results indicated that the quantity of food consumed without vomiting increased and subjective discomfort after eating decreased when exposure-plus-response-prevention treatment was applied sequentially to each class of food. Complete cessation of vomiting and binging and minimal discomfort subsequently were achieved when the client was directed to practice response prevention at home over a period of 44 days. A 10-month follow-up showed maintenance of this therapeutic improvement. Moreover, Rosen and Lei-

---

[5] I have experimented with asking the client to use different coping strategies (e.g., relaxation or relabeling) during exposure, although there is no clear evidence showing that this enhances treatment efficacy.

tenberg (1982) add that "other positive effects of the treatment were reported by the subject. She was no longer obsessed about her weight (despite a 7-pound weight gain), and she noted she ate what she wanted. Also, she reported an improvement in self-esteem and a decrease in mood swings" (p. 123). By way of follow-up on this single case report, Brody (1981) reports that Rosen and Leitenberg claim "to have completely stopped the binge-and-purge syndrome in a dozen patients treated thus far, with minimal weight gain afterward" (p. C5).

These results not only indicate the promise of exposure and response-prevention as a form of treatment, but they also lend support to the conceptualization of binge eating and vomiting in terms of an avoidance conditioning model, put forward by Rosen and Leitenberg (1982) and Wooley and Wooley (1981). The former's findings apply only to binge eaters who then vomit; however, the model can be extended to cover those clients who binge without vomiting.[6] In these cases the binge itself can be viewed as the escape/avoidance response that reduces the different sources of emotional distress or food stimuli that would be hypothesized to trigger the urge to overeat. Treatment would involve prolonged exposure to cues that elicit the urge to binge, without allowing the client to engage in the binge. Among the many cues that might trigger a binge are those that accompany the actual ingestion of specific foods, particularly forbidden fruits. The logic of the treatment would require exposure to these internal cues as in the case of external stimuli such as the sight or smell of specific foods. The direct analogy is to Hodgson and Rankin's (1976) treatment of alcoholism, in which the alcoholic is given a small priming dose of alcohol to elicit internal cues (craving) and then not permitted to consume any additional alcohol until the craving passes. There is some similarity between this procedure and the use of programmed binges insofar as both focus on the consumption of food from which the client has tried to abstain. An important difference is that the objective of exposure and response-prevention treatment is to extinguish the urge to eat, whereas the rationale behind programmed binge eating as described by Loro (Chapter 8), for example, is that of overcoming resistance or countercontrol on the part of the client. Furthermore, whereas the stimulus-exposure model requires a small "priming dose" of a particular food(s), the programmed binge eating strategy calls for something approaching a regular binge.

[6]The vast majority of obese binge eaters I have seen have not resorted to vomiting.

Where Do We Go from Here?

The recent upsurge of interest in the problems of binge eating has produced systematic attempts to conceptualize the disorder and many clinically creative strategies for treating it, as the preceding chapters amply demonstrate. It seems clear that we are on the brink of burgeoning clinical and research interest in all facets of binge eating, including its biological, psychological, and social dimensions. In my view, there is no more pressing need at this point than careful evaluations of therapeutic outcome in ways that also will allow the examination of the theoretical mechanisms that are responsible for the maintenance and modification of binge eating.

Despite the wealth of clinical detail and therapeutic suggestions in the preceding chapters and elsewhere, relatively little can be said about the efficacy of different treatments. Virtually all available information on treatment outcome is at the level of uncontrolled, anecdotal reports. Among the few exceptions to this state of the art are the single-case experimental designs of Monti, McCrady, and Barlow (1977) and Rosen and Leitenberg (1982), the controlled study of the effects of Dilantin by Wermuth, Davis, Hollister, and Stunkard (1977), and the brief report by White and Boskind-White (Chapter 4) in which they compared their experimental–behavioral treatment with a waiting list control group. If we are to make advances in the treatment of binge eating, careful evaluation of therapy outcome is a necessary next step.

There are several directions along which evaluation of treatment effects might proceed. Given the rudimentary and fragmentary state of our therapeutic knowledge, ambitious, tightly controlled group studies might be premature at this stage. A most useful contribution would be a systematically conducted clinical trial in which the clients and their specific problems are described adequately, the particular treatment methods are defined well (so as to be replicable by other investigators), and measures of therapeutic effects are detailed carefully. The description of the clinical sample should meet the minimal requirements that I indicated earlier in this chapter, and multiple outcome measures should provide specific information on actual binge behavior and weight changes, as well as other relevant aspects of psychological and social functioning such as depression, anxiety, self-efficacy, body image, interpersonal skills and assertiveness, sexual adjustment, and marital satisfaction. Clinical trials, lacking appropriate control groups, never can provide definitive evidence on therapeutic efficacy, but this is not their primary purpose. If well executed and thoroughly reported, the value of clinical trials lies in illustrating the use of specific treatment strategies applied to particular problems, thus allowing other investigators to carry out the necessary replications and refinements. As Barlow (1980) has pointed out, timely and informative clinical trials were chiefly responsible for initiating the impressive therapeutic advances that have been made in the treatment of anxiety disorders (i.e., Wolpe, 1958) and sexual disorders (i.e., Masters & Johnson, 1970) over the past two decades.

In addition to the specification of assessment and treatment methods and the inclusion of multiple measures of biobehavioral functioning, clinical trials (and all other forms of evaluation) must involve long-term follow-up of clients. The probability of relapse is a characteristic feature of all addictive disorders, and there are sound theoretical and clinical reasons for anticipating problems with maintenance of therapeutic change in binge eaters. White and Boskind-White (Chapter 4) already have demonstrated the importance of including appropriate follow-up evaluation. Detailed clinical reports of treatment outcome that provide information about individual clients also will facilitate the search for all-important prognostic factors. There is much to be learned from a systematic analysis of treatment failures aimed at isolating client or treatment variables that determine outcome (Foa & Emmelkamp, in press). Investigations along these lines are needed to follow up on observations such as White and Boskind-White's (Chapter 4) finding that maintenance of improvement is "contingent upon initiating, maintaining, and enhancing the quality of . . . interpersonal relationships, particularly with men" (p. 98).

Single-case experimental designs are a suitable methodology for evaluating and developing the treatment of binge eating. The usefulness of this methodology is evident in the studies by Monti et al. (1977) and Rosen and Leitenberg (1982). Rau and Green's (Chapter 6) use of clients as their own controls in assessing the specific pharmacological impact of Dilantin on binge eating is also consistent with the philosophy of single-case experimental designs. Two characteristics of this methodology seem particularly pertinent in view of our current lack of precise knowledge about the treatment of binge eating. The first is the personalistic emphasis on the individual client. Until conceptual and definitional issues surrounding binge eating and purging are resolved, explicit recognition of the possibly crucial differences among different clients will be beneficial. Are there differences between obese binge eaters and their underweight and normal-weight counterparts? Might not the treatment strategies differ? The second characteristic is the flexibility that single-case experimental designs offer. Hersen and Barlow (1976) describe this advantage as follows: "If a particular procedure works well in one case but works less well or fails when attempts are made to replicate this in a second or third case, slight alterations in the procedure can be made immediately. In many cases, reasons for the inability to replicate the findings can be ascertained immediately, assuming that procedural deficiencies were, in fact, responsible for the lack of generality" (p. 59). This flexibility is especially important in the beginning stages of the evaluation of treatment methods, because it facilitates the development and refinement of therapeutic intervention.

As we learn which methods have what effects on binge eating it becomes necessary to use one of several between-group experimental designs (Kazdin, 1980) to establish the specific efficacy of a treatment program. As in the case of uncontrolled clinical trials, multiple measures of outcome and adequate follow-up are required. Between-group designs are necessary to test the effects of experimental treatment strategies such as White and Boskind-White's (Chapter 4) approach. In view of the consistent emphasis that is placed on sex-role conflict as a critical ingredient of binge eating and vomiting, its therapeutic implications should be isolated and evaluated explicitly. Does group therapy confer any advantage over individual sessions? It would be most unusual to find that group treatment was reliably superior to individual therapy, given the pattern of findings from a wide range of other disorders. A case can be made for a blend of individual and group treatment, since there are hints in the obesity literature that group support might help to sustain initial improvement.

Finally, there is enough evidence on the therapeutic potential of Dilantin to warrant better-controlled evaluations of its effects. Rau and Green (Chapter 6) outline some of the requirements for an unambiguous test of their hypothesis, including the selection of suitable clients, the mandatory EEG assessments, and other neurological measures. Investigators in this area also might consider more sophisticated controls for disentangling psychological from pharmacological treatment influences. Specifically, the use of what has come to be called the balanced placebo design (Marlatt & Rohsenow, 1981), where feasible, permits definitive conclusions about the separate or interactive effects of psychological variables such as placebo influences and the clients' expectations about receiving drug therapy on the one hand, and the pharmacological properties of the drug on the other. Moreover, it is possible to implement the logic of this balanced placebo design in single-case experimental designs as well as the more usual between-group comparative outcome study (Wilson, 1981).

References

American Psychiatric Association. *Diagnostic and Statistical Manual of Mental Disorders,* 3rd ed. Washington, D.C.: American Psychiatric Association, 1980.

Bandura, A. *Principles of Behavior Modification.* New York: Holt, Rinehart & Winston, 1969.

Barlow, D. H. Behavior therapy: The next decade. *Behavior Therapy,* 1980, *11,* 315–328.

Beck, A. T. *Cognitive Therapy and the Emotional Disorders.* New York: International Universities Press, 1976.

Blakey, R., & Baker, R. An exposure approach to alcohol abuse. *Behavior Research and Therapy,* 1980, *18,* 319–326.

Booth, D. Acquired behavior controlling energy intake and output. In A. J. Stunkard (ed.), *Obesity.* Philadelphia: W. B. Saunders, 1980.

Boskind-Lodahl, M., & White, W. C. The definition and treatment of bulimarexia in college women: A pilot study. *Journal of American College Health Association,* 1978, *27,* 2.

Brody, J. E. An eating disorder of bingeing and purging reported widespread. *New York Times,* October 20, 1981, page C1.

Burns, D. D. *Feeling Good.* New York: Morrow, 1980.

Cannon, D., Baker, T., Wehl, C. Emetic and electric shock alcohol aversion therapy: Six and 12 month follow-up. *Journal of Consulting and Clinical Psychology,* 1981, *49,* 360–368.

Derogatis, L. *SCL-90, Administration, Scoring, and Procedures Manual for the R(evised) Version.* Baltimore, Md.: Johns Hopkins University, School of Medicine, 1977.

Dubbert, P., & Wilson, G. T. Treatment failures in behavior therapy for obesity: Causes, correlates, and consequences. In E. Foa & P. M. G. Emmelkamp (eds.), *Treatment Failure in Behavior Therapy.* New York: John Wiley, in press.

Ellis, A. Rational–emotive therapy: Research data that supports the clinical and personality hypothesis of RET and other modes of cognitive–behavior therapy. *The Counseling Psychologist,* 1977, *7,* 2–42.

Foa, E., & Emmelkamp, P. M. G. *Treatment Failure in Behavior Therapy.* New York, John Wiley, in press.

Franks, C. M., & Wilson, G. T. (eds.). *Annual Review of Behavior Therapy*, Vol. 7. New York: Brunner/Mazel, 1980.

Gormally, J., Black, S., Daston, S., & Rardin, D. The assessment of binge eating severity among obese persons. *Addictive Behaviors*, 1982, 7, 47–55.

Hawkins, R., & Clement, P. Development and construct validation of a self-report measure of binge eating tendencies. *Addictive Behaviors*, 1980, 5, 219–226.

Hersen, M., & Barlow, D. *Single-Case Experimental Designs*. New York: Pergamon Press, 1976.

Hodgson, R., & Rankin, H. Modification of excessive drinking by cue exposure. *Behaviour Research and Therapy*, 1976, *14*, 305–307.

Kazdin, A. E. *Research Design in Clinical Research*. New York: Harper & Row, 1980.

Lazarus, A. A., & Fay, A. Resistance or rationalization? In P. Wachtel (ed.), *Resistance in Psychodynamic and Behavioral Therapies*. New York: Plenum, in press.

Lichtenstein, E., & Rodrigues, M. P. Long-term effects of rapid smoking treatment for dependent cigarette smokers. *Addictive Behaviors*, 1977, *2*, 109–112.

Mahoney, K., & Mahoney, M. J. Cognitive factors in weight reduction. In J. Krumboltz & C. E. Thorensen (eds.), *Counseling Methods*. New York: Holt, Rinehart & Winston, 1976.

Mahoney, M. J. Psychotherapy and the structure of personal revolutions. In M. J. Mahoney (ed.), *Cognition and Clinical Science*. New York: Plenum, 1980.

Marks, I. M. *Cure and Care of the Neuroses*. New York: John Wiley, 1981.

Marlatt, G. A. Alcohol use and problem drinking: A cognitive–behavioral analysis. In P. Kendall & S. Hollon (eds.), *Cognitive–Behavioral Interventions: Theory, Research, and Procedures*. New York: Academic Press, 1979.

Marlatt, G. A. *Relapse Prevention*. New York: Guilford Press, in press.

Marlatt, G. A., & Rohsenow, D. J. Cognitive processes in alcohol use: Expectancy and the balanced placebo design. In N. K. Mello (ed.), *Advances in Substance Abuse: Behavioral and Biological Research*. Greenwich, Conn.: JAI Press, 1981.

Masters, W. H. & Johnson V. E. *Human sexual inadequacy,* Boston: Little, Brown, 1970.

Meichenbaum, D. Resistance: From a cognitive–behavioral perspective. In P. Wachtel (ed.), *Resistance in Psychodynamic and Behavioral Therapies*. New York: Plenum, in press.

Meichenbaum, D. *Cognitive Behavior Modification*. New York: Plenum, 1977.

Meyer, R. G. *Delay Therapy: Two Case Reports*. Behavior Therapy, 1973, *4*, 709–711.

Mischel, W. *Personality and Assessment.* New York: John Wiley, 1968.

Monti, P. M., McCrady, B. S., & Barlow, D. H. Effect of positive reinforcement, informational feedback, and contingency contracting on a bulimic anorexic female. *Behavior Therapy,* 1977, *8,* 258–263.

Olson, R. P., Ganley, R., Devine, V., & Dorsey, G. Long-term effects of behavioral versus insight-oriented therapy with inpatient alcoholics. *Journal of Consulting and Clinical Psychology,* 1981, *49,* 866–877.

Polivy, J. Perception of calories and regulation of intake in restrained and unrestrained subjects. *Addictive Behaviors,* 1976, *1,* 237–244.

Rachman, S. The primacy of affect: Some theoretical implications. *Behaviour Research and Therapy,* 1981, *19,* 279–290.

Rachman, S., & Hodgson, R. *Obsessions and Compulsions.* Englewood Cliffs, N.J.: Prentice-Hall, 1980.

Rachman, S., & Wilson, G. T. *The Effects of Psychological Therapy.* Oxford, England: Pergamon Press, 1980.

Rathus, S. A. A 30-item schedule for assessing assertive behavior. *Behavior Therapy,* 1973, *4,* 398–406.

Rau, J., & Green, R. S. Compulsive eating: A neuropsychologic approach to certain eating disorders. *Comprehensive Psychiatry,* 1975, *16,* 223–231.

Rosen, J. C., & Leitenberg, H. Bulimia nervosa: Treatment with exposure and response prevention. *Behavior Therapy,* 1982, *13,* 117–124.

Ullmann, L. P., & Krasner, L. *A Psychological Approach to Abnormal Behavior,* 2nd ed. Englewood Cliffs, N.J.: Prentice-Hall, 1975.

Welch, G. J. The treatment of compulsive vomiting and obsessive thoughts through gradual response delay, response prevention and cognitive correction. *Journal of Behavior Therapy and Experimental Psychiatry,* 1979, *10,* 77–82.

Wermuth, B., Davis, K., Hollister, L., Stonkard, A. J. Phenytoin treatment of the binge-eating syndrome. *American Journal of Psychiatry,* 1977, *134,* 1249–1253.

Wilson, G. T. Booze, beliefs and behavior: Cognitive factors in alcohol use and abuse. In P. E. Nathan, G. A. Marlatt, & T. Loberg (eds.), *Alcoholism: New Directions in Behavioral Research and Treatment.* New York: Plenum, 1978.

Wilson, G. T. Perceived control and the theory and practice of behavior therapy. In L. C. Perlmuter & R. A. Monty (eds.), *Choice and Perceived Control.* Hillsdale, N.J.: Lawrence Erlbaum, 1979.

Wilson, G. T. Behavior therapy and the treatment of obesity. In W. R. Miller (ed.), *The Addictive Behaviors: Treatment of Alcoholism, Drug Abuse, Smoking and Obesity.* New York: Pergamon Press, 1980.

Wilson, G. T. Expectations and substance abuse: Can basic research facilitate clinical research and practice? *Addictive Behaviors,* 1981, *6,* 221–232.

Wilson, G. T., & Evans, I. M. The therapist–client relationship in behavior therapy. In A. Gurman & A. Razin (eds.), *The Therapists Contribution to Effective Psychotherapy: An Empirical Approach.* New York: Pergamon Press, 1977.

Wilson, G. T., & O'Leary, K. D. *Principles of Behavior Therapy.* Englewood Cliffs, N.J.: Prentice-Hall, 1980.

Wolpe, J. *Psychtherapy by reciprocal inhibition.* Stanford, Calif.: Stanford University Press, 1958.

Wooley, S. C., & Wooley, O. W. Overeating as substance abuse. In N. Mello (ed.), *Advances in Substance Abuse,* Vol. 2. Greenwich, Conn.: JAI Press, 1981.

Wooley, S., Wooley, O., & Dyrenforth, S. Theoretical, practical, and social issues in behavioral treatments of obesity. *Journal of Applied Behavior Analysis,* 1979, *12,* 3–26.

Zajonc, R. Feeling and thinking. *American Psychologist,* 1980, *35,* 151–175.

Index